Podcasting in a Platform Age

BLOOMSBURY PODCAST STUDIES

Series Editors:
Martin Spinelli and Lance Dann

Series Editorial Board Members:
Martin Spinelli, University of Sussex, UK
Lance Dann, University of Brighton, UK
Mia Lindgren, University of Tasmania, Australia
Kathleen Collins, John Jay College, USA
Richard Berry, University of Sunderland, UK
Ann Heppermann, Sarah Lawrence College, USA
Tiziano Bonini, Università di Siena, Italy
John Sullivan, Muhlenberg College, USA
Belén Monclús, Universitat Autònoma de Barcelona, Spain

Podcasting in a Platform Age

From an Amateur to a Professional Medium

JOHN L. SULLIVAN

BLOOMSBURY ACADEMIC
NEW YORK • LONDON • OXFORD • NEW DELHI • SYDNEY

BLOOMSBURY ACADEMIC
Bloomsbury Publishing Inc
1385 Broadway, New York, NY 10018, USA
50 Bedford Square, London, WC1B 3DP, UK
29 Earlsfort Terrace, Dublin 2, Ireland

BLOOMSBURY, BLOOMSBURY ACADEMIC and the Diana logo
are trademarks of Bloomsbury Publishing Plc

First published in the United States of America 2024

Copyright © John L. Sullivan, 2024

For legal purposes the Acknowledgments on pp. ix–xi constitute
an extension of this copyright page.

Cover design: Andrew Walker

All rights reserved. No part of this publication may be reproduced or transmitted
in any form or by any means, electronic or mechanical, including photocopying,
recording, or any information storage or retrieval system, without
prior permission in writing from the publishers.

Bloomsbury Publishing Inc does not have any control over, or responsibility for,
any third-party websites referred to or in this book. All internet addresses given
in this book were correct at the time of going to press. The author and publisher
regret any inconvenience caused if addresses have changed or sites have ceased
to exist, but can accept no responsibility for any such changes.

A catalog record for this book is available from the Library of Congress.

ISBN:	HB:	978-1-5013-8070-9
	PB:	978-1-5013-8069-3
	ePDF:	978-1-5013-8067-9
	eBook:	978-1-5013-8068-6

Series: Bloomsbury Podcast Studies

Typeset by Integra Software Services Pvt. Ltd.
Printed and bound in Great Britain

To find out more about our authors and books visit www.bloomsbury.com
and sign up for our newsletters.

CONTENTS

List of Figures vi
Series Preface viii
Acknowledgments ix

Introduction: Podcasting in Transition 1

1 Podcasting as a Twenty-First-Century Cultural Form 19
2 Podcasting as a Media Industry—Formalization from Above and Below 45
3 Distribution and Exhibition Shifts—The Platformization of Podcasting 81
4 Professionalism and the Myth of Meritocracy 103
5 Podcast Conventions and the Entrepreneurial Dream 121
6 Market Information Regimes in Podcasting: Formalization and Audience Metrics 143
7 "This Episode Is Brought to You by …": Advertising and Podcast Monetization 173

Conclusion: Platformization and Podcasting's Third Decade 207

References 225
Index 263

FIGURES

1.1 "Global Podcast Listener Forecast 2022–6 Podcast Popularity Varies by Region—and So Do Growth Rates." © eMarketer, 2023. Reprinted with permission 21
1.2 Adapted from "The most crowded categories in Apple Podcasts (April 2021 edition)." © Pacific Content, 2023. Reprinted with permission 39
1.3 "Weekly Insights 1.11.2023—Top Podcast Genres in the US Q3 2022." © Edison Research, 2023. Reprinted with permission 41
2.1 Adapted from "Libsyn Statistics, visualized" on *Livewire Labs*. © John Spurlock. Reprinted with permission 60
2.2 "Top Podcast Publishers." © Podtrac, Inc, 2023. Reprinted with permission 61
2.3 Adapted from "Top Podcast Hosting Companies by Episode Share (May 2023)" on *Livewire Labs*. © John Spurlock. Reprinted with permission 63
2.4 Adapted from "Buzzsprout Platform Stats," by Buzzsprout Podcast Hosting. Reprinted with permission 68
2.5 "Major Acquisitions in the Podcasting Industry." Author's own 73
3.1 Adapted from "Podcast Media Hosting Services by New Episode Share (May 2023)" on *Livewire Labs*. © John Spurlock. Reprinted with permission 92
3.2 Google search interest for "RSS" (2004–Present). *Google Trends* 95
5.1 Podcast Movement 2016 Logo. Author's own photo 132

FIGURES

6.1 "Monthly Podcast Listening (2008–23)." © Edison Research, 2023. Reprinted with permission 155
7.1 "Patreon payouts for podcasting (2016–23)." © Graphtreon, 2023. Reprinted with permission 184
7.2 "Top 15 Podcast Advertisers in September 2022." © Magellan AI, 2023. Reprinted with permission 194

SERIES PREFACE

The Bloomsbury Podcast Studies Series sets out to establish Podcast Studies as its own distinct field which spans the Humanities and Social Sciences. It offers granular political, cultural, historical, economic, literary, and data-driven analyses of podcast genres, production practices, institutions and platforms, narratives and semiotics, and national and regional currents by leading scholars and practitioners. With commitments to both accessibility and rigor, the series promotes research and knowledge creation about, through and with podcasting, and offers insights to policy makers, academics, and creatives alike. Its underlying intention is to develop the practical yet sophisticated vocabularies, methodologies, and critical tools needed to fully appreciate the depth and dynamism of our newest audio medium and what it contributes to the broader world.

Martin Spinelli & Lance Dann
Series Editors

ACKNOWLEDGMENTS

The road to the end of this project has been long and has taken many unexpected twists and turns, not the least of which was the worldwide COVID-19 pandemic and lockdown in 2019–20. There were some days when I thought this book would never see the light of day, but I am grateful to so many people for helping me to complete this project.

First, I would like to thank Martin Spinelli and Lance Dann for giving me the opportunity to include this work as part of the podcast studies book series for Bloomsbury Academic. Both of them have been unfailingly supportive and encouraging, and I feel fortunate to be working with pioneers in the academic study of podcasting. Special thanks to the reviewers of my original proposal and to the careful reviews for the draft by Lance Dann and Richard Berry. I would also like to thank the staff at Bloomsbury for their editorial support, especially Katie Gallof and Alyssa Jordan. The text has been greatly improved thanks to their efforts, though of course all errors and omissions remain mine alone.

There were many people at Muhlenberg College who were also instrumental in bringing this project to a successful conclusion. I am appreciative of my colleagues in the department of Media and Communication who continue to foster an environment of collegiality and intellectual curiosity despite our heavy teaching and service responsibilities. I would also like to thank my research assistant, Kat Dickey, for her careful reading and editing of some of the early drafts of the chapters. Additionally, I would like to thank the Muhlenberg College Provost and the Faculty Development and Scholarship Committee, who approved several summer grants to allow me to access resources for this research. The indexing of the book was generously supported by the Daniel J. and Carol Shiner Wilson Grant. My students in my Introduction to Podcasting course also read and commented on early drafts of several chapters, and I am grateful to have had this helpful feedback.

My understanding of podcasting as a cultural, social, and economic phenomenon was greatly enhanced by the many kind and generous people from the podcasting community who spoke with me and provided me with their insights about the medium. My sincere thanks to Lee Anderson, Bryan Barletta, Mignon Fogarty, Stephanie Fuccio, Rob Greenlee, Sean Kneese, Jennifer Longworth, John Luckenbaugh, Amanda McLoughlin, Eric Nuzum, Joe Pardo, Paul Riismandel, Lynn Smargis, Jay Soderberg, Jenna Spinelle, Evo Terra, Naresh Vissa, Rob Walch, Keith Weinhold, and Shereen Lani Younes.

As I have been conceptualizing and writing this book over the past five years, I have also greatly appreciated the intellectual engagement and feedback from colleagues across the globe. The genesis of the book's core argument about the platformization of podcasting was developed in Toronto in 2018 at a workshop on platforms and cultural production that was organized by Brooke Duffy, David Nieborg, and Thomas Poell. I will always be grateful to them for one of the most productive and intellectually stimulating scholarly encounters I have ever experienced. I was thrilled to exchange ideas with some of the most talented and generous scholars in the field there, including Arturo Arriagada, Sophie Bishop, Tiziano Bonini, David Craig, Daniel Joseph, David Hesmondhalgh, and Jeremy Morris. Cogent critiques and suggestions from these and other colleagues at that workshop had a profound impact on my work.

I am also thankful for the growing international community of podcast scholars who have influenced my knowledge of this nascent field and whose scholarship and friendship have provided invaluable support and guidance as I have worked to complete the book. Some of these fellow travelers on my intellectual journey include Lori Beckstead, Richard Berry, Kim Fox, Nicholas John, Aske Kammer, Dario Llinares, and Tzlil Sharon.

Finally, I would like to thank my extended family for their patience and understanding during the years that I have been working on this project. Thanks go to Mary Jane Gilchrist, Jack Sullivan, Vickie Sullivan, Sue Anne Basu, Krisna Basu, Linnea Basu, Joshua Krell, Sarah Krell, and Joseph Krell. None of this would be possible without the love and support of my family. To my wife, Andra, and to my daughters Cindy and Niva, I thank you from the bottom of my heart. This book is dedicated to you.

John L. Sullivan
Allentown, PA, USA
June 2023

Introduction: Podcasting in Transition

Leo Laporte is a longtime radio and television talk show host who began interviewing guests about computers and new technology in the early 1990s. In 2005, Laporte and a few of his former colleagues from the defunct ZDTV program "Tech TV" were fascinated by the relatively new technology of podcasting and created an experimental technology-oriented online podcast entitled "This Week in Tech," or TWiT for short. The show featured weekly informal discussions about technology-related topics between Laporte and a variety of guests and regular commentators. TWiT quickly developed a loyal online following with thousands of downloads for each episode. Capitalizing on the apparent interest in computer and technology-related issues, Laporte began recording weekly episodes of TWiT which he distributed on his website. He also leveraged his experience in radio and television to begin selling advertising on the podcast and eventually expanded the operation to include fifteen different weekly shows about specific niche technology topics. With his distinctive radio voice, Laporte had invented a new online programming format that he dubbed "netcasting" (a cross between broadcasting and the Internet). Laporte shocked audiences during his keynote address at the 2009 Online News Association Conference when he announced that the TWiT netcasts had amassed $1.5 million in revenue for the previous year (Ali 2009). In a message posted on Reddit.com in 2012, Laporte noted that he had grossed $3.75 million in 2011 and was on track to pass $4 million in 2012 thanks to listener donations and advertising.

Back in 2005, Laporte was one of only a small handful of early pioneers to bring broadcast radio aesthetics, routines, and a scheme for monetization to the emerging medium that we recognize today as podcasting. Almost two decades later, the financial success of Laporte's TWiT Network is no longer an anomaly in the podcast ecosystem. Instead, podcasting has begun a rapid transformation from a largely amateur, homegrown cultural form into a bona fide cultural industry. Encouraged by the huge success of the 2014 podcast sensation *Serial*—which was downloaded more than 80 million times in the first six months after its release (Mallenbaum 2015)—entrepreneurs and so-called legacy media companies (those with commercial interests in broadcast radio and television) have rapidly expanded their interests in podcasting as a business, bringing professional standards and the logics of capital with them. In the United States, for example, well-resourced public radio stations like New York City's WNYC, for example, started their own podcasting divisions (Sisario 2015) and advertising firms like Midroll and legacy radio companies like iHeartMedia and SiriusXM have specialized in bundling popular podcasts for sale to advertisers. E.W. Scripps, a company which owns a diverse portfolio of legacy media such as newspapers, broadcast radio, and television stations, bought Midroll in 2015 for $10 million, purchased podcasting app company Stitcher for $4.5 million in 2016, and then sold both of these to satellite radio giant SiriusXM in 2020 (Lafayette 2020). These companies are motivated not simply by the creative possibilities of the medium, but also by the potential to cultivate mass audiences. A survey conducted by Edison Research and Triton Digital, for instance, estimated that 164 million Americans had listened to a podcast in 2023, up from 45 million in 2015 (Edison Research 2023). Breakout podcast hits such as *S-Town* (the 2016 follow up to *Serial*), *This American Life,* Aaron Mahnke's *Lore,* and *WTF with Marc Maron*—just to name a few—have demonstrated to both programmers and advertisers the potential for podcasting to emerge as a commercially viable media industry (O'Connell 2015). Thus, despite podcasting's roots as a forum for user-generated content (UGC), the recent expansion of the podcast audience and interest from traditional media has begun to transform it "from a do-it-yourself, amateur niche medium into a commercial mass medium" (Bonini 2015, 27).

Understanding Podcasting

Podcasting is the focus of this book, but what is it, exactly? Podcasting can be understood as "a technology used to distribute, receive, and listen, on-demand, to sound content produced by traditional editors such as radio, publishing houses, journalists, and educational institutions ... as well as content created by independent radio producers, artists, and radio amateurs" (Bonini 2015, 21). The term "podcasting" was coined by journalist Ben Hammersley back in 2004 (he also floated the term "audioblogging") as a means to describe a mode of distribution similar to radio broadcasting, but delivered via portable digital devices, of which the Apple's iPod was the most well-known at the time (2004). At the time, podcasting's popularity was limited due to the relative niche status of portable digital audio players like iPods and the necessity for those devices to be continually plugged into computers in order to access new downloaded content.

In its early history, podcasting appealed primarily to technology enthusiasts who were especially adept at locating and manually subscribing to RSS feeds. Much of the early content available, such as Adam Curry's *Daily Source Code* and the TWiT network mentioned above, catered to this particular male-dominated audience of early tech adopters. Podcasting broadened its listener base and content significantly following the 2008 introduction of the iPhone, which allowed audiences to access and consume digital media on mobile devices anywhere and anytime. Thus, podcasting's rise in popularity is at least partially due to its technological features: its availability, convenience, and near ubiquity thanks to global adoption of mobile smartphones. Podcasts are widely available either via streaming or direct downloading to digital devices via helper software (such as podcatchers like iTunes, Google Play, or other third-party desktop and mobile applications). Podcatchers have made it relatively simple to locate, subscribe, and listen to on-demand audio files. When Apple decided to include RSS aggregation into their iTunes Music Store in Spring 2005, their market dominance in digital audio sales opened the floodgates for millions of iTunes users to easily locate and download podcasts (Sterne et al. 2008a). The key benefits of podcasts over traditional broadcast media are their portability, and their ability to time-shift other forms of media (such as radio broadcasts). Second, because podcasts are on-demand, they are very much in line with media consumption habits of most twenty-first-century audiences who have come of age in an era of other on-demand online media such as YouTube, Spotify, Netflix, and Pandora.

To say that podcasting is essentially a method for easily distributing audio files online, while technically accurate, doesn't capture how it has evolved into a medium with its own unique culture, aesthetics, and listening. As Markman and Sawyer (2014, 21) noted, while the "podcasting as distribution" model is a good description of how broadcast radio networks like National Public Radio (NPR) essentially allowing for easy time-shifting of programs, the popular fascination with podcasting stems mainly from the homegrown, grassroots nature of its content. Thanks to the thousands of independent and amateur creators producing new podcast episodes on a continual basis, podcasting has developed a powerful ethos of authenticity and creative empowerment (see Murray 2009). Since the economic and technological barriers to podcast production as low, tens of thousands of podcast shows have mushroomed, covering extremely "niche" topics such as "The Pen Addict" (about the finer points of writing pens: fountain vs. ballpoint), "Gilmore Guys" (two friends watch the entire series of *Gilmore Girls* with commentary), and "Witch, Please" (two literature professors discussing the Harry Potter books from a feminist perspective) (Basu 2017). Listeners have discovered in podcasts what they may have found wanting in commercial media content: compelling, real stories from people from all walks of life, unburdened by the necessity to cultivate large, mainstream audiences.

Podcasting and the Politics of "Spreadable" Media

Podcasting emerged at a time of popular euphoria surrounding the enablements of Web 2.0. Given its relatively low barriers to entry (a computer and a cheap microphone), serialized online audio broadcasting became a popular form of amateur media in the early 2000s, though its existence was greatly overshadowed by the advent of video sharing via YouTube (which launched 2005 and was purchased by Google in 2006), and audio streaming (Pandora launched its music streaming service in 2005). Nevertheless, podcasting shared a great deal in common with other forms of UGC in that it ignited a culture of participatory creativity online (Jenkins 2006; Lobato, Thomas, and Hunter 2012). Scholars excitedly cataloged the cultural shift that was enabled by new content-sharing platforms online, toward amateur media creations, arguing that online digital distribution had effectively leveled the playing field between media corporations and everyday citizens, allowing for a more democratic, "grass roots" economy (Freedman 2012). Clay Shirky (2008), for example, has argued that we are witnessing the "mass amateurization" of cultural production. Benkler (2006) pushed this claim even further, arguing that human beings face a historical tipping point when the ubiquity of networked computing in the most advanced economies of the world is creating a new mode of production by transforming passive information receivers into engaged information producers. This new breed of media entrepreneurs have also been described as "produsers," a term meant to underscore the "the communities which engage in the collaborative creation and extension of information and knowledge" (Bruns 2008, 2).

Jenkins and Green (2011) have adopted the term "spreadable media" to more accurately conceptualize how forms of online media can spread quickly online via distribution platforms and social media. The key difference between "spreadable media" and traditional, legacy media is not only the speed at which cultural messages can be distributed online (by becoming "viral"), but also the market orientation of cultural production. Whether commercial or noncommercial, traditional mass media orients itself toward the consumer marketplace. Scholars argued that online UGC, on the other hand, was instead driven by users' desires to explore their creativity and make connections with others (see Benkler 2006; Bruns 2008; Jenkins 2006; Tushnet 2007). The notion here is that these forms of amateur media imagines the public "not as simply consumers of preconstructed messages but as people who are shaping, sharing, reframing, and remixing media content in ways which might not have been previously imagined" (Green and Jenkins 2011, 2).

The low barriers for creating user-generated online content have also greatly expanded the potential diversity of cultural production. Subsequently, the sheer variety of online products has allowed for much smaller, niche media products to find an audience (and potentially a source of revenue). Chris Anderson (2006) famously dubbed this trend the creation of a "Long Tail" market. Online storage and distribution, he argued, has made smaller, niche content economically viable, and this is in turn reshaping how content providers are imagining the audience. As I will explore later in the book, the richness and diversity of the podcasting ecosystem offers us a glimpse into a quintessential Long Tail media environment. Indeed, podcasters often proudly proclaim their creative independence from the strictures of the mainstream, and this newfound abundance of content options has promised to mark the "death of the blockbuster economy" (Freedman 2012). As journalist Ben Hammersley (Ulanoff 2015) noted, "I don't think there is a mainstream anymore ... Mainstream success is really a twentieth century artifact." As a distinctly Long Tail medium, the audiences for each show are tiny in comparison to legacy media like television and radio. For example, market research firm Edison Research has reported that podcasting's "Share of Ear" in 2022 (the percentage of American audio consumers aged 25–54 who listen to podcasts) was only 18 percent, though up from 6 percent in 2017. AM/FM Radio share of ear, by contrast, was 54 percent (Mayer 2023).

Despite the wild utopian enthusiasm that has accompanied the surge in UGC, however, something important is changing: these amateur, online media producers are developing professional practices found in traditional media, and some are even abandoning their existing occupations to rely on their online activities for financial support. While many popular forms of UGC are generated by amateurs, there is in fact a vast range of competencies and purposes behind these creative productions, ranging from individuals running their own news or gossip blogs, to semi-skilled producers, many of whom were once directly involved in commercial media production, to highly skilled media professionals who are employees of media corporations. Thus, the intermixing of this collection of production experience and competency, from amateurs to semi-skilled to professionals, is a defining feature of the kind of hybridized forms that are appearing with greater frequency online. Indeed, many of the most popular websites for distributing UGC, such as Facebook, YouTube, craigslist, and Yelp, are essentially platforms that generate income from this content

(Hetcher 2012). Hybridized media like podcasting incorporate both commercial and noncommercial aspects, often existing on a continuum between more formal and informal economies (Lobato, Thomas, and Hunter 2012).

Method and Scope of Analysis

This book explores the transition underway in podcasting by considering how the influx of legacy broadcasting media and Big Tech interest in the medium has introduced professional and corporate logics into what had been largely an amateur media form. In particular, I map out the institutional structures surrounding podcasting, paying close attention to the distribution of power and resources. The distribution of resources in podcasting is a continually moving target, however, making it even more challenging to assess the "state of play" within the medium. I have been writing this book on and off since 2016, and whenever I seem to have emerged with a grasp on the dynamics of the industry, a new podcasting technology, service, merger, acquisition, or issue emerges to disrupt the status quo.

My approach to the many shifts in podcasting can be described as "critical media industry studies" (Havens, Lotz, and Tinic 2009). Specifically, I aim to understand the underlying dynamics of the emergent podcasting industry by focusing both on broad "macro" trends by noting the structural and economic dynamics of the medium and the "micro" conditions of production among both professional and amateur practitioners. The methods underpinning this analysis leverage what John Thornton Caldwell (2011, 201) calls an "integrated cultural-historical method of analysis." Caldwell describes a "synthetic" approach to data gathering about production cultures, relying upon four key modes of analysis (2011, 201):

1 Textual analysis of trade and worker artifacts
2 Interviews with film/television workers
3 Ethnographic field observation of production spaces and professional gatherings
4 Economic/industrial analysis

Podcasting in a Platform Age utilizes all four of these analytical modes to bring clarity to the shifts underway in podcasting. Chapters 2 and 3, for instance, offer a broad overview of the industrial structure of the industry in line with the fourth approach above. Here I outline key market players, mergers and acquisitions, and the increasingly important role of advertisers for the flow of capital within the podcasting ecosystem. Since podcasting is quite a self-referential and self-reflexive cultural form, I look closely at how podcast practitioners talk about expectations and "best practices" for podcasting in Chapter 4 (approach #1 above). Just as Caldwell (2008) found within the movie industry, the industry-related talk and industrial narratives among podcast practitioners are similarly instrumental in creating a sense of what podcasting is all about. Scholars have uncovered similar cultures of production, for example, among YouTubers (Burgess and Green 2009) and fashion bloggers (Duffy 2015; 2017). Through these informal mechanisms, professional and social norms are discussed and perpetuated. Mining the content of podcasting itself for insights into production practices and expectations can be understood as "listening in" to industrial discourses among practitioners of a craft (Corrigan 2018).

This analysis is also informed by interviews with industry practitioners (approach #2) and ethnographic observations of professional spaces where podcasters gather to talk about what they do and why (approach #3). Unlike the film and television industries, where studying media elites is often fraught due to the reticence of these elites to engage with outside academics wishing to understand their industry (see Ortner 2009; 2010, for example), podcasting has fewer such institutional boundaries to thwart outside scholars. In the process of researching this book, I formally interviewed eighteen podcast industry practitioners (and two more on an informal basis), some of whom were independent podcasters, and others who worked full time either as entrepreneurs or full-time for a larger podcasting production company. While I initially intended these interviews to be primary sources of data, they served instead as sources of background on industry trends and as a "reality check" on my continually evolving analysis of the changes underway in podcasting. These interviews are referenced throughout the book at various points. Finally, as discussed in Chapter 5, I attended a number of annual podcast conventions beginning in 2016, especially Podcast Movement, and conducted ethnographic observations of these gatherings as another source of "listening in" (Corrigan 2018) to industrial discourses about podcasting and the changes underway.

One final note on method and scope: My analysis of platformization and the shifts in podcasting is heavily US-centric since it incorporates data mainly from US-based podcasters and companies. Given the fact that much of the industry expansion and consolidation has taken place among companies located within the United States (except for Swedish audio giant Spotify, of course) and that the major platforms for producing, hosting and exhibiting podcasts (such as Apple Podcasts, Amazon, Google) are all located within the United States, this somewhat limited field of view is not necessarily as limiting as it might seem. That said, podcasting is developing in some unique and exciting ways internationally, and much more cross-national research is sorely needed to better understand how the three institutional forces I outline below are affecting podcast production and consumption in different regions and countries around the globe.

Formalization, Platformization, and the Structural Formation of a Cultural Industry

Leaning on the above sources of data, I outline how the efforts of industry players to transform podcasting into a profitable medium are beginning to challenge the very definition of podcasting itself. The book focuses on three major aspects of this transformation: *formalization* (including *platformization*), *specialization*, and *monetization*. Podcasting has its roots at the dawn of the Web 2.0 era in the early 2000s. Its technical structure emerged directly out of blogging, chiefly via the technology of RSS, or Really Simple Syndication, which allowed web users to easily keep up with their favorite blogs and websites by "subscribing" to them. As I discuss in the next chapter, the open architecture of RSS protocol was key to its adoption by enabling its integration into other forms of software, most importantly Apple's iTunes in 2005. The technology of podcasting remains unchanged from the early days of the web. What has undergone dramatic change, however, is the variety and type of content available. With the release of the Apple Podcasts app in 2016, the number of podcast listeners skyrocketed to 13.7 billion episode downloads on that platform in 2017 alone (Locker 2018), though that figure decreased somewhat to approximately 11.8 billion downloads in 2022 (Triton Digital 2023). Major public radio providers such as NPR have begun offering their programming for download via podcasting (essentially, timeshifting) as well as developing programs specifically as podcasts that are not available on air. Former public radio alums like Alex Blumberg launched their own commercial ventures to create new podcasts and capitalize on emerging advertiser interest in the platform. Podcasting is no longer just a hobby activity, but a potential career for millions of disaffected creative professionals in the gig economy. Podcasting is looking less and less like a small backwater for amateur content and more and more like a commercial media industry.

This transformation is what scholars refer to as *formalization*. Formalization describes the process by which "media systems become progressively more rationalized, consolidated and financially transparent. It can happen because of increased state intervention in a particular industry, which finds itself dragged into the light of regulation and accountability. Alternatively, it can occur when formerly small-scale media concerns become integrated into larger-scale structures" (Lobato and Thomas 2015, 27). In the case of podcasting, the latter style of formalization is found, whereby well-known amateur podcasters with sizable audiences are being recruited to join podcast networks, lured by the potential for a larger percentage of advertising sales revenue and the ability to expand their audience via cross-promotion with other shows on the same network. New players like technology companies, advertisers, venture capital firms, talent agencies, and other ancillary services are also moving into the podcasting space, making for a complex and inter-dependent media landscape.

While the concept of distinct industries may be increasingly outdated in a world of online media, the structural dynamics of production, distribution, and exhibition remain critical tools for understanding the dynamics of power in new media markets. As a student of so-called legacy media industry studies in the 1990s, I came to appreciate the grounded frameworks offered by political economic and cultural theories of media production. Even though those frameworks emerged during an era of distinctive industrial histories and economic structures, in modified form they can provide the theoretical scaffolding for our understanding of the changes underway in podcasting.

A second major transformation has also shifted the balance of power in podcasting: *platformization*. Platforms are digital infrastructures that allow groups, individuals, organizations, and companies to interact in an online space (Gillespie 2010). In the first decade of the twenty-first-century, internet denizens were largely reliant on web browsers to navigate the web and locate content. With the advent of social media, photo sharing, video chatting, online shopping, and other services, our access to the internet is increasingly mediated through platforms like Facebook, Twitter, Instagram, Amazon.com, and YouTube. The launch of Apple's iPhone in 2007 and the rise of mobile adoption have only increased consumers' reliance on platforms by mediating their interactions with the internet via mobile apps (Morris and Murray 2018). Just as they have with other forms of media, platforms have begun to assume more importance in podcasting as well. Through corporate acquisitions, for example, large platform services like Spotify, Apple Podcasts, SiriusXM, Google, and iHeartMedia have suddenly become major players in the podcasting ecosystem. As more and more audiences discover podcasting via their interactions with these platforms, their role in shaping the future of the medium will only increase. Along with providing access to content via discovery algorithms, these platform providers also serve as sophisticated surveillance machines. Platforms regularly harvest specific data about listener habits and choices that go far beyond what is typically available via download data. This, coupled with the fact that platforms require user accounts at minimum as the price of admission to their services, means that listener profiles and precise advertising targeting are now available for podcasting. As I will discuss later in the book, the explosion of audience data has fueled a gold rush of "ad tech" for podcasting, thereby altering the relationship between creators and their listeners. This is yet another consequence of the platformization of podcasting.

Specialization of Labor in Podcasting: Produsers, Pro-Ams, and Professionals

While formalization and platformization processes are occurring at the macro-level, a second major transformation has occurred at the level of podcasting production: the emergence of specialization of labor roles most found in legacy forms of commercial media. What was once a bastion of "do-it-yourself" production ethos has now diversified into a constellation of new professional roles, including editors, advertisers, networks, technology companies, support software vendors, and a host of other ancillary services. Podcaster personalities like Joe Rogan, Marc Maron, and others have also routinized and largely professionalized the production of podcasts. As will become clear later, this process was accelerated thank to the influx of existing media producers post-*Serial*—many of them from legacy media such as commercial or public radio. The image of the podcast creator is thus being altered. This is having some recursive effects on the medium. For example, the production values, audio quality, content genres, distribution methods, and monetization structures are becoming standardized, and are beginning to inform the production practices of amateurs. Podcasting is therefore in the slow process of transitioning from a largely informal, amateur medium to one that looks more similar to traditional media industries like television, radio, and motion pictures, though the path of that transition is complex, multi-faceted, and sometimes contradictory.

The book charts the professionalization of podcast labor mainly via the discourse that occurs among players in this emerging industry. In particular, podcasts, blogs, and self-published "how to" books work to actively construct a particular view of podcasting as an emergent, commercially viable industry that can serve as a full-time occupation for entrepreneurial amateurs. Underlying this discourse is a powerful and seductive message of meritocracy: that amateur podcasters can successfully compete with established industry players thanks to the absence of industry gatekeepers. Unlike broadcast media, podcasters are encouraged to offer a more personal and "authentic" perspective on the world. As I will outline in the book, amateur podcasters face a deeply contradictory landscape: on the one hand, they can experience a level of empowerment thanks to low entry barriers to the medium; on the other hand, amateurs' ability to compete financially with larger media producers for audiences (and, by extension, advertisers) is largely dependent upon their ability to adopt professional formats, technical standards, and topics that are similar to those in traditional media. The belated entry of broadcast radio into the podcasting space may further challenge the meritocratic ideal that drives much of the "how to" discourse. These professional narratives are also beginning to affect the production practices of amateurs as well by encouraging them to adopt specific technologies, production techniques, formats, and aesthetics to ensure commercial success in the marketplace. In this way, the professionalization of podcasting is also having recursive effects on the very definition of podcasting itself.

Monetization and Audience Metrics

The third major trend in the formalization process is the expansion of *monetization* schemes into the podcasting space. Monetization describes the process whereby audiences for an online medium are translated into revenue for the media producer or distributor. The introduction of monetization schemes for podcasting and other online cultural products is not new. Even since the early days of the medium in 2004–5, podcasts hosts (like Leo Laporte) developed rudimentary mechanisms for underwriting their efforts, such as selling merchandise to their audience (T-shirts, mugs, and other paraphernalia) and "direct response" advertising (whereby podcasts offer their listeners a reduced rate with a special promotional code for the services of an underwriting sponsor). Today's podcast ecosystem has dramatically expanded the use of brand advertising spots as a form of monetization, bringing with it an avalanche of money into the ecosystem. Indeed, in the United States alone, the total podcast advertising revenue for 2023 is projected to top $2.2 billion, up from $220 million in 2017 (Main 2017; Spangler 2023). Large corporate players like Spotify, iHeartMedia, SiriusXM, and even public broadcasters such as NPR and the BBC have made significant financial gambles on the promise of future growth in podcasting, and these moves have emboldened venture capitalists to inject the space with major startup cash. Brand advertisers are also beginning to explore podcasting as an outlet for their messages, which has the potential to rapidly formalize the structure of podcasting firmly around revenue models found in broadcast media (Kafka 2017b).

Advertisers are not jumping into podcasting with blind faith in the commercial potential of the medium, however. Rather, they are insisting that their advertising buys in podcasts are backed up by the reliable audience metrics. In the emergent industry of podcasting, measurements of audience exposure are still contested and in flux, despite the efforts of entities like the Interactive Advertising Bureau (IAB) to standardize those metrics. Thus, there is a spirited and sometimes contentious debate among different players within podcasting about which metrics should become the standard, or whether there is any prospect for standardization. These debates, explored in a later chapter, underscore the contested dynamics of industry formalization.

The Rise of Podcast Studies

Podcasting as a media form is in the midst of what Bonini (2015, 22) calls its "second age" characterized by its transformation into "a commercial productive practice and medium for mass consumption." Indeed, the medium itself is rather mature by new media standards, having just reached the twentieth anniversary the first RSS feed transmission in early 2021. Despite podcasting's relative maturity as a medium, however, the field of "podcast studies" is still in its nascent stages. Important early scholarly interventions (Berry 2006; Crofts et al. 2005; Menduni 2007; Sterne et al. 2008a) sought to conceptualize and contextualize podcasting as similar to, yet distinct from radio. Two early book-length explorations of podcasting, *Podcasting: New Aural Cultures and Digital Media* (Llinares, Fox, and Berry 2018) and *Podcasting: The Audio Media Revolution* (Spinelli and Dann 2019), have helpfully mapped out the theoretical terrain and provided the groundwork for the development of what can be called "podcast studies." Podcasting sits at the nexus of a number of related areas of inquiry within media studies such as radio studies, sound studies, pedagogy studies, and new media studies.

Much of the extant work on podcasting has examined it as a unique panoply of storytelling that creates strong bonds between creators and audiences through the intimacy of spoken audio (see Euritt 2022). Podcasting, argues Llinares (2018, 126), is distinct from its radio forebear because it has "created new audio practices and experiences that can and should be understood instrumentally, artistically and socio-culturally." Indeed, as Spinelli and Dann (2019) have persuasively argued, even though it shares its aural storytelling DNA with radio, there are some key features of podcasting such as the intimacy of its consumption via headphones, which creates a different kind of relationship between podcaster and listener; the fact that podcasting is almost entirely mobile-centric; the hyper-niche nature of the content; the absence of scheduling constraints and timing; the lack of institutional gatekeepers; and the "freemium" model of content. To Spinelli and Dann's criteria I would also add that the open architecture of RSS has been the key backbone of the first twenty years of podcasting and an important part of its technological and cultural DNA. However, some of the more recent developments in the wider podcasting industry pose significant challenges for this method of distribution. These definitional questions about podcasting are directly addressed in the next chapter.

To be sure, understanding podcasting as an artistic, documentary, and informational medium is key to grasping its social and cultural significance around the globe. But there are other transformations happening around online media that are also important to podcasting's story, and those are the ones that occupy the central focus in this book. My attention here will be squarely on the institutional and organizational dynamics of podcasting as a twenty-first-century cultural industry. Like blogging, vidcasting, social media, and other forms of online media, podcasting is largely driven by the thousands of amateur and semi-professional creators who develop new content on a regular basis. The rapid formalization and platformization of the medium promises to reshape the medium in important ways, and an analysis of these changes can also reveal how both technological and institutional barriers can challenge this uniquely open medium. Thus, my aim here in this book is to continue to expand upon the growing corpus of academic research into podcasting by drawing attention to these shifts by leveraging the tools of institutional and political economy to examine podcast production, distribution, audiences, and industry structures.

Plan of the Book

This book approaches podcasting as both a unique, vibrant form of cultural production and as an increasingly formalized cultural industry. While each chapter explores a different facet of the podcasting industry, it is expected that readers may prefer to skip around to those particular issues of most concern to them. Given this fact, I do loop back to some of my core arguments throughout each chapter, so a small amount of repetition there is to be expected.

Chapter 1 situates podcasting within a much broader historical context of audio distribution via the internet and includes a discussion on the importance of RSS as the key mechanism for distribution syndicated audio online. Podcasting emerged as a viable medium as a result of a confluence of several interrelated factors: advancements in technology (the introduction of Apple's iPod and, later, its iTunes music directory as well as the introduction of web syndication via the RSS standard in 1999), personal factors (early efforts by radio personalities Adam Curry and Dave Winer), and structural factors such as the desire to find alternatives to an increasingly homogenized content available on commercial radio, at least in the United States. Chapter 2 utilizes Turow's power roles framework to map the current landscape for podcasting. In particular, I note the increasing importance of platforms and networks to the distribution of podcasting, as well as the introduction of new players (such as advertisers and broadcast radio stations) into the ecosystem.

Chapter 3 looks carefully at the landscape of distribution in podcasting, in particular the curious centrality of Apple to the podcast universe, despite Apple's largely hands off approach. Rival distribution platforms such as SiriusXM, iHeartMedia, Amazon, Spotify, Google, and NPR have also emerged as competitors to Apple. Meanwhile, the radio-centric notion of networking has taken hold in podcasting. The notion of professionalism in podcasting is considered in Chapter 4. Here I analyze two well-regarded "how to" podcasts, *School of Podcasting* with Dave Jackson and *The Audacity to Podcast* with Daniel J. Lewis and the types of productions expectations that they develop a particular notion of professionalism for podcast producers. Chapter 5 amplifies the theme of entrepreneurism and provides an on-the-ground look at how discourses of formalization and specialization come together at the largest annual convention of podcasters in the United States: Podcast Movement. Based upon participant observations and interviews of participants at the 2016 Podcast Movement convention and several other podcasting conventions, this chapter explores how discourses of authenticity and creative freedom are often in conflict with the professional realities of today's podcast landscape.

The movement of commercial media into podcasting has brought with it some initial interest from brand advertisers. In Chapter 6, I explore the debate over audience metrics in podcasting and what that means for the future of the medium. The standardization of audience data is a key element of the formalization process, and the open architecture of podcasting has made efforts in this area somewhat scattershot. The movement of online platforms into podcasting has the potential to revolutionize the gathering and processing of listener data, though at the cost of privacy and the close relationships between creators and their audiences. Chapter 7 moves this discussion further by examining the key form of monetization in podcasting: advertising. Here I will explore how podcasting has historically differed from commercial radio in its approach to sponsored messages, opting less for pre-produced advertising "spots" and more for host-read advertisements. The emergence of key players in the podcast advertising scene such as podcast-specific ad agencies has largely institutionalized the process of buying and selling advertising for the medium. Major platforms like Anchor, Google, and Spotify are beginning to shift the terms of the market by pursuing "dynamic ad insertion," whereby advertising is digitally inserted into podcasts (postproduction), much as it is done in commercial broadcast radio. Through this pursuit of programmatic advertising, advertisers can spread their ad messages over a wide range of podcasts in an efficient manner, much as they do on other forms of media. Lastly, Chapter 7 explores some of the ways in which the content of podcasting itself is become part of "branded" experiences for companies. Major retailers such as Trader Joe's and McDonalds, for example, are creating original podcast content in order to draw attention to their brands.

In the conclusion I consider what these shifts mean for the future of podcasting. Podcasting's role as a forum for independent, amateur, and "authentic" cultural expression is being challenged by distinct formalization processes: the increased focus on effective methods of audience monitoring, monetization via advertising, standardization of production techniques, and aggressive forms of self-branding found in other forms of online cultural production. Podcasting is at a historic crossroads: formalization, specialization, and monetization may fundamentally challenge the democratic ethos of the medium, and it is imperative that we consider what might be lost.

CHAPTER ONE

Podcasting as a Twenty-First-Century Cultural Form

The stage was set in Cupertino, California on June 28, 2005, with a crowd of Apple faithful waiting excitedly for the latest announcements from then-Apple CEO Steven P. Jobs about the latest innovations in personal and portable computing at the Apple World Wide Developers Conference (WWDC). Jobs jaunted onto the stage in his signature black turtleneck and wasted little time launching into a celebration of Apple's new venture into brick-and-mortar retail stores, followed by an update on Apple's hit portable music playing device, the iPod, which at the time held a 75 percent market share of digital music devices. For our purposes, however, the most significant announcement at the 2005 WWDC was Jobs' announcement that podcasts would be integrated into Apple's popular iTunes desktop music management software. Jobs used two metaphors for described podcasting to the audience. First, he noted that podcasts could be understood as "TiVO for radio," allowing for radio broadcasts to be delivered to listeners on demand and asynchronously for greater access and convenience. He also referred to podcasting as "Wayne's World" for radio, a nod to podcasting's status as a largely amateur medium, much like the two public access TV amateurs depicted on the humorous *Saturday Night Live* sketch.

In 2005, Apple boasted that its iTunes podcasts directory featured "over 3,000" unique shows for listeners to select (Apple

2005). Fast forward sixteen years to 2021, and there are now over 2 million podcasts listed in the Apple Podcasts directory (Cridland 2021a). But this staggering growth since Steve Jobs' WWDC announcement has not been methodical. Instead, the medium that had relatively slow and steady year-on-year growth from 2005 up until about 2014 has grown exponentially since 2019. In fact the number of podcasts available has more than doubled in size (in terms of the number of unique podcasts available) since 2019, with recent data showing more than 2.5 million unique podcasts on the Apple Podcasts directory (Cridland 2023). This is meteoric growth in the production of podcasts, though some industry insiders have noted that 44 percent of those podcasts have three or fewer episodes, making the total number of regularly updated podcasts closer to 1.2 million (Goldstein 2021). Newly founded companies, legacy media from broadcast radio, and tech giants like Amazon, Google, and Spotify have all made major investments in podcasting since 2018, leading to something of a "Gold Rush" mentality.

The supply of new podcast content has also been met with rising audience demand around the world. Each year, more and more listeners discover that a wealth of free, exciting audio content on their mobile phones and begin to turn podcast consumption into a regular habit. Podcast growth is a global phenomenon. Survey data collected in August 2022 by eMarketer, a market research company, projected that the share of podcast listening in all regions of the world will continue to rise through 2026, with the United States seeing the largest percentage growth, followed by Western Europe (see Figure 1.1). Interestingly, these data indicate a much lower adoption rate in China, though the trend line is similarly upwards as more Chinese listeners discover podcasting.

In the United States, Edison Research and Triton Digital—two online audience research agencies—have tracked a growing consumer awareness of podcasting in their annual survey called *The Infinite Dial*. In their 2023 report, for example, they noted that 64 percent of respondents aged twelve and up reported having ever listened to a podcast, which amounts to an estimated 183 million listeners (Edison Research 2023). To place this in perspective, the same report in 2016 found that only 36 percent of Americans had ever listened to a podcast (or 98 million), so the total US podcast

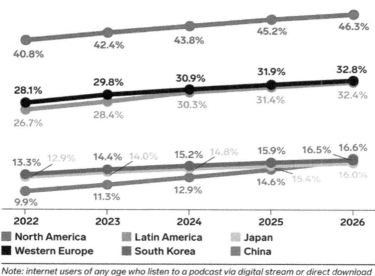

FIGURE 1.1 *Podcast listeners worldwide, by region/country, 2022–26 (percentage of internet users).*

Source: eMarketer. https://www.insiderintelligence.com/content/global-podcast-listener-forecast-2022–2026.

audience has essentially doubled since then (Edison Research 2016). Industry trackers project that the US podcast audience alone will reach 100 million in 2024 (Statista Research Department 2021b). While the podcast audience is still quite small when compared with broadcast radio, the growth in podcast listening has attracted the interest of advertisers, who are beginning to include podcasting in their media plans for brands, pumping more than US $800 million into the medium in 2020, with estimates that this spending will double to US $1.7 billion by 2024 (Adgate 2021). As this book will explore, the interest from major online content platform services like Spotify, Apple, Google, and Amazon is beginning to reshape the medium in important ways. On the one hand, the recent expansion of podcasting is a welcome development, since it is bringing new voices and audiences into a medium that was once dominated by a few, tech-savvy White men. While these platforms have expanded access to the medium, however, they have also inserted themselves into the ecosystem as powerful intermediaries. They have become erstwhile gatekeepers in a medium that had once celebrated its independence from the strictures of commercial media.

Radio Remediated? Defining Podcasting as a Unique Medium

Podcasting has become a powerful part of the cultural Zeitgeist, but what is it exactly? While the question seems rather straightforward, there is some complexity—and indeed disagreement—about what constitutes a "podcast" among scholars and practitioners alike. The "meaning of the medium" is not an idle, purely academic question, either. In fact, how we understand the experience known as "podcasting" is shaped by multiple forces, including the underlying technologies involved in producing and distributing audio, listeners' expectations and experiences, the social roles of the individuals who create podcasts (and those who support them in other professional roles), and, increasingly, large online platforms that help connect creators and audiences. As I will argue throughout this book, the fundamental structures that underlay the medium of podcasting are shifting thanks to the massive infusion of money into the industry by legacy media companies like iHeartMedia, SiriusXM, and National Public Radio, tech giants like Amazon, Google, and Spotify, and brand advertisers. Public broadcasters like National Public Radio (NPR) in the United States (Cwynar 2019), the Canadian Broadcast Corporation (CBC) (Cwynar 2015), the British Broadcast Corporation (BBC) (Berry 2020), and the Australian Broadcasting Corporation (ABC) have all invested heavily in expanding their podcast offerings (Murray 2009). Audiences' expectations for what podcasting should be—including what it should sound like—have also been shifting because of the rapid expansion of the medium in the past five years. All of these institutional changes are folding back onto independent podcasters, shaping their ideas about their own creative process, expectations for their labor, and aspirations for the future. Indeed, podcasting is currently at something of a historical inflection point that will shape the trajectory of the medium for the next decade.

As an audio medium, there is no question that podcasting shares a deep historical, psychic, and aesthetic connection to broadcast radio. As Andrew Bottomley (2020, 16) argues in his recent book *Sound Streams*, forms of internet audio stretching back to the dawn of the internet in the early 1990s up to and including podcasting "are all radio. That is, these are new radio practices rather than each being a separate new medium." Bottomley's argument that all forms of internet audio are radio leverages the theory of remediation (Bolter and Grusin 2000), wherein newer forms of media continually represent and extend earlier media forms, though the immediacy of these newer forms actively work to erase those linkages to the past. For Bottomley (2020, 3), "radio at its core represents a sonically mediated set of cultural relations that produce a social space that structures our everyday lives." Radio, then, is something he defines as "any nonmusic sound medium that is purposefully crafted *to be heard* by an audience." This definition of radio is extremely broad, of course, and captures a wide variety of sonic practices and outputs. The goal here is laudable, which is to move our collective attention away from the specific technology apparatus, and instead to understand audio technologies "as a set of cultural relations that is identifiable by a composite of textual codes and representational strategies, cultural and industrial structures, and production and listening practices" (Bottomley 2020, 25). But I will argue here that podcasting is distinct from radio, and understanding these points of difference is key for grasping why podcasting faces such major crossroads in the wake of formalization and platformization.

Extant scholarship on podcasting has rightly noted the close connections between the genres, sonic structures, and listening communities of podcasting with early radio enthusiasts in the 1920s and 1930s, particularly the DIY ethos surrounding the early years of radio's amateur period (Douglas 1999; Hilmes 1997). Early internet radio pioneers—the forerunners of the medium we understand today as podcasting—were keen to essentially extend the functions of broadcast radio into the newly launched internet. The fact that podcasting has become a business focus for large "legacy" media companies like iHeartMedia, SiriusXM, and Sony offers still more evidence that the medium is shaping up to be "Radio 2.0." As Menduni (2007) and Berry (2006) argued in early podcasting research, the mobility of podcasting coupled with its flexibility in terms of its liberation from the strict adherence to radio's hourly time clock presented the opportunity for podcasting to perhaps become a bridge between legacy and new online media. However, as I argue below, there are some good reasons for drawing some finer distinctions between radio and podcasting, particularly because the fundamental architecture, the distribution mechanisms, the production ethos, and the producer-listener relationship mark podcasting as something unique in our media landscape. While noting the similarities to radio, Berry (2016, 9) argued that "the 'radio' label might help the uninitiated, but it is not conducive to innovation and may actually distract us from attempts to fully theorize and investigate the form of podcasting on its own terms as it becomes more ingrained in our lives." In a similar vein, this book takes the uniqueness of podcasting as its entry point into a closer analysis of the sociocultural character of podcasting and the existential challenges it is facing from platform-based online media. How podcasting is integrated within an online ecosystem dominated by social media and platform-centered services will determine how the medium will survive and change in the next ten years and beyond.

Podcasting's Structures: Technology and Sonic Qualities

In brief, podcasting can be understood as "a technology used to distribute, receive, and listen, on-demand, to sound content produced by traditional editors such as radio, publishing houses, journalists, and educational institutions ... as well as content created by independent radio producers, artists, and radio amateurs" (Bonini 2015, 21). Bonini's definition here focuses on two specific aspects of a podcast: first, the technology of distributing audio over the internet, particularly its ability to deliver on-demand, asynchronous audio to listeners; and two, the nature of the content and its roots as an amateur medium that caters to niche interests from a wide variety of creators. Software programmer Dave Winer (who is integral to the history of podcasting) likewise offers a technical explanation for podcasting, describing it as "a series of digital media files made available over the open web through an RSS feed with enclosures" (Winer 2019). Similarly, Hansen (2021, 195) argues that a podcast is "a collection of downloadable files, of any format, served with accompanying metadata via an open updatable internet feed, primarily RSS." Here the focus is exclusively on the technical infrastructure for distributing audio via the internet, specifically RSS. One of the distinguishing features of podcasting is the openness of its distribution mechanism. Indeed, as Berry (2021) argues, it is difficult to imagine the creation and popularization of podcasting without the open infrastructure of RSS, which essentially lowered barriers to entry for producers and listeners alike, allowing for "the flowering of user generated content that characterized the medium's early development." The rise of online file sharing for audio is a key aspect of podcasting as well, since the advent of decentralized MP3 directories online like Napster and Gnutella paved the way for the exchange of audio files via the internet (Menduni 2007; Sterne 2012).

Podcasting, then, is clearly a technology for distributing audio files asynchronously over the internet, but there is clearly more to the ethos of podcasting than the nature of its distribution. Podcasting scholarship pioneer Richard Berry (2021) has provided some clarity on the definitional question by surveying the scholarly literature on podcasting. He locates three types of arguments on the meaning of a podcast: technical, sociocultural, and sonic. First, as outlined above, podcasting is a technology that leverages RSS and the portability of MP3 files to deliver audio content to listeners. But this integral factor of the medium, argues Berry, is inextricably intertwined with sociocultural environment that has emerged around podcasting. The "DIY spirit" of podcast content is largely a result of the grassroots, amateur content that attracted many to the medium, which was made possible largely due to the open architecture of podcasting and lack of institutional gatekeepers. Some of podcasting's most popular programs, he (2021) points out, would have been quickly rejected or heavily edited by the professional standards of commercial or public radio. Many shows are even somewhat voyeuristic in nature, with listeners encouraged to essentially "listen in" to everyday conversations among podcasts hosts about a variety of weighty or even taboo topics. Podcasting also offers a plethora of hyper-niche content that would likely never find a critical mass of listeners to make it commercially viable on broadcast radio. One look at the twenty-two different podcasts on the "Horse Radio Network"[1]—a group of podcast shows completely dedicated to horses, their care, and how to manage horse shows—demonstrates this truism. With over 2 million podcasts and counting, there seemingly is a podcast for every listener taste and preference. Podcasting's ability to "thrive on niche global audiences" is one of its key distinguishing characteristics (Spinelli and Dann 2019, 8).

But there is more to podcasting than a set of protocols and tools for distributing audio over the internet. The medium has developed some sonic features that are instantly recognizable as "podcasting" and distinguish it from contemporary radio as well (McHugh 2016). First, there is a relative freedom from oversight of its language, argues Berry (2021, 7) because radio must adhere to broadcast standards set by regulators to protect a station's license. Podcasts can tackle difficult or taboo topics (Anna Sale's podcast *Death, Sex, and Money* handles three such topics regularly, for example), and casual profanity lends the medium a kind of raw, unfiltered character that sounds more like an overheard conversation than a typical radio interview program. This sense of expressive freedom offered by podcasting is also evident in the ways that podcasts regularly remix different types of audio genres in unique ways. Dan Carlin's popular podcast *Hardcore History* (2006–), for example, blends a traditional historical journalism approach with dramatic styles of storytelling found more often in fan fiction (Salvati 2015). Second, because podcasts are typically consumed via headphones or earbuds, the individualized nature of this interaction leads to a close, intimate connection between the podcaster and the listener. Lindgren (2016), for example, notes that personal audio narratives have become a popular and identifiable genre format in podcasting, with shows such as *This American Life* (1995–), *Invisibilia* (2015–), and *Planet Money* (2008–), and of course *Serial* (2014) all blurring the typical boundaries between journalistic and intimate, personal storytelling. Podcasts also display a kind of narrative self-reflectivity

---

[1] https://www.horseradionetwork.com/

(Dowling and Miller 2019) and "critical (self)interrogation" (Llinares 2018) that brings audiences into the production process itself. These podcasts draw listeners into the narrative by making the on-air host an integral part of the story. Because podcasting has also become integrated (once again) with forms of social media, audiences are typically more actively engaged with podcasting content than other forms of media (Spinelli and Dann 2019, 8), which has become important for podcast advertisers and marketers seeking to similarly engage listeners in their brands and messaging.

Along with the sonic qualities of the medium, podcasting has rediscovered a number of audio content genres from broadcast radio's heyday such as dramas, crime and mystery shows, and even science fiction. Small, independent podcast productions like *Welcome to Night Vale* (2012–) have revived interest in radio drama (Bottomley 2015b), something that was a mainstay of US broadcast radio during its heyday in the 1930s (Verma 2012). Gimlet Media's *Homecoming* (2016–) skillfully deploys audio effects, atmospheric noises, and talented voice actors to create a sense of audio-realism and tension for listeners (Hoover 2022), similar to classic radio dramas like *The Shadow* (1937–54) and *Inner Sanctum* (1941–52). Berry (2015) notes that podcasting's 2014 breakout hit *Serial* unfolded much like a detective or crime series, with specific plot elements revealed slowly to create a fuller picture of a murder. Crime and police procedurals occupied a prominent place in the programming diet of commercial radio in the 1930s through the late 1950s in the United States, which was itself a re-interpretation of pulp magazines and serialized dime novels of an earlier era (Cheatwood 2010). The revival of these older radio program genres in podcasting—related of course to the copyright restrictions on playing commercial music in podcasts without express written permission (Lang 2006)—has served to distinguish the medium from contemporary radio, which is predominately devoted to playing recorded music.

Podcasting Cultures

Third, along with the technical and sonic qualities of podcasting, there are sociocultural features of the medium that distinguish it from radio. The question of who produces (or can produce) podcast content is also distinctly different from more professionalized media like television or broadcast radio. As Berry (2006) argued in one of the earliest scholarly work on the medium, podcasting has very low barriers to entry because anyone with a computer, a microphone, and an internet connection (which can now all be achieved via a smartphone) can essentially create and distribute podcasts to listeners. This, in turn, has encouraged a wide variety of individuals—from amateurs and pre-professionals to career-oriented content producers—to create new audio content. Because podcasting's growth in its first decade was driven largely by amateur, user-generated content (UGC), it shares some important similarities with other forms of online media production such as YouTube (Burgess 2012; Burgess and Green 2009) and blogging (Bruns 2008; Bruns and Jacobs 2006; Chia 2012; Duffy 2015; Lenhart and Fox 2006).

The practice of podcast listening is also something distinct from broadcast radio. As Berry (2016) notes, radio simply requires listeners to turn on the apparatus and then instantly encounter content, though the type of content will be entirely determined by the station at that given moment and subject to scheduling constraints. Podcasting, by contrast, "is not constrained by such fixed-point linearity" (Berry 2016, 12) because listeners can access specific types of content whenever they want, from a list of "self-curated" audio files that have been pre-selected. Additionally, unlike radio, podcasts are typically consumed via headphones for a more individualized, personal experience. A report from RAJAR (2020) in the UK, for instance, found that 57 percent of podcast listening occurred via headphones, as opposed to only 12 percent for live radio. Podcasting therefore creates a quite different atmosphere for the listener—one that encompasses a more intimate relationship between the audience and the content (Swiatek 2018). As some research has noted (Nadora 2019; Schlütz and Hedder 2021; Zuraikat 2020), this can also result in a parasocial relationship between listeners and podcast hosts, something that has begun to cause some concern within the podcast creator community (Euritt 2022; Williams 2019).

The producer-listener relationship is also a key marker of the podcasting experience, often because it forms the basis of the fragile economic ecosystem surrounding podcasting (to be discussed more in the next chapter). Since amateur productions take place outside of institutional structures of financial support, content creators often rely on direct support from listeners in the form of crowdfunding, merchandising, premium content, or even ticket sales for live performances. This provides yet another feature of podcasting that distinguishes it from mainstream commercial radio, namely the creation of a community of listeners around podcast content. For example, Black podcasters have created the sonic equivalent of "enclaved Black spaces like barber/beauty shops and churches" through their frank, uncensored, and intimate conversation style (Florini 2015). Similarly, Fox et al. (2020) found that Black podcasts like *The Read* (2013–) and *Still Processing* (2016–) provided a "potent articulation of Black identity and experience" which created a forum for broader social conversations about race in society. Early research on podcast producers also found that one of the prime motivations for these creators to continue their largely unpaid production work was "the relationships they had formed, the networking opportunities they discovered, and very frequently, the sense that they were part of a community of listeners" (Markman 2012, 557). The community ethos surrounding podcasting is an important aspect of the medium's identity and purpose.

Finally, as I outline in this book, there is an *institutional* and *structural* argument to be made for the uniqueness of podcasting as a medium. While Berry's (2021) overview imagines distinct categorical dimensions of podcasting (technical, sociocultural, and sonic), these dimensions interact with one another in important ways. In other words, the technological infrastructure of podcasting—its open ecosystem built on top of the essentially Web 1.0 technology of RSS—and the time period in which it emerged (in the early years of the 2000s) fostered a particular decentralized institutional structure for the medium. The emergence of an institutional structure for podcasting can be best understood by considering the dense thicket of interrelationships among technology and broader social, economic, and sonic contexts. My approach here draws from theories of the social construction of technology (W.E. Bijker 1997; Pinch and Bijker 1987) as well as actor-network theory (Latour 2005). These theorists argue that technologies are not distinct elements somehow outside of human social relations, but are instead actors that operate within complex systems of social interactions. Similar to Sterne's (2006, 826) approach to the MP3 file format, technological artifacts or processes such as podcasting must be considered as "a crystallized set of social and material relations." The social constructivist approach is particularly crucial for understanding podcasting because the meaning of the medium itself has shifted during its history as users and organizations have leveraged the technology and content in different ways.

For instance, podcasting was the direct beneficiary of broader movements of cyberlibertarianism that emerged during the 1990s (Turner 2006), captured in its essence by John Perry Barlow's 1996 online essay (2019), the "Declaration of Independence for Cyberspace." The explicit promise of the World Wide Web was to free society from the constraints of both corporate domination and governmental regulation. Podcasting's promise was that it could provide an outlet for creative audio expression without the influence of institutional gatekeepers or regulatory oversight and control (Spinelli and Dann 2019, 8). The fact that broadcast radio is federally regulated in the United States, UK, and many other nations provides a contrast to the essentially unregulated arena of podcasting. The expressive freedom of podcasting to capture more unfiltered, raw conversations and expression, noted above by Berry (2021), can be understood in this broader historical context. The open nature of RSS, the underlying distribution mechanism for podcasting, is a key element of the medium because its nonproprietary nature spurred technical innovations that were instrumental to the early growth of the medium. Software hacks like former MTV VJ Adam Curry's iPodder software—which updated new audio files into Apple's iTunes software to transfer the files to an iPod—were indicative of the type of software development common among the free, open source software (F/OSS) movement that was flourishing thanks to the dot com boom (Bollier 2008; Kelty 2008). The open architecture of RSS also fostered a culture of entrepreneurism that resulted in the early launch of independent podcast hosting companies (such as Libsyn and Blubrry/Rawvoice, among others).

Platforms and Podcasting

In *Podcasting: The Audio Media Revolution*, Spinelli and Dann (2019) highlight the distinguishing features of podcasting mentioned above such as its mobile character, the sense of intimacy associated with listening, the asynchronous nature of content access and listener control, the ease of content creation and distribution without the necessity of institutional gatekeeper, as well as the active engagement of listeners. They added two other unique features of podcasting: The fact that the content is "evergreen" and available in perpetuity online (unlike "live" media such as broadcast radio) and that podcasting is associated with a "freemium" model of monetization, whereby the core product (the podcast) is distributed for free and income, is earned via secondary means such as advertising, crowdfunding, and merchandising. In a sign of the dramatic transformations that have reshaped podcasting even in the short time since the publication of Spinelli and Dann's book, subscription-based podcasting has become much more common. Spotify (2020), for example, has begun making exclusive content deals with a number of popular podcasts such as *The Joe Rogan Experience* and *Armchair Expert with Dax Sheppard* (Carman 2021d). These podcasts will no longer be distributed via RSS but will be streamed directly and exclusively from Spotify's web servers. In 2021, both Apple (Perez 2021) and Spotify (Carman 2021c) also launched their own premium podcast subscription services, whereby creators can charge listeners a recurring subscription fee to access their shows. Podcasting networks such as Luminary, Stitcher Premium, Wondery, PodcastOne Premium, and Audible, among others, offer bundles of podcasts for a monthly subscription fee, much like video streaming services such as Netflix, Amazon Prime, and Disney Plus.

Additionally, we can no longer take for granted that podcasting remain free and available for download on the internet "in perpetuity," as Spinelli and Dann suggest. As the above examples illustrate, some podcast content is being stored behind paywalls and inaccessible to listeners as part of the open RSS ecosystem. As the number of podcasts has exploded in the past several years, so too has the number of "podfaded" shows, or shows that are abandoned by their creators. A recent analysis by podcast journalist James Cridland (2021b) found that 81 percent of all shows hosted by Anchor.fm (now Spotify for Podcasters), the largest podcast hosting platform (mainly because it offers free content hosting for creators) had not been updated in the past ninety days. Looking across all podcast hosting providers, 44 percent of podcasts have produced three or fewer episodes (Goldstein 2021). While podfaded content may be stored on online servers for some period of time, there is no guarantee that it will always be available. As Morris (2017) discovered, for example, when Dropbox changed its terms of service and disabled links for files stored in public folders, access to podcast content was disrupted. Locating archival audio content from podcasts as recent as fifteen or twenty years ago has become quite challenging for scholars, leading podcasting historian Andrew Bottomley (2021) to lament that archives from radio in the 1930s are often more accessible to scholars than podcasting content from the early 2000s. The fragility of RSS for the purposes of locating online podcast content—a necessity for any archival research on the medium—has spurred efforts the PodcastRE project, which aims to archive podcasts for future audio historians (Morris 2017). The fact that some new podcast content is being released on proprietary online platforms outside of the distribution mechanism of RSS makes the task of archiving podcast content even more challenging.

In the wake of these dizzying changes, many industry observers have asked: If a serialized audio program is locked behind a paywall, available only via a specific online platform or service, and available to listeners only via a streaming app and not as a downloaded MP3 file, *is it still a podcast?* The question of whether or not these new forms of audio distribution veer away from the aforementioned definitional boundaries of podcasting is not altogether that important. What is important, however, is that these distributional shifts are altering the structural dynamics of the medium. Instead of audio distributed freely via an open web standard, platform services are now courting popular podcasters with the promise of large paydays for the exclusive rights to their content. While open ecosystem of RSS allowed the medium to be "plugged in" to new apps and features during its long maturation, the goal of platform services—whether social media or audio—is to make sure that audiences stay locked into their services for all of their information and entertainment needs. As I explore in Chapter 3, platforms are also sophisticated surveillance machines that carefully monitor every user interaction, which makes them tailor made for the creation and monetization of audience activity. These platforms also rely heavily on sophisticated algorithms to serve up recommended content in one seamless interface. These are conveniences for the listener, to be sure, but added together these changes amount to nothing less than a sea change in how podcasting is being experienced by audiences. The new model privileges a "push" model wherein content is actively served up to the listener, in contrast to podcasting's earlier "pull" model of active discovery and curation by the audience. In addition, the rapid influx of capital into the ecosystem via acquisitions, brand advertising, and cross-media synergies are introducing corporate logics to the production of content. This folds back onto independent podcast creators as well, as cultures of entrepreneurism and professionalism begin to shape their labors.

RSS: An Infrastructure of Openness

The distinct character of podcasting as a medium emerges from a variety of technical and sociocultural factors. That being said, it's worth getting technical for a moment and focus some attention briefly on the distributional infrastructure of podcasting, RSS, because it has played a vital role in helping to shape podcasting's identity and broader industrial ecosystem up to this point in its existence. It also serves as an important counterpoint to the platformization processes that are slowly remaking the medium, as later chapters will explore. Podcasting entered the popular lexicon relatively early in its history, having been names the "Word of the Year 2005" by the New Oxford American Dictionary (Bierma 2005). However, the underlying infrastructure that allows podcasting to function—RSS—is less well understood by the public. For example, an early Infinite Dial report released in 2006 found that 22 percent of a nationwide sample of Americans were familiar with the term "podcasting" (Rose and Rosin 2006). A Pew Research nationwide survey of Americans from 2005, on the other hand, found that just 9 percent of respondents had any idea what "RSS feeds" were (Rainie 2005). RSS remains perhaps the least well-understood aspect of podcasting, in part because it is now largely invisible to listeners, buried deep within in the code and protocols of the apps that serve up audio content.

RSS emerged on the cusp of the twenty-first century before the advent of social media and the cloud. The concept for behind RSS, known as "Rich Site Summary" (or, "Real Simple Syndication," though its original name was itself a hyphenated acronym of "RDF Site Summary"), was to allow users to subscribe to blogs or other text-based information on websites and get updated when new content was released without having to navigate to the website itself (for an excellent overview of RSS history, see Hansen 2021). This was important in the 1990s, when many websites with images or large amounts of text were often quite slow to load due to relatively low bandwidth capabilities. The first 0.90 version of RSS was initially developed by Dan Libby and Ramanathan V. Guha at Netscape in March of 1999 as a value-added feature for the browser (RSS Advisory Board 2021). RSS was actually first developed by Guha at Apple Computers in 1995, though it was called the MCF (Meta Content Format) at the time (Wittenbrink 2005, 25). RSS allowed any web portal or browser to display headlines and URLs from other websites within the same page, which was a strong value-added feature at a time when bandwidth was relatively scarce (Hammersley 2003, 3). The RSS standard is based upon the XML file format, an open text-based format for presenting information on the web. At its most basic level, RSS is a set of XML elements and attributes for those elements, along with a hierarchical connection between them. UserLand Software CEO Dave Winer was one of the original contributors to the RSS code and advocated that it be kept as simple as possible in order to encourage user adoption and more widespread use. After Netscape abandoned the development of RSS, it was forked into two separate development projects, one with RDF code (Version 1.0) developed by Rael Dornfest at O'Reilly Media and the other by Dave Winer (Version 0.91) which eschewed RDF code for a simpler XML-only standard (Hammersley 2003, 4).

The simpler version of RSS maintained by Dave Winer is key for the development of what became known as podcasting. The idea to leverage the ease of RSS to assist the distribution of online content was originally hatched by RSS developer Dave Winer and independent radio broadcaster Adam Curry. The key innovation for podcasting occurred in the October 25, 2000 0.92 release of RSS when Dave Winer and UserLand Software included the <enclosure> tag, which allowed both text-based and media files to be directly referenced by the RSS feed (RSS Advisory Board 2021). This allowed audio files to be referenced from anywhere on the internet and solved the problem of audio streaming latency that had bedeviled proto-podcasting services in the 1990s (Bottomley 2020). Users could leverage the enclosure feature of RSS to access and download updated content overnight or when data usage was low. In 2004 former MTV VJ Adam Curry used Apple's iTunes API to write a brief AppleScript program to link the RSS feed to iTunes, thus allowing the MP3 files to transfer directly into iTunes and, subsequently to an iPod for consumption. Curry's programming hack, appropriately called "iPodder," opens the gates to casual users to subscribe to syndicated audio content and forever linked the medium to Apple's mobile platform (later called iOS when the iPhone was unveiled in 2007). The code for RSS has changed little over the years, and version 2.0 of the specification, written by Winer, has been essentially frozen in place since March 30, 2009 (RSS Advisory Board 2021).

There are several important facets of RSS that bear on the nature of how podcasting has developed over time. These bear mentioning here because these technical affordances of RSS feeds have enabled specific types of development and innovation that have shaped the medium throughout the first two decades of its existence. RSS feeds are vital for podcasting because they allow for:

Distribution—At its core, RSS is a distribution technology, acting like a sophisticated telephone book that connects listeners with audio content, regardless of where that content is stored on the internet. RSS has served as a core element of the medium since its inception, and even twenty years after its birth continues to be the core of the medium, driving the discoverability of content via major directories like Apple Podcasts, Google Podcasts, and Spotify (Morris 2021). The distribution infrastructure of RSS has also driven the development of server-side metrics for the medium, which is discussed in detail in Chapter 6.

Syndication—RSS feeds are ingenious in their highly functional simplicity. It seems bewildering that even in today's complex online environment featuring powerful tech platforms like Google, Amazon, Facebook, and Apple that are interconnected via APIs, a simple text-based XML file can alert millions of listeners to updated audio content and facilitate access to that content from anywhere on the web. In one of the earliest scholarly treatments of podcasting as a media form, Sterne et al. (2008a) pointed to this aspect of RSS which "creates an expectation of seriality which shapes both production and consumption practice: podcasts are supposed to repeat over time, so listeners subscribe to 'shows' and podcasters make 'shows'." Thus, the notion of podcast "shows" with updated "episodes" with new content is a consequence, at least in part, of the underlying technology for distributing the content. While the medium is slowly evolving to include more short-form audio stories and even social audio with services like Clubhouse, Spotify Green Room, and Twitter Spaces, among others (Skinner 2021), the legacy media structure of "shows" and "episodes" continues to define podcasting today.

Transparency—RSS feeds are plain text XML files that can be viewed and downloaded by anyone on the web. There is nothing secretive or proprietary about RSS feeds, as they reveal the exact URL addresses where the content (in the case of podcasting, audio files) is stored as well as other information about that has been uploaded or added by the feed creator. This transparency is lost when cloud-based platforms offer audio files via their own systems, since the original source files are hidden behind proprietary software. As Hansen (2021) outlines, the transparency of RSS feeds also tells the podcatcher software what kind of content is referred to, what genre or category the content fits into, content links (show notes), and even a full transcript of the content (in other words, it contains useful *metadata*). This allows for ease of organization and even sorting and identification of content that is distributed via these feeds. Directories and third-party podcasting apps make use of this information to allow users to sort podcast content by genre, author, keywords, or other criteria. The transparency of the XML file also makes it possible for other software to ensure that the RSS feed is valid by ensuring that it contains the basic elements of a <channel> parent item along with a <title>, <link>, and <description> information, along with an <enclosure> item with an audio file to download.

Flexibility—Although the RSS specification has essentially remained frozen since version 2.0.11 in 2009 (RSS Advisory Board 2021), the functionality of RSS can be greatly expanded without changing the fundamental nature of the underlying code itself thanks to the addition of namespaces. Namespaces are essentially prefixes in the tags that allow the user to further specify elements within the feed by appending a keyword descriptor in front of an existing item to clarify its meaning (Hemenway 2002). In this way, even though development on the core RSS specification is essentially frozen, RSS can continue to be expanded through the deployment of new namespaces, though these typically require that feed readers and podcatching software adapt to recognize these new namespaces in order to allow end user to benefit for them. A new project to expand the utility of RSS is Podcasting 2.0, launched by podcasting pioneer Adam Curry and developer Dave Jones (2020). The project has added a new <podcast> namespace to RSS along with the ability to add transcripts, chapters, and other useful features to RSS. This type of volunteer software development around podcasting would not be possible without the flexibility and openness of RSS.

Decentralized control—Finally, perhaps the most important feature of RSS—and by extension the podcasting ecosystem as a whole—is its decentralized structure. This makes it difficult for one organization or individual to guide the evolution of podcasting for self-serving purposes. This is partly a result of programmer Dave Winer's orientation to information. As podcasting veteran Eric Nuzum (2019, 234) remarks, "Dave believed in making systems open, democratic, and easily accessible, going against the prevailing tide to make material on the Internet as proprietary, controlled, and commercialized as possible." As a result of this decentralization, podcasting's institutional dynamics are fluid and continually shifting, with new companies, services, and producers coming into the medium almost daily. While this fast-paced development makes the prospect of writing a book on podcasting daunting at best, it is a sign of the medium's relative health and competitiveness. As the next two chapters outline, however, the investment of large tech and media companies like Spotify, Google, iHeartMedia, and SiriusXM in podcasting in the past several years has begun to shift the decentralized nature of the business toward more platform-driven services. Platforms offer centralized hubs for content distribution and consumption and generally connect to partner services mainly via proprietary APIs (Bodle 2011), which are closed systems that are governed by the needs and desires of the platform. Individuals and businesses that have thrived in the context of podcasting's decentralized industrial model are beginning to push back against what they regard as the threat of platform-based media and the resulting loss of institutional freedom they represent.

Podcasting Today: Trends in Spoken Word Audio

Podcasting continues to grow as a medium, continually adding more listeners, more content, and more investment from advertisers and media firms alike. In spite of its unique structure and heritage, as noted above, podcast content nevertheless bears strong similarities to content found on talk radio today. Many of podcasting's most recognized shows are the stock and trade of traditional broadcast radio: Celebrities interviewing other celebrities (*The Joe Rogan Experience, Conan O'Brien Needs a Friend*), news magazines (*The Daily*), political talk programs (*The Rachel Maddow Show, Pod Save America*), documentaries (*This American Life, Serial*), and even general interest programming (*Freakonomics Radio, Hidden Brain, Radiolab*). The amount of podcast listening is also increasing with each year. According to the 2023 Edison Research Infinite Dial (2023) report, US podcast listeners reportedly listened to an average of nine podcast "shows" per week, eight shows per week from the previous year.

What types of content define the podcasting medium today? This straightforward question is tricky to answer, mainly because there isn't a single source of universal data about the medium. This has complicated the process of gathering easily comparable statistics about what is being produced and who is listening (a key topic to which I return in Chapter 6). There are also differences in content between the *production* and *consumption* of podcast content. On the production side, when creators upload their content to major directories such as Apple Podcasts (Apple n.d.), they must specify a specific content genre and sub-genre for their podcast. A podcast on personal finance decisions might select "Business: Investing" as the closest category and sub-category that matches the content, for example. An overview of all podcast content conducted by Pacific Content's (former) Head of Audience Development Dan Misener (2021) examined over 1.5 million unique podcasts listed in Apple's directory and found that the content categories with the largest number of podcasts were "Education" and "Society & Culture," followed by "Arts" (see Figure 1.2). As the Apple Podcast category listings demonstrate, the vast majority of podcasting content is oriented toward education and discussion of topical content. When

Content Category	Podcasts
Education	213,558
Society & Culture	213,530
Arts	158,274
Religion & Spirituality	152,827
Business	149,647
Comedy	118,227
Health & Fitness	95,943
Leisure	81,295
Music	81,064
News	72,967
TV & Film	44,797
Kids & Family	33,257
Technology	31,221
Science	31,107
History	28,349
Fiction	22,102
Sports	20,723
Government	10,709
True Crime	6,876
TOTAL	**1,566,473**

FIGURE 1.2 *Most popular content genres in Apple Podcasts, ranked by size (April, 2021).*

Source: Misener, D. (2021, April 1). The most crowded categories in Apple Podcasts (April 2021 edition). *Medium.* https://blog.pacific-content.com/the-most-crowded-categories-in-apple-podcasts-april-2021-edition-273b3d59866e.

Misener sorted the categories based upon episode count rather than podcast show, however, the picture changed dramatically, with "Religion & Sprituality" episodes accounting for a whopping almost 8.27 million, far and away the most common episode category, followed by "Society & Culture" episodes in distant second place at almost 3.64 million.

The *consumption* side of podcasting—or the categories of content to which users are actually listening—looks quite different from the above trends in the types of content available. For example, a nationwide survey of almost 12,000 US podcast listeners in 2021–2 conducted by Edison Research (see Figure 1.3) found that the podcasting genres of greatest interest were Comedy and Society & Culture, followed by News, True Crime, Sports, and Business. Podcasting has also revived a number of narrative forms that were once popular on radio such as scripted dramas, though their consumption is relatively small when compared to the other topical, talk-based genres.

Podcasting during COVID-19

The global pandemic of 2019–20 violently reshuffled much of our media landscape, from shuttered movie theaters to dramatic decreases in broadcast radio usage thanks to the loss of the in-car "drive time" commute (Inside Radio 2020). A number of industry insiders began to sound the alarm early in 2020 that podcasting too would likely experience a significant drop in listenership thanks to the pandemic and the profound disruption in daily routines that resulted. But something interesting happened with podcasting during the pandemic—it not only survived the profound disruption of COVID-19, it actually rebounded and displayed impressive growth. As journalist Nicholas Quah (2021) observed, one of the reasons for the relative strength of podcasting in comparison to other media during the same period that "[podcasting] lent well to remote production workflows, which in turn attracted more participation from creators and celebrity talent and media companies, which in turn led to the creation of more podcasts and greater recruitment of their respective followings into the medium." Early in the pandemic in March of 2000, for example, major podcasting production organizations like NPR along with public radio stations in the

U.S. Top Podcast Genres, By Reach
Weekly Podcast Listeners Q4 2021 – Q3 2022

#	Genre
1	Comedy
2	Society & Culture
3	News
4	True Crime
5	Sports
6	Business
7	Arts
8	History
9	Religion & Spirituality
10	Education
11	Health & Fitness
12	TV & Film
13	Music
14	Science
15	Technology
16	Fiction
17	Leisure
18	Kids & Family
19	Government

How The Study Was Conducted: The Edison Podcast Metrics Q4 2021- Q3 2022 Top Podcast Genres, By Reach is based upon 11,675 online interviews with weekly podcast consumers in the United States, ages 18 and older. Interviews were conducted in English and Spanish from 10/1/2021 – 9/30/2022. Genres are based on the information podcast shows report to the Apple API. All respondents reported listening to podcasts in the last week. Data weighted using The Infinite Dial from Edison Research, Wondery and ART19.

FIGURE 1.3 *Leading podcast genres in the United States (Q3 2022).*
Source: Edison Research. 2023. "Weekly Insights 1.11.2023—Top Podcast Genres in the U.S. Q3 2022." Edison Research (blog). January 11, 2023. https://www.edisonresearch.com/weekly-insights-1-11-2023-top-podcast-genres-in-the-u-s-q3-2022/.

United States shifted abruptly to remote-based recording and editing in order to comply with the necessities of social distancing (Quah and Crampton 2020). Independent producers, many of whom conducted interviews for their podcasts, adjusted to the limitations of online video conferencing platforms like Zoom and Google Meet, with reduced audio quality on recordings. Some podcasting-related services were poised to take advantage of the forced shift to remote recording, however. Salt Lake City company Zencastr, which offers end to end high quality recording of interviews for remote podcasters, expanded its platform to include video with millions of dollars in venture capital funding (Heater 2021), while rival Squadcast.fm secured its own outside funding (Ganguly 2021).

Conclusion

As this chapter has explored, podcasting has emerged as a major cultural and media form in the early twenty-first century. As an aural medium featuring numerous interconnections with radio, especially the similarities in genres of spoken word content such as current events, sports, comedy, and journalistic documentaries—all of which are staples of broadcast radio—it is tempting to imagine podcasting as the next evolutionary iteration of radio itself. However, as I have argued in this chapter, podcasting has unique technical, sonic, and institutional qualities that distinguish it from radio. The production practices of the medium are distinct in the sense that they are distributed among both professional and amateur producers (and all shades in between) due to the traditional absence of formal aesthetic and organizational gatekeeping. The podcasting experience is also characterized by a greater sense of intimacy due to the fact that most listening occurs with headphones. This creates a close psychic bond between the podcaster and the listener that is distinct from more casual radio consumption. Podcasting shares a culture of participation that engages audiences to build communities of interest around shows and their hosts.

Without veering into the conceptual trap of technological determinism, I have also argued here that the distribution mechanism for podcasting—RSS—is integral to the definition of the medium. The fact that podcast audio files are distributed via the open architecture of RSS carries with it a number of important consequences and expectations for the medium, such as the notion of seriality (the structure of "shows" and "episodes"). The transparency, universality, and simplicity of XML—the core of RSS—has served as a base for key technical innovations, such as podcast directories like iTunes (now Apple Podcasts) as well as entrepreneurial investments in the medium, especially during the past decade. There are significant changes on the horizon, however, and podcasting sits at the precipice of another inflection point in its relatively short history. Specifically, major investments from big tech and legacy media companies, along with the emerging prominence of major online platforms, are beginning to challenge the primacy of RSS for the medium. As the next chapter on the industrialization of podcasting will explore, these moves are beginning to change the essence of the medium itself.

CHAPTER TWO

Podcasting as a Media Industry—Formalization from Above and Below

Built upon the infrastructure of RSS, podcasting is a unique cultural form that has enjoyed a somewhat meteoric rise following both the popular success of *Serial* and the inclusion of a default podcast app in iOS, both of which occurred in 2014. While some scholars such as Henry Jenkins, Axel Bruns, and Yochai Benkler have argued that the web provides unparalleled possibilities for democratic participation thanks to low entry barriers, this chapter analyzes market data to demonstrate that corporate gatekeepers are moving into the podcasting ecosystem and beginning to privilege specific types of content and audiences, which moves them into the position of becoming tastemakers for a growing audience of listeners.

The changes underway in podcasting are chiefly the result of industry *formalization.* Formalization describes the process by which "media systems become progressively more rationalized, consolidated and financially transparent. It can happen as a result of increased state intervention in a particular industry, which finds itself dragged into the light of regulation and accountability. Alternatively, it can occur when formerly small-scale media concerns become integrated into larger-scale structures" (Lobato and Thomas 2015, 27). In the case of podcasting, the latter style of formalization is found, whereby well-known amateur podcasters with sizable audiences are being recruited to join podcast networks, lured by the potential for a larger percentage of advertising sales revenue and the ability to expand their audience via cross-promotion with other shows on the same network. There is another aspect to the formalization of podcasting as well, however. Namely, existing media producers—many of them from legacy media such as commercial or public radio—are entering the podcasting space with existing (e.g., time-shifted) content or new content and directly competing with those amateurs. This is having some recursive effects as well. Namely, the production values, audio quality, content genres, distribution methods, and monetization structures are becoming standardized, and are beginning to inform the production practices of amateurs. Thus, podcasting is in the slow process of transitioning from a largely informal, amateur medium to one that looks more similar to traditional media industries like television, radio, and motion pictures: several large players dominating the production and distribution of products, and controlling the lion's share of the revenue as well.

This chapter examines the formalization of podcasting through the lens of media industry studies in order to map the current landscape for podcast production, distribution, and exhibition. First, I briefly sketch out the contours of a critical media industries approach to podcasting, being careful to note the differences in industries such as podcasting where amateurs compete directly with professionals for audience attention. Next, Joseph Turow's "power roles" framework is leveraged to outline the key players in podcasting today. The podcasting ecosystem is undergoing seismic changes thanks to a wave of mergers and acquisitions by large media corporations and platform services. Monetization of podcast content via subscription-based services, paywalls, and advertising are key factors that are contributing to the rapid formalization of the medium. These forms of "top down" formalization are being accompanied by different forms of "bottom up" formalization through the emergence of professional organizations, labor collectives, unions, and podcast trade journalism. As I argue in this chapter, we can better understand the changes taking place within the medium by applying the analytical framework of critical media industry studies.

Podcasting as a Hybrid Media Industry

As the previous chapter outlined, podcasting emerged as an important cultural form in the twenty-first century, but can it be understood as a media *industry*? To answer this question, we need to reach back into the rich tradition of scholarly inquiry into the structures of media production and distribution stretching back to the early twentieth century. Scholars in this tradition have explored the impacts of industrial conditions on the production of culture. As a student of so-called legacy media industry studies in the 1990s, I came to appreciate the grounded frameworks offered by political economic and cultural theories of media production. The industrial tradition draws attention to the economic, structural, and organizational processes that shape the production of cultural texts and the impacts of those processes on both the texts themselves and their reception by audiences. The industrial tradition of cultural production typically includes the following in its empirical gaze:

- Cultural production by large, complex organizations (those that are both capital- and labor-intensive, therefore requiring sophisticated management structures)
- Mass communication technologies (Broadcast and cable television, radio, film, print books, magazines, newspapers)
- Formal economic systems of exchange (market systems, profit-driven, resource-driven, competition, relatively high economic risk)
- A professionalized labor force with highly specialized skills
- Established legal frameworks (copyright, monopoly and corporate ownership restrictions, free speech protections, etc.)
- Mass audiences (large, heterogeneous audiences who offer relatively limited forms of feedback to media producers).

The scope of analysis in the industrial tradition encompasses both the structures of an industry and the organizational dynamics (including production and distribution practices) within those industries. In this context, an industry has been understood as "a conglomeration of organizations that work together in a regulated fashion to create and distribute products or services" (Turow 1997, 12). In *Media Systems in Society*, Turow argued that media industries are responsible for mass communication, which he defined as "the industrialized production, reproduction, and multiple distribution of messages through technological devices" (1997, 12). This places the emphasis on institutionalized production, though today's online digital environment is marked by much more fluid boundaries between professional and amateur productions. A more ecumenical definition is that of "cultural industries," or industries which "make and circulate texts" (Hesmondhalgh 2007, 3). Hesmondhalgh's definition shifts the focus away from the conditions of production (via large organizations) and places it on the outputs of production. Since cultural industries produce and distribute media texts, they are therefore "most directly involved in the production of social meaning" (2007, 12). Herbert, Lotz, and Punathambekar (2020, 5) point to some distinctions of media industries that have been pointed out by economists, such as "high first-copy costs, their status as public goods, and low-to-no marginal costs" for reproduction. But because the products of these industries are *cultural* in nature, examining how they are produced and distributed is instrumental in grasping how our notions of self and society are circulated via these products.

Key to media industries scholarship in the industrial tradition is an understanding the how power structures and control of resources shape the dynamics of that industry, especially media content. Havens and Lotz (2011), for example, outline an "industrialization of culture" framework which identifies several important aspects of media industry operations such as "mandates" (commercial and government regulations), conditions (technological structures, regulatory structures, and economic concerns), and practices (professional roles). Havens and Lotz's notion of practices is an extension of Joseph Turow's "power roles" framework. These models for understanding cultural production—conceptualized long before the popularization of the internet—are premised on the type of industrialized cultural production outlined above, and calibrated to an environment in which key resources are limited. Companies with control over these resources can leverage them in order to reach their goals, achieve profitability, and to gain access to more resources and market power.

Many of the core assumptions of the approaches of the industrial model—the systematized production and distribution of cultural products by large organizations, the specialization of labor practices into clearly definable roles, the necessity of large amounts of capital, and the clear differentiation between producers and audiences—have been fundamentally challenged by the rise of so-called amateur media in the twenty-first century. In an era wherein the reproduction and distribution costs of information are negligible thanks to the internet, the traditional power dynamics of cultural production industries are dramatically changing. Today's online media are essentially *hybrid industries* in the sense that they incorporate both formal and informal production and distribution structures. Lobato and Thomas (2015, 26) have defined the "informal economy" as "an analytic concept that refers to a range of activities and processes occurring outside the official, authorized spaces of the economy." The informal economy essentially incorporates all economic activity that occurs "beyond the view of the state" (p. 27), such as domestic housework, non-market production, garage-based technological innovation, and of course illicit or black market activity. Formal and informal economies are not separate spheres of activity, argue Lobato and Thomas (2015), but are instead interdependent, with each element shaping the other. In the sphere of media, for example, the industrialized production of a blockbuster motion picture like the *Lord of the Rings* trilogy, for example, can incorporate fan activity such as blogs and social media to extend the marketing for the film. Indeed, circulation of these types of media "paratexts" (Gray 2010), some of which are created by amateurs, has become a vital part of the commercial media production process.

Informal economic activity can occur within formal media organizations, for example, when businesses crowdsource their innovations to some of their best customers (so-called lead users) as a means for harnessing the innovations taking place outside of institutional contexts (Von Hippel 2005). The reverse process can also occur when amateurs begin to develop formal processes and structures to guide their own activities, also known as formalization. As I will outline in this chapter and the balance of the book, processes of formalization are well underway in podcasting, much as they are in other cultural forms found on YouTube (Burgess 2012; Burgess and Green 2018) and social media (Cunningham 2012; Cunningham and Craig 2021). These formal and informal processes are continually dynamic, and can be found at various stages of a continuum from one to the other. Lobato et al. (2012) argue that forms of media that rely upon user-generated content (UGC) occupy a "spectrum" that extends across multiple dimensions, each of which is also shifting over time. Moreover, the boundaries between formal and informal are often fluid and difficult to disentangle.

Lobato and Thomas (2015, 67) identify three categories of interactions in media industries—functions, effects, and controls—that are useful for delineating the boundaries between formal and informal. *Functions* refers to ways in which informal elements get used within formal media markets, such as the use of freelancers or informal processes to solve specific internal problems. *Effects* refers to the impacts of informal processes being incorporated into more formal systems. One example they provide of this effect is the substitution of the free, online crowdsourced website Wikipedia for the Encyclopedia Brittanica. In the case of podcasting, the distribution of radio programs via RSS in the form of podcasts—such as NPR has done with its lineup of time-shifted radio shows—has expanded the reach and popularity of existing programs while creating anxiety for traditional radio stations about their future (Bilton 2014). Finally, *controls* refers to the "ways of managing, organizing, or understanding informality" (Lobato and Thomas 2015, 67). Controls are ways of restricting, codifying, systematizing, or otherwise managing informal processes through governance structures or socially enforced rules. In the absence of the kind of formal regulatory structures that have been established for legacy media in most countries, emergent media forms such as podcasting, vidcasting, and social media entertainment will experience the introduction of controls as they formalize over time. As I will discuss below, the changes underway in podcasting can be more fully understood by considering the ways in which its informal and formal aspects are shifting over time.

Podcasting can be understood as a kind of hybrid media industry that incorporates both formal and informal economies. The medium has strong roots as an amateur endeavor borne of innovators excited by the potential of the internet to syndicate the distribution of sound. At the same time, however, podcasting has clearly grown out of the formal and institutional traditions of radio. From its beginnings, podcasting incorporated a mixture of amateur and professional voices. That there was any space for amateurs and tech enthusiasts at all in podcasting is in part due to "existing mainstream media's hesitancy to invest heavily in internet radio (and internet media, more generally)" (Bottomley 2020, 101). With this in mind, it is still clear that we can understand production practices in the fledgling medium "in the context of the long history of radio dissemination and radiophony, particularly the tradition incorporating amateur radio, community radio, and other manifestations of the citizen voice" (Madsen and Potts 2010, 34). Indeed, many of the early pioneers in internet radio were "early adopters were technologists or entrepreneurs coming from completely outside the broadcasting field," which worked to distinguish online audio as a realm for experimentation and exploration outside of the boundaries of traditional institutional gatekeepers. KYCY, a San Francisco radio station and one of the earliest innovators, even experimented with an all-podcast format beginning in May of 2005 (Bonini 2015). The BBC began releasing some of its own programs, such as *In Our Time*, as podcasts in October 2004, and launched a dedicated podcasting service in 2007 (Bonini 2015).

Given the hybrid nature of podcasting, how should we endeavor to investigate these shifts? I argue that the analytical tools developed by critical political economic and media industries scholars are still valuable in helping to understand the dynamics of the podcasting industry today. To this end, I will leverage Turow's (1997) power roles framework to outline the players within the key roles in this industry. Turow describes power roles as "resource-controlling relationships" within a media industry as a means to grasp the ways in power operates through the collection and leverage of resources. The key power roles for any media industry—the production, distribution, and exhibition of content—are outlined below for the podcasting industry. The emergence of other key players within podcasting such as advertisers, mobile apps, and professional organizations to systematize and authenticate the skills of freelance labor is all features of a rapidly formalizing medium.

Mapping the Production Cycle in Podcasting Today

The process of producing and distributing a podcast to audiences can be accomplished in a number of different ways. In some cases, specific companies and providers are involved at various stages of the value chain from production through distribution and exhibition. Increasingly, however, thanks both to consolidation and to the rise of platform services, podcasters today may be required to interact with only a single company or service in order to distribute their content to audiences. This has brought podcasters closer than ever to their audiences thanks to *disintermediation*, or "the elimination of intermediaries in the distribution chain" (Arditi 2021, 35). What was once a fragmented and complex chain of production and distribution, then, has given way to a more streamlined process of reaching audiences, resulting in the emergence of new platform gatekeepers in a medium that has been traditionally known for its stubborn independence from such gatekeepers (see P. M. Hirsch and Gruber 2015). This institutional dynamic—an explosion of new and diverse content thanks to low entry barriers coupled with an increasing formalization and consolidation among distribution mechanisms within the industry—forms one of the central paradoxes of the podcasting industry today and is the key source of tension for creators and audiences alike. To better understand this complex media ecosystem, Turow's power roles can serve as an important analytical tool to disentangle some of the industrial relationships among players, since it draws our attention to functions and resources that allow for the operation of the medium rather than toward specific companies or individuals.

Podcast Production: Independents and Freelancers

Media industry producers are responsible for creating original content to be distributed for consumption by audiences. Similar to the popular video sharing site YouTube, podcasting's public identity has been associated with independent content creators who typically operate outside of media institutional structures, but even from the emergence of the medium in the early 2000s, this picture of podcasting as a largely amateur medium was considerably more complex. Early scholarly investigations of podcast producers (Markman 2012; Markman and Sawyer 2014) highlighted the role of independent content creators, noting enthusiasm for the technology tools and desire for interpersonal connections via their podcasting efforts. An international survey of podcast over 1,600 podcast producers in 2007 (Mocigemba and Riechmann 2007) identified a good deal more "private" or independent podcasters than professionalized or "corporate" podcasters. They discovered that these independent podcasters were largely white, male, and highly educated, and that these individuals typically focused their efforts on the production of a single podcast (or "monocasting"). A much more recent report on podcasters in the United States compiled by Edison Research and the *Sounds Profitable* newsletter called *The Creators* (2022) found that little about the demographics of creators had changed: 69 percent of the respondents in the group of 617 podcasters surveyed were male, likely to have full time jobs, and live in high earning households. However, *The Creators* study also found that the self-described podcasters are slowly becoming more diverse, with 51 percent of the respondents describing themselves as White, as compared to the their comparative proportion in the population (63 percent, according to the US Census) (Edison Research and Sounds Profitable 2022). Another recent survey of 654 regular podcast creators in Germany revealed similar demographics, with an average age of thirty-eight years and 73 percent self-identifying as male (Attig 2020). Attig discovered that female podcasters generally produced fewer podcasts and had been podcasting for a shorter period of time. The vast majority of the podcasters in her sample (76.8 percent) also did not monetize their podcast content (Attig 2020). These types of amateur, hobbyist creators are the driving force behind what Lobato, Thomas, and Hunter (2012, 4) call "informal media systems" or "those which fall largely or wholly outside the purview of state policy, regulation, taxation and measurement."

Freelancers are also part of the production apparatus of podcasting. As the medium has expanded, freelancers who specialize in specific aspects of podcasting production have emerged. For instance, the boom in podcast production has created a market for podcast editing, and content producers may outsource the editing of an episode to a freelance editor. Freelancers have also begun providing support for other production tasks as well such as scriptwriting, producing, and marketing. Quill, an online marketplace for vetted podcast freelancers, was founded in November 2019 with a plan to create a vibrant online clearinghouse where individuals and companies could locate trained podcast production personnel (Quill 2019). Several months into the global pandemic of 2020, however, Quill's plans shifted abruptly due to the impending shutdown of numerous in-person conferences and professional gatherings. Quill shuttered the freelancer marketplace, pivoting to become a full-service podcasting production agency that caters to businesses wishing to launch branded podcasts (Moore 2020). Podcast production freelancers are currently found most often on online gig labor websites such as Fiverr.com and even social media sites like Facebook and Twitter. Quill's centralized marketplace has been replaced by AIR,[1] a website that bills itself as a "global community of independent podcast producers," with job postings, training sessions, and mentorship opportunities for podcast freelancers. Finally, entrepreneurs offering mentorship and podcast launch support services have also emerged as cultural intermediaries, something I explore in a later chapter. A number of these podcasting guides or experts have start up podcast consulting agencies and generally host their own podcasts as well.

Podcast Production: Publishers

In the post-*Serial* era, large-scale podcast production has become a much more prominent feature of the podcasting landscape. These firms—often dubbed "publishers"—are the hubs of production for multiple podcasts, all of which may be produced at a central facility with high quality audio equipment. Unlike the independents, podcast hosts, producers, editors, and other support staff are employed directly by the publisher. Some early entrants into podcast publishing came from public service broadcasters like National Public Radio (NPR) in the United States and the British Broadcasting Corporation (BBC) in the UK. There are other traditional media companies with extensive production interests

---

[1] https://airmedia.org/

in radio content that have also expanded rapidly into podcasting, including iHeartMedia—the largest single radio station group owner in the United States—and satellite radio provider SiriusXM. News organizations have become major podcast publishers as well, with *The New York Times* launching its own podcasting division in 2016 (Owen 2016), and *The Washington Post* introducing a slate of news-oriented podcasts in 2018 (Willens 2018). These media companies have substantial resources and capacity to create content on a regular basis and have often leverage their existing content outlets to provide material for their original podcasts. These publishers typically have substantial audiences that have carried over from their other media properties and they have been pushing the development of advertising to provide revenue for their podcasts. While they may have production facilities and staff solely dedicated to podcasting, for these larger audio production companies, podcasting is simply another distribution outlet for their programming.

Large media companies are not the only large-scale publishers creating original content for podcasting, however. Instead, a number of independent, podcast-only publishers were launched following the success of *Serial* in 2014. Some well-known radio shows, like *This American Life* and *Serial*, both originating from public radio in the United States, separated from their parent organizations to form their own independent production companies (Sheikholeslami 2017). Other "boutique" or creator-focused publishing companies were formed in the aftermath of Serial, such as Wondery (now owned by Amazon), which was founded by former Fox International CEO Hernan Lopez in 2016 (Littleton 2016), and Gimlet Media, a company co-founded by former *This American Life* and *Planet Money* producer Alex Blumberg and entrepreneur Matt Lieber in 2014 (now owned by Spotify) (Zinsli 2014). These creator-oriented publishers are profit-driven, typically funded by other media companies or venture capital investments, and monetize their podcasts via advertising. A number of these independent, boutique publishers have also been acquired by larger media companies as well. For example, Parcast, an audio production studio specializing in crime and mystery content, was acquired by Spotify in 2019 (Reuters 2019). This is a sign both of the increased profitability of podcasting and of the formalization of the medium as a whole.

Some independent podcasters with extremely large audiences have become their own publishers as well. A good example of this type of publisher is *The Joe Rogan Experience* (JRE), an interview and chat-based podcast built upon television celebrity Joe Rogan which is usually ranked the number one podcast in terms of monthly downloads. When rap music star Joe Budden struck a deal with audio streaming giant Spotify to release his new episodes exclusively on that platform in 2018 (Saponara 2018), a number of high-profile independent podcaster-publishers began securing their own exclusive platform deals, including celebrity Dax Sheppard and podcasting's number one star, Joe Rogan in 2020 (Spotify 2020). While these podcasters are "independent" in the sense that they produce their own podcasts, they generally have developed a large audience from another medium making them highly atypical of other independent podcasters.

Finally, there has been a boom in podcast publishers that cater to corporate clients. These "business-to-business" podcast publishers will produce content for other companies that wish to promote their products or services via a freely distributed podcast. These shows are dubbed "branded podcasts" because the production costs are entirely underwritten by a single sponsor and are used as means to create positive brand awareness or to explicitly market a product or service to an audience (much like "advertorials" in newspapers or "informercials" on television). The market for branded podcasting has grown rapidly, with 2020 branded podcast revenues reaching almost $379 million in 2021 (Interactive Advertising Bureau 2021b). Advertising and branded content have become so integral to the formalization of podcasting that they are discussed more fully in a later chapter.

In a medium that often celebrates the relative absence of institutional gatekeepers as barriers to new and innovative content, large publishers have nevertheless emerged as significant players in the process of scouting new talent and content. In 2020, for example, iHeartMedia created a competition for aspiring podcasters entitled "The Next Great Podcast" and received nearly 1,800 submissions (Spangler 2021b). The winning podcast, called "Tossed Popcorn" (a movie reviews podcast), was awarded $1,000 and distribution on the iHeartMedia network, along with substantial publicity and marketing. Similarly, Gimlet Media launched its own competition and podcast entitled *Casting Call* in 2018, which narrowed down more than 5,000 entries to three finalists, each of which was paired with a producer from the company to create a pilot episode of their proposed podcast (Sturges 2018). The market power of these large publishers has encouraged independent podcasters to form their own production collectives, also known as content networks.

Podcast Production: Content Networks

The concept of networks is a hold over from the broadcast era, but the term has emerged once again as a prominent feature of modern podcasting, albeit in slightly different form. The broadcasting notion of networks served mainly as a distribution mechanism for radio and television content through interconnected stations, and typically required large amounts of capital investment, resulting in an oligopolistic market structure. In the case of podcasting, however, the open architecture of RSS obviates the need for sophisticated distribution institutions. Instead, podcast networks comprise collectives of podcasts or podcast producers. These networks are typically built around a core theme that links their podcasts together as a means to pool and expand audiences for all of the podcasts within the network. Individual podcasts within a network will often cross-promote on each other's shows, and may share organizational resources as well such as production facilities, editing costs, and advertising sales personnel. Content networks can lend a brand identity to podcasts under their umbrella, which can help those podcasts grow their audience by encouraging listeners to discover new content within the network. Typically, networked podcasts feature more recognizable hosts, have high production values, and are advertiser-supported. Barstool Sports, for example, is one of the largest content networks with ninety-nine active podcasts. Their most downloaded podcast, *Pardon My Take*, features two high-profile sports commentators, Dan "Big Cat" Katz and Eric Sollenberger (also known as "PFT Commenter" for "Pro Football Talk" Commenter).

Podcasts connected to a content network often fit into a similar theme or genre, though networks can also simply refer to a specific company (like Gimlet Media or Wondery) that produces the podcasts. The HowStuffWorks podcast network, for example, features thirty-five different thematically linked educational podcasts such as *Stuff*

You Should Know, *Stuff You Missed in History Class*, and *BrainStuff*, among others (HowStuffWorks 2000). Its parent company, Stuff Media, was purchased by American radio company iHeartMedia in 2018 for $55 million (Spangler 2018). Podcast networks can run the gamut from a loose collection of independent podcasters who agree to consolidate their efforts under a shared banner to highly formalized companies like Gimlet Media or Wondery, which are staffed by full-time employees with considerable expertise in audio production. For example, Heeremans (2018) analyzed the podcast network *The Heard*—now rebranded as Great Feeling Studios[2]— which is a collection of independent podcasters who met at the Third Coast International Audio Festival in 2016. Similarly, New York City podcaster Amanda McLaughlin created an independent production collective in 2017 with her podcast co-hosts called Multitude Productions,[3] which has since grown to eight podcasts, a podcast consulting service, and even a studio space for independent podcasters to rent by the hour. For independent podcasters, the "the benefits of being part of the network mostly pay out in the form of social or cultural capital, or at least the exchange of other forms of capital" (Heeremans 2018, 65).

While the concept of creating content-oriented collectives or "networks" might seem a throwback to an earlier era of broadcast radio, there are some distinct benefits for grouping podcasts together under a single production company or banner. As Quirk (2015) argued in her overview of the podcast industry in 2015, podcasts that are part of networks can take advantage of cross-promotional opportunities across partner shows in the network to grow their audience base. Theme-oriented networks (like HowStuffWorks network of informational podcasts) can also create a brand identity around their podcasts to stand out to audiences. Additionally, as Quirk (2015) noted, since most podcasts typically feature rather small, niche audiences, combining them together in a network can help with the problem of scale. This allows them to approach potential advertisers with a much larger combined audience across all of their affiliated podcasts for easier monetization. Finally, more prominent podcast networks have also begun operating as erstwhile

---

[2]https://greatfeelingstudios.com/about
[3]https://multitude.productions/about

gatekeepers for new and aspiring podcasters by either soliciting proposals for new podcasts to add to their network, or by actively recruiting podcast talent (or poaching from other networks) for new shows. Google, for example, has partnered with non-profit Public Radio Exchange (PRX) to launch the "Google Podcasts Creator Program" which offers a competitive twelve-week training program, equipment, and a $12,000 stipend to "foster podcast development among underrepresented voices in podcasting around the world"[4]. Podcasters gain more visibility and larger audiences by being listed on networks thanks in part to the cross-promotion they receive from other in-network shows. Some networks will also provide production staff, funding, and advertising revenue sharing for their affiliated podcasts. Approaches to independent podcast labor and communities of podcast practice are discussed in a later chapter.

Independent podcasting remains one of the key defining features of the medium. Recent data released by Edison Research revealed that 49 percent of all US podcast listeners (or roughly 39 million listeners) consumed at least on independent podcast per week (T. Webster 2021). While numbers like this speak to the enduring appeal of indies, Edison's data point obscures a larger reality about podcasting today: audience distribution is heavily concentrated among a few larger podcasts, forming a classic "Long Tail" market much like those found in other media industries (Anderson 2006). For example, data provided by Libsyn in March 2023 revealed that the top 1 percent of podcasts receive almost 99 percent of the downloads—an average of 30,000 downloads per episode—with the remaining almost 2.4 million podcasts dividing the rest of the audience (see Figure 2.1). By stark contrast, the median number of podcast downloads per episode is 153, representing the top 50 percent of all podcast downloads on Libsyn's hosting service. These small download numbers are much more typically for the vast majority of independent podcasters.

Along with the skewed download distributions, the podcasts with the largest audiences are also generally associated with the larger publishers and content networks. Podcast measurement firm Podtrac, for example, ranks the top podcast publishers each month

---

[4] https://googlecp.prx.org/apply

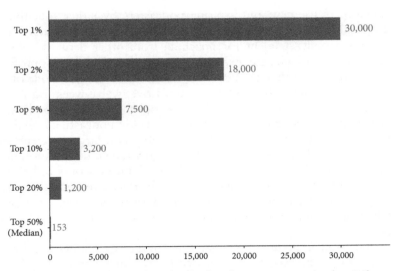

FIGURE 2.1 *Podcast download distribution per episode (Libsyn, March 2023).*
Source: Spurlock, John. 2023. "Libsyn Statistics, Visualized." Livewire Labs. May 17, 2023. https://livewire.io/libsyn-stats-visualized/.

based upon their audience size (see Figure 2.2). For October 2021, for example, broadcast radio firms such as iHeartMedia and NPR topped the list of downloads with 252 million and 158 million, respectively, followed by major publishers such as Wondery (now owned by Amazon) and *The New York Times*. These audience numbers are huge in comparison with the median audience for podcasts, which is 153 downloads per episode, according to Libsyn (see Figure 2.1). As these numbers indicate, podcasting has become a means to reach very large audiences, despite its reputation as a primary vehicle for independents and small-time entrepreneurs.

Facilitators: Podcast Hosts

Turow (1997, 26) defines industry facilitators as organizations that "help production firms carry out or evaluate mass media material." These entities act essentially as intermediaries in the production process. For the podcasting industry, podcast hosting companies

PODCAST INDUSTRY RANKING HIGHLIGHTS
TOP PODCAST PUBLISHERS
US AUDIENCE: MAY 2023

RANK	PODCAST PUBLISHER	US UNIQUE MONTHLY AUDIENCE	GLOBAL DOWNLOADS & STREAMS	ACTIVE SHOWS	SALES CONTACT
1	iHeartPodcasts	32,997,000	374,046,000	788	iHeartRadio
2	Wondery	24,102,000	169,302,000	214	Wondery Brand Partnerships
3	NPR	18,973,000	168,474,000	49	National Public Media
4	NBC News	10,859,000	65,476,000	69	
5	New York Times	10,392,000	106,677,000	12	
6	DailyWire+	9,240,000	77,804,000	14	
7	The Walt Disney Company	8,193,000	42,344,000	132	Disney Ad Sales
8	Barstool Sports	6,813,000	34,386,000	99	Barstool Sports Sales
9	PRX	6,649,000	57,776,000	128	Soundrise
10	Vox Media	6,113,000	35,155,000	60	Vox Media
11	PodcastOne	5,324,000	30,613,000	168	PodcastOne Sales
12	Fox Audio Network	5,007,000	39,390,000	106	Fox Ad Solutions
13	Paramount	4,569,000	34,773,000	109	
14	WNYC Studios	3,743,000	20,895,000	34	
15	CNN	3,714,000	36,349,000	57	WarnerMedia Ad Sales
16	Blaze Media	3,621,000	34,715,000	18	Blaze Media
17	This American Life	3,259,000	10,650,000	1	
18	American Public Media	2,839,000	14,843,000	59	
19	BBC	2,670,000	#	848	Acast
20	TED	2,560,000	38,299,000	20	

Total mobile and desktop US podcast audience.

Unique Monthly Audience:
Total of unique audience members who stream or download publisher's podcast content across all shows they produce.

Unique Streams & Downloads:
Total unique streams and downloads of podcast content for the month across all shows produced by publisher.

Active Shows:
Count of shows produced by publisher and measured by Podtrac which contribute to the totals in the Ranking.

Podcast Publisher:
An entity or individual which owns, creates and publishes podcasts.

Ranking data only includes publishers that participate in Podtrac measurement for the full month for which the ranking is being released.

49,964,000 for March 2023 based on data for 859 shows (BBC's Global Streams and Downloads are published after each quarterly financial report)

PODTRAC

FIGURE 2.2 *Rankings of the top podcast publishers (May 2023).*
Source: Podtrac. (2023, May). *May 2023—Top Podcast Publishers.* https://analytics.podtrac.com/podcast-publisher-rankings.

are critical facilitators, though they are often not as visible as major publishers or networks. These companies perform a number of essential tasks for podcasters related to the mechanics of the podcast. They may store the MP3 audio file (media hosting), generate the RSS feed (feed generator), and store and deliver the RSS feed (feed hosting) (Zohrob 2018). Most of the time, the same company provides all of these features for podcasts. The role of podcast hosts in the industry is typically much more expansive than this, however. As I will discuss in a later chapter, podcast hosts are integral to the monetization of content because they carefully monitor the consumption of podcasts, including the number of downloads for specific episodes, the geolocation of those downloads, as well as information about the user agents (operating system and/or apps) that are requesting the download.

Podcasts hosts that cater to the business of independent podcasters—called "retail hosts"—often offer value-added features for podcasters, such as a dedicated website and specialized audience consumption analytics. Their primary sources of income are the monthly fees they charge individual podcasters, which can range from US$5.00 to $50.00 depending upon the number of episodes and regular downloads (bandwidth traffic) for the podcast. Podcast hosts were some of the earliest entrants into the medium, and have long championed the development of the industry. Indeed, because their core business depends upon a thriving ecosystem of independent creators, these companies have positioned themselves as champions of the everyday podcaster. Some of these podcast hosts, like Libsyn or Blubrry, were some of the earliest entrants into the medium. Enterprise podcast hosting, by contrast, offer their services mainly to other companies or are part of larger media companies, providing hosting for in-house podcasts. National Public Radio (NPR) and the British Broadcasting Corporation (BBC), for example, host all of their podcasts themselves while Omny Studio (owned by Triton Digital) offers hosting services to business and large corporations.

A large number of hosting companies typically compete for business among independent podcasters (journalist James Cridland keeps a running list here: https://podnews.net/article/hosts). Given this high degree of competition, there is a healthy amount of churn in the industry, with independent podcasters moving their content and feed from one host to another where there may be lower rates or better services. James Cridland of Podnews.net tracks the number of podcast shows that have moved from one hosting company to another over the past seven days based upon changes in the RSS feed. His data[5] reveal a fairly robust degree of churn in podcast hosting. One of the largest podcast hosts in terms of feeds is Anchor, which was purchased by Spotify in 2019 (and renamed Spotify for Podcasters in 2022). The introduction of Anchor caused an initial disruption to the hosting business when it launched since it offered podcasters free media and RSS hosting, along with a free website for each podcast (though with Anchor branding on the show's cover art). The only other large free hosting platform is SoundCloud, which also hosts a large number of podcasts. Determining the relative size of each host in terms of the number of podcasts they carry is tricky, but one industry watcher (Spurlock 2021) compiled a ranking of top podcasts hosts from October 2021, based upon the release of new episodes during that month as cataloged by The Podcast Index (see Figure 2.3). As the rankings make clear, Spotify-owned free

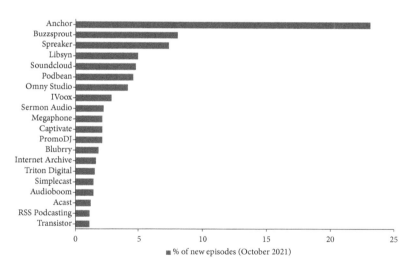

FIGURE 2.3 *Top 20 rankings of podcast hosts by new episodes (October, 2021).*

Source: Spurlock, John. 2021. "Podcast Host Rankings by Episode Share (Sept 2021)." Livewire Labs (blog). October 7, 2021. https://livewire.io/podcast-hosts-by-episode-share/.

---

[5] https://podnews.net/article/hosts/changes/

podcasting host Anchor was by far the largest host, with 24 percent of all new episodes uploaded during the month, followed by more traditional paid hosting companies such as Buzzsprout, Spreaker, and Libsyn. The dramatic expansion of new podcasts on Anchor represents a major power shift in the podcast hosting business, as many new podcasters have flocked to the service due to its free hosting and the ability to be instantly cross-listed in major podcast directories such as Spotify, Apple Podcasts, and Google Podcasts.

Distribution—Podcast Directories

The key linchpin in any media industry is the ability of producers to connect their content to the end user or listener. As Turow (1997, 26) describes, distributors "select and coordinate dispersal of material to the point of exhibition." Questions of media distribution are central to critical media studies because they directly address the availability and accessibility of content to consumers. As Braun (2014, 27) notes, "perhaps even more directly than questions of production or content, the study of distribution cuts straight to the heart of who has access to culture and on what terms." Indeed, the shifting landscape of podcast distribution and exhibition is so central to the future direction of the medium that it is discussed in much more detail in the next chapter. The largest single distributor of podcasts has traditionally been Apple, with over 2.39 million podcasts listed in its directory as of November 2021 (Lewis 2021). However, in 2020, podcasting pioneer Adam Curry and developer Dave Jones launched The Podcast Index, an independent, open directory of podcast RSS feeds designed to preserve an open ecosystem of links to content outside of the dominance of corporate platforms (Cridland 2020a). The Podcast Index[6] currently indexes over 4 million unique podcast RSS feeds in its service, far eclipsing Apple despite being on the scene for a very short time.

As I discuss in the next chapter, distributors are vital to the medium because they serve as the primary means for listeners to discover new content. While the open web standard of RSS is the key distribution mechanism that drives podcasting, online directories such as Apple Podcasts (formerly iTunes), Google

---

[6]https://podcastindex.org/

Podcasts, and Spotify have emerged as key distributors for the medium mainly because these directories make it easy to discover and subscribe to podcast RSS feeds. Apple's historical dominance via iTunes and iPods gives it unique clout and the ability to affect subscriptions through selective promotion, though other companies such as Google (via its Google Play service), Spotify, Amazon, and Stitcher play a similar role. These online platforms are more than distributors as well, since their podcast directories are directly linked to their mobile apps, where the vast majority of podcast consumption takes place.

Some distributors have begun to change the primary advertising-based revenue model for podcasting by introducing paid subscriptions for content. Early moves in this direction came from distributors such as Earwolf, which launched a premium services called Howl in 2015 with extensive show archives and bonus content (Nagy 2015), and Stitcher, which launched its own Stitcher Premium subscription-based service in 2016 (Thorpe 2016). One of the first distributors places its entire catalog of podcasts behind a paywall was Luminary, a podcast distributor that launched in April 2019 with US $100 million in venture capital funding, a $7.99 per month subscription fee to access its exclusive podcasting content, and a provocative message for the rest of the industry: "Podcasts don't need ads" (Carman 2019a). Luminary's launch was riddled with missteps, leading many in the industry to initial question the viability of paid subscriptions as a revenue model. However, in 2021 both Spotify (Carman 2021c) and Apple (Perez 2021) launched their own podcast subscription services whereby individual podcasters could charge listeners a monthly subscription fee to access their podcast episodes, leading to what some in the industry have called the "paywall wars" (Fischer 2021). Aside from the expanded ability to monetize podcasting, the most significant aspect of these recent developments in podcast distribution has been the central role played by platform services as key intermediaries in the industry.

Exhibition—Apps and Platforms

Spurred by the launch of smartphones beginning in 2007, podcasting has transformed itself into a mobile-centric medium. Research from 2019 found that 65 percent of podcast listeners access feeds and content via dedicated apps on mobile devices (smartphones and tablets) instead of desktop computers or laptops (25 percent), a distinct shift from the earliest days of the medium (Statista Research Department 2021a). A similar podcast listener survey—TechSurvey 2019—found that 77 percent of all podcast listening occurs via mobile apps, as opposed to desktop and laptop computers (Inside Radio 2019). Moreover, analysis by Dan Misener (2019a) uncovered evidence that listeners are much more engaged with podcast content delivered via mobile apps than via a webpage or other desktop interface. Mobile apps, therefore, have become vital intermediaries in the podcast production cycle. Since podcatching apps are the last stage in the cycle by actually delivering the audio file to the listener, they are best understood as *exhibitors* within Turow's power roles framework. Exhibitors "offer material for public viewing or purchase" (Turow 1997, 26). In broadcast media such as radio and television, local stations occupy the exhibitor role, are relatively scarce and expensive to operate, and are generally governed by broader regulatory structures (such as the Federal Communications Commission in the United States). Podcatcher mobile apps, on the other hand, are easy to program, largely ungoverned, numerous, and are available for purchase through one of the major mobile app stores, Google Play and the Apple App Store. In addition, thanks to the open standard of RSS, all of these apps have the capability to perform the essential function of a podcatcher: to locate and subscribe to podcasts via and RSS feed.

In the first decade of podcasting, Apple's iTunes operated as both a central distribution directory for RSS feeds and an exhibition endpoint for consumers who leveraged desktop software to download and transfer audio files to a portable device such as an iPod. Other erstwhile competitors, such as Microsoft's Zune player, performed the same functions but were never able to overcome Apple's head start and deep market penetration (Rosenthal 2020). Following the introduction of mobile smartphones, podcatching apps have become increasingly important to the medium, since this is where the vast majority of listeners discover new content, manage their subscriptions to RSS feeds, and listen. These apps have become ubiquitous since access to the core distribution backbone of the medium—RSS—is a free, open standard. Additionally, major directories such as Apple Podcasts, Spotify, Listennotes, and now the Podcast Index have all allowed free access to their respective podcast directories via the use of Application Programming Interfaces (APIs), which allows any app developer to instantly tap into millions of podcast feeds that are distributed on any one of these directories. Podcast hosts such as Podbean, Anchor, and Spreaker also offer their own dedicated apps which privilege access to podcasts hosted on their services. Some content networks are also launching their apps as a means to further bundle and promote their content. Amazon-owned network Wondery, for example, recently launched their own mobile app in a bid to attract more subscribers for their podcasts (Spangler 2020).

Because there are numerous podcast mobile apps in competition with one another for potential users thanks to the low barriers to entry, the app ecosystem is fluid and highly dynamic, with apps continually changing to introduce innovative features in order to attract new users. For example, in the past several years, podcatching apps such as Airr, Notecast, Momento, and Podverse have been enabled listeners to capture short selections of audio from podcasts, tag them, transcribe them, and share them with the broader community of the app's users much like social media. Other apps and podcatching services such as Hark, ListenNotes, Goodpods, Podyssey, Breaker, and Podchaser (among others) allow for both editorial and user-based curation of podcast episodes around specific themes, much like Spotify, Apple Music, and other music apps allow for user-generated playlists.

With literally hundreds of different podcasting apps available, one might expect the use of those apps by listeners to be more or less evenly distributed and that users might regularly switch from one app to another due to improved functionalities or features. Instead, podcast app usage is concentrated among a handful of apps, with platform apps by Apple and Spotify dominating the top spot in an essential duopoly. Spotify rapidly gained ground on Apple's decade-long head start by leveraging its sizable music user base to drive up podcast usage in a relatively short period of time. Download statistics for podcast host Buzzsprout echo this essential duopoly structure for podcast apps. During the month of May 2023, for instance, Buzzsprout reported that 41.3 percent of podcast downloads originated from Apple Podcasts, followed by 30.2 percent for Spotify (see Figure 2.4). The next closest download source that month was web browsers (4.0 percent) and Google Podcasts at 2.6 percent, with many more podcast apps representing a "Long Tail" usage model.

These numbers demonstrate the power of platforms to "capture" podcast consumption even in spite of rapid innovation and competition among podcast apps. Apple's position as the monopoly provider of the iOS mobile platform via its iPhone and iPad product lines, coupled with the company's decision to install the app by default on all new versions of iOS beginning in 2014, led to an 18 percent growth in podcast consumption over the next year (Marsal 2015). The power of Apple's platform has propelled podcast usage on its mobile devices, but mainly via Apple's pre-installed Podcasts app. Since Apple has not developed its podcatcher app for Android, those users (which represent 70 percent of all mobile users worldwide as of December 2021) had to rely upon other apps to subscribe to podcasts ("Mobile Operating System Market Share Worldwide" 2022). Spotify's music app was already available on both iOS and Android mobile operating systems, and leveraged

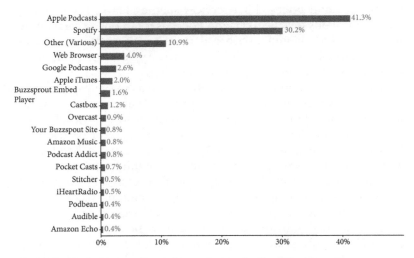

FIGURE 2.4 *Most commonly used apps for listening to podcasts.*
Source: Buzzsprout Platform Stats. 2023 May. https://www.buzzsprout.com/global_stats.(% app listening, Buzzsprout, May 2023).

its large music listener base to expand the podcasting audience once it began offering podcast subscriptions via its app in 2015 (Titlow 2015). Since that time, Spotify's podcasting growth has increased dramatically, with many industry analysts expecting that its podcast listener base will surpass Apple's by the end of 2021 (Lebow 2021). The launch of YouTube podcasts in 2023 may begin to shift this duopoly dynamic due to the enormous build-in user base of YouTube worldwide (Amadeo 2023).

Podcast exhibition is a critical intermediary in the industry, and not just because it is the last stop in the production cycle. As Morris and Patterson (2015, 222) argue, for example, that the evolution of podcasting is being affected "app-ification," or "the ways in which the design and function of podcatcher apps shape podcasting's production and reception." The functions and design of apps may constrain listener choices and skew the consumption of podcasting by canalizing listening into a narrow range of "featured" podcasts via the app. As the endpoint in the consumption of content, apps also provide vital data to the distributors, the podcast host, and to the podcaster about how much of their content is being consumed, and by whom. Apps are therefore explicitly designed as "people-catching technologies, drawing in an otherwise dispersed audience in an attempt to make them economically viable" (Morris and Patterson 2015, 222). The centrality of apps to the business of measuring and capturing audiences is discussed in detail in Chapter 6.

Top-Down Formalization in Podcasting

As Lobato and Thomas (2015) note, formalization can occur from two different directions. It can occur from above—*top-down*—when existing companies incorporate informal modes of production, use crowdsourced labor as a means of product testing, or leverage social media to market products or services. Alternatively, formalization can occur *bottom-up* when informal labor practices are codified or restricted, or when informal media are subjected to high levels of surveillance via standardized measurement. Both types of formalization are evident in the podcasting industry and warrant a brief discussion here.

Clients—Advertisers and Advertising Firms

First, media industries often rely on advertisers—what Turow calls the "client" power role—to produce cash flow in exchange for exposure in the finished media product. Advertising has been a feature of podcasting from its earliest days, with show hosts often utilizing direct response techniques to raise revenue, typically by offering promotional discount codes for online services like Audible or Squarespace and being paid by those services when a listener makes a purchase using the code. As the size of the podcast audience has grown, marketers and brand advertisers are showing increasing interest in podcasting as a medium to provide them with niche marketing opportunities. According to the Interactive Advertising Bureau (IAB), 2020 US podcast advertising revenues rose to $842 million, a 19 percent year-on-year increase with an expected revenue of $1 billion by the end of 2021 (Interactive Advertising Bureau 2021b).

The emergence of podcast-specific ad agencies has largely institutionalized the process of buying and selling advertising for the medium. Major platforms like Anchor, Google, and Spotify are leveraging their role as key intermediaries by pursuing "dynamic ad insertion," whereby advertising is digitally inserted into podcasts (post-production), much as it is done in commercial broadcast radio. Through this pursuit of programmatic advertising, advertisers can spread their ad messages over a wide range of podcasts in an efficient manner, much as they do in other forms of media. Podcast advertising firms have also merged or been acquired by larger media companies with interests in online audio, thereby further institutionalizing the development of advertising markets within the medium. The importance of advertising for platform-era podcasting is explored in more detail later in Chapter 7.

Facilitators—Audience Measurement Services

Second, the explosion of advertising in podcasting, particularly programmatic advertising, is fueling a push for more extensive metrics on the size and character of the audience. Established media research firms such as Edison Research, Triton Digital, and The Pew Research Center have all begun regularly tracking the growth of podcast listening, at least in the United States, and have used these data to demonstrate the market viability of podcasting as an advertising medium. Podcast hosts have offered podcasters their own metrics of audio file downloads as measures of consumption, and the launch of measurement firm Podtrac in 2005 marked the beginning of an industry-wide effort to standardize the measurement of podcast downloads in order to streamline the advertising buying process. More recently, the IAB, a major online media trade organization, established a working group of representatives from podcasting hosts and networks to codify a set of guidelines for ensuring the accuracy and comparability of podcast download statistics. The efforts of these major industry facilitators have been a key formalizing force by establishing standards for audience metrics.

Linking Pins—Cross-licensing of Podcasting Content

Another sign of the formalization of podcasting has been the incorporation of content into other forms of media as a source of intellectual property. This migration of original content from production in one industry to another in the form of cross-licensing deals is what Turow (1997) calls a "linking pin," and it is quite common in other media industries. In a sign of the growing cultural and commercial significance of podcasting—as well as the television industry's continual hunger for novel content—the rights to some podcasts are being purchased by other media companies and turned into television series.

For example, *Alex, Inc.* was a short-lived 2018 television series on American TV network ABC starring Zach Braff. The series was a fictionalized portrayal of the real-life experiences of former *This American Life* producer and Gimlet Media CEO Alex Blumberg, who cataloged his efforts to found a podcast-centric media company in his own podcast, *Start Up* (Rao 2018). There is an increasingly long list of podcasts optioned for television deals, including Aaron Mahnke's horror podcast *Lore*, which was optioned for television by Amazon in 2016 (Sarkar 2016) and ran for two seasons on Amazon Prime before being canceled (Fingas 2019), the British comedy podcast *My Dad Wrote A Porno*, which premiered on HBO in 2019 (White 2018), and Wondery-backed true crime podcast *Dirty John* was optioned for television and premiered on the Bravo network in 2018 (Turchiano 2018). Television industry interest in adapting podcast content into new series was reportedly so fierce, that Spotify's Head of Studio's and Video Courtney Holt described it as a "feeding frenzy" (White 2020). In something of a reversal of the typical production cycle, podcast production company Cadence13 released two feature-length podcast "movies" starring the voices of Hollywood actors in 2021, further blurring the lines between podcasting and legacy media forms like film and television (Ugwu 2021b).

Mergers and Acquisitions within Podcasting

Lastly, the podcasting ecosystem has been radically transformed over the past several years by a flurry of major mergers and acquisitions (see Figure 2.5). This development, above all else, is the most visible sign of a rapidly formalizing industry. Between 2019 and 2021, media and technology companies spent over $1 billion on podcast content and technology in a deluge of merger activity under the theory that it is "easier to buy than it is to build" (Jarvey 2021). The deluge of merger activity began in earnest in early 2019 when Swedish audio platform Spotify announced that it would spend a breathtaking $340 million combined to acquire two very different podcast startups: Gimlet Media, a boutique podcast production company co-founded by Alex Blumberg, a former producer for *This American Life*; and Anchor, a podcast hosting platform that offered free file storage and accounts for podcasters in exchange for selling advertising against their content, much like YouTube (Spangler 2019). This level of spending in an otherwise sleepy niche medium shocked industry observers. Spotify CEO Daniel Ek publicly made it clear at that time that Spotify intended to spend up to $500 million during that year on acquisitions in podcasting, noting that podcasting represented a unique business opportunity for the audio streaming company. Podcasting, he noted, offered advertisers "increased user engagement, lower churn, faster revenue growth, and higher margins," particularly via the potential of platforms like Spotify to acquire and produce exclusive content (Kafka 2019).

PODCASTING AS A MEDIA INDUSTRY

Purchasing Company	Company Purchased	Date	Amount ($ millions)
Amazon	Wondery	December 2020	300
	Art19	June 2021	undisclosed
	Smartless (podcast)	June 2021	80
Apple	Scout FM	September 2020	undisclosed
Audacy (formerly Enteroom)	Cadence 13	August 2019	50
	Pineapple Street	August 2019	18
	Podcorn	March 2021	22.5
	WideOrbit Digital Streaming	October 2021	40
iHeartMedia	Stuff Media	September 2018	55
	Jelli	November 2018	undisclosed
	Voxnest	October 2020	55
	Triton Digital	February 2021	230
Libsyn	Auxbus	February 2021	undisclosed
	Advertisecast	June 2021	30
	Glow	April 2021	1.2
	Podgo	November 2021	undisclosed
The New York Times	Audm	March 2020	undisclosed
	Serial Productions	July 2020	25
	The Athletic	January 2022	550
SiriusXM	AdsWizz	May 2018	66.3
	Simplecast	June 2020	28
	Stitcher/Midroll	July 2020	325
	99% Invisible (podcast)	April 2021	undisclosed
Spotify	Gimlet Media	February 2019	230
	Anchor	February 2019	110
	Parcast	April 2019	56
	The Ringer	February 2020	196
	The Joe Rogan Experience (podcast)	May 2020	100
	Megaphone	November 2020	235
	Podz	June 2021	53
	Whooshkaa	December 2021	undisclosed

FIGURE 2.5 *Major acquisitions in the podcasting industry.*

There have generally been two types of acquisition activities in podcasting. First, large companies with extensive media portfolios like Spotify, SiriusXM, iHeartMedia, and Audacy (formerly Entercom) have spent tens of millions of dollars on acquiring either podcast production, advertising-related companies, or podcast app developers (or all three). The primary aims of these types of acquisitions have been to secure access to podcast content (which is clear from the Gimlet Media, Cadence13, and Wondery acquisitions, for example) and to streamline the process of monetizing the podcasts through the delivery of advertising (which is clear from the Megaphone, Advertisecast, and AdsWizz acquisitions). The second type of podcast acquisition has been exclusive contract deals with popular independent podcasts. One of the first such deals was hip hop artist Joe Budden's exclusive distribution agreement with Spotify in 2018 (Saponara 2018). By far the largest and most consequential of these types of acquisitions, however, was Spotify's $100 million deal for an exclusive license to distribute *The Joe Rogan Experience*—the number one podcast in terms of audience size—on its platform in 2020 (Cramer 2020). Other blockbuster exclusive content agreements have followed, including a another reported $100 million Spotify three-year exclusive license for comedian Dax Shepard's *Armchair Expert* in May 2021, a $60 million exclusive deal for Alex Cooper's *Call Her Daddy* podcast on Spotify in June 2021 (Spangler 2021a), and the purchase of the production company behind Roman Mars' popular architecture podcast *99% Invisible* in April of 2021 (Ugwu 2021a). This deluge of mergers and acquisitions is the most visible sign of top-down formalization, and has begun to prompt concerns among media reform organizations about the emergence of a new "podcast oligopoly" that will make it all the more difficult for smaller, independent producers to find an audience (Hunt 2021).

Bottom-up Formalization in Podcasting

The process of formalization, as Lobato and Thomas (2015) have outlined, is not only a top-down process whereby established institutions assert control over informal or amateur productions. Instead, alongside the types of formalization outlined above, forms of bottom-up formalization are also occurring within podcasting. Here the primary mode of formalization is under the category of what Lobato and Thomas (2015, 78) call "controls," or "strategies by formal actors that seek to manage, contain, organize, systematize, or curtail informal activities." This takes several forms, including what they term *restriction*, or direct enforcement of rules in informal economies; *codification*, or "creating new categories, rights, and limitations around informal activities"; *authorization*, which includes licensing schemes, classifications or other official recognition; and measurement, or forms of information collection about informal economic activities (pp. 78–80). These types of control mechanisms are beginning to emerge in podcasting, though they are not necessarily always imposed from above by commercial media firms. Instead, informal networks of cooperation and recognition have in some cases created institutional structures that have shaped the medium in important ways. This type of formalization is not unlike platform cooperatives that have emerged in forms of gig labor such as Uber drivers (see Scholz 2016), and indeed in some cases has resulted in full-fledged movements for unionization.

Facilitators—Professional Organizations

One of the hallmarks of amateur or independent podcast production has been the formation of communities or practice to help share knowledge, address issues of concern, set standards, and to provide mentorship. During the "second era" of podcasting, these informal communities have formalized their interactions—much of which takes place via social media channels—to form professional organizations. These organizations act much like other professional associations in that they aim to provide institutional and material support for podcasters by connecting them with one another in more structured settings. These professional organizations also act as clearinghouses of information about training, auxiliary services, and mentorship opportunities.

Podcasting conventions and other types of formal "meetups" are one important example of this type of professional organization. For example, Podcast Movement, one of the largest annual conventions for podcasters, was launched with a crowdfunded Kickstarter campaign by Dan Franks, Jared Easley, Gary Leland, and Mitch Todd in 2014 and made its target funding goal of $11,000 within 24 hours, and would go on to triple that amount (Corcoran 2014). A similar conference dubbed Podfest Expo was organized by independent podcaster Chris Krimitsos and launched the following year after another crowdfunding effort. The number of podcast conventions and meetups have since grown exponentially, with events launching all around the world such as Third Coast International Audio Festival, PodX, Podcon, PodSummit, Independent Podcast Conference (formerly Mid-Atlantic Podcast Conference), OzPod (Australia), ShePodcasts, Evolutions, Afros & Audio Conference, and Asian Podcast Festival, among many others. While the global pandemic of 2020–1 challenged the ability of groups to hold in-person meetings, it nevertheless created a boon in virtual podcasting conference meetings, effectively lowering costs for organizers and attendees alike.

Independent podcast entrepreneurs have also offered their services as podcasting consultants, creating their own businesses to provide mentorship and consulting to both individual and institutional podcast producers. These podcast consulting agencies may contract with companies who wish to enter podcasting, offering podcast concept design, scripting, and even production services. Some of these agencies offer other services such as hosting, production facilities, booking agents for guests, and even podcast management software. Some independent podcasters have launched consulting businesses that serve their fellow podcasters, acting as ersatz mentors and guides to assist neophyte podcasters in launching and growing their podcasts.

Facilitators—Podcast Journalism

Another sign of the maturation of podcasting is the emergence of more formal types of trade journalism that covers the medium as a growing business concern. One of the earliest regularly updated online publications dedicated to podcasting was Nicholas Quah's *Hot Pod*, a free email subscription newsletter founded in 2014 with news and longer essays about the medium ("About Hot Pod" 2022). *Hot Pod* was purchased in 2021 by Vox Media and has been folded into the online tech news website *The Verge*. James Cridland was the first to launch a daily email newsletter completely dedicated to the podcasting industry in June 2017, which now has over 21,000 active subscribers and is financially supported by premium subscriptions from companies, executives and even independent podcasters (Cridland 2018c). Modeled stylistically on *Billboard* and *Rolling Stone* and appearing both in print and online, *Podcast Magazine* launched in 2019. There are a number of other important online newsletters and websites dedicated to the podcast industry as well, including *Sounds Profitable* (dedicated to covering podcast advertising), *PodMov Daily* (a publication linked to the annual Podcast Movement conference), *Podcast Business Journal* (originally published by Blubrry, a podcast hosting company, and then sold to

Podnews in 2023), *I Hear Things* (a personal newsletter published by former Edison Research Vice President Tom Webster and now published as part of *Sounds Profitable*), and even *Podcast Reader*, an online service that publishes full transcripts of podcasts (Hill 2021). Finally, it is no surprise that there are numerous podcasts that regularly discuss the shifting dynamics of the podcasting business as well. Podcasts such as the *New Media Show*, *The Feed (The Official Libsyn Podcast)*, *BuzzCast (The Official Buzzsprout Podcast)*, *Podland News*, *Podnews*, *Podcast Pontifications*, *Q'd Up Podcast*, *Podcast Junkies*, and *Sounds Profitable*, among others, all focus attention on trends within the podcasting industry and often feature in-depth interviews with professionals.

Unions—Specialization and Organizing Podcast Labor

As the number of podcasts has expanded dramatically in the past five years, podcast producers have begun conceptualizing their own cultural labor in new ways by forming shared collectives and even standardizing some of the practices involved in producing podcasts. Turow's (1997, 26) *Media Systems in Society* defines the union power role as any type of organization that "regulate(s) the provision of personnel to producers." Unions typically have a central role in setting work standards, defining and regulating roles within media production environments, providing worker protections, and negotiating salary rates with producers through collective bargaining. Similarly, podcast creator communities have begun to share their experiences with podcasting, including production techniques, monetization strategies, skills building, and mentorship, some of which are described in Chapter 4. These kinds of informal creator collectives share many of the same goals and purposes as more formal unions, though without the more tangible and material benefits of trade unionism. While there are some examples of explicit labor unionization within podcasting, these efforts are in their infancy and are fraught given the fact that most podcast creative workers are independents and freelancers.

The provision of creative labor is a fundamental aspect of any creative industry, and podcasting has witnessed several bottom-up initiatives to create standards and definitions around this labor.

One recent example is Quill, a Toronto-based company launched in 2019 that built an online marketplace to serve as a clearinghouse for podcast creative freelancers (Quill 2019). As CEO and founder Fatima Zaidi explained in a podcast interview:

> [Quill is] the one-stop shop Fiverr or UpWork equivalent to the podcasting community. So if you're looking to start a show or outsourced elements of your existing show, you can go onto our platform and hire podcasting experts at a range of different price points for whatever services you're looking at.
>
> (Passy 2020b)

Quill's online labor marketplace was noteworthy in that it vetted the resumes of all freelancers before they were posted to the website as a means of quality control. Quill also restricted their site to feature only those living in North America which, according to Zaidi, "protects freelancers from being price cut in places like India and Eastern Europe, where people can do it for a fraction of the cost." Quill eventually shuttered its online marketplace and pivoted to creating branded podcasts, but this effort represented a type of labor formalization by placing a third party as a gatekeeper for creative talent in the industry.

Another hallmark of the bottom-up formalization of podcasting is the increasing specialization of labor roles. Specifically, as the number of podcasts has expanded and with it the number of independent producers, freelancers have begun to specialize in particular aspects of the industry, such as editing, social media marketing, or consulting. Steve Stewart and Mark Deal founded the Podcast Editor Academy,[7] for example, which offers training and job boards for freelance audio editors. The group has also begun scheduling their own conferences and meetups such as the Podcast Editors Conference in March 2021. This drive toward specialization is also evident in the Podcast Taxonomy,[8] a project started by Podchaser and online freelance marketplace UpWork in partnership with a multiple publishers and hosting companies. The purpose of the Podcast Taxonomy is to both name and describe

---

[7] https://www.podcasteditoracademy.com/
[8] https://podcasttaxonomy.com/

specific labor roles within podcasting. The broader goals, according to the White Paper released by the project in December 2020, are to "further professionalize the podcast industry" by adopting standard roles, to "help with job searching and creation in podcasting," and "Ensure the taxonomy of podcast roles is inclusive, representing people of all backgrounds, including women, people of color, and marginalized voices." This taxonomy not only allows for individuals carrying out similar functions at different organizations to exchange knowledge and network, but it also facilitates the easier movement of professionals from one organization to another due to the shared understandings of specific occupational titles and responsibilities.

Finally, among some podcast publishers, full-fledged unionization of creative workers has emerged. Shortly after it was acquired by Spotify, employees at Gimlet Media pushed to codify a set of work and pay standards with the Swedish audio giant, as had other Spotify-acquired publishers The Ringer and Parcast (Jaffe 2021). The unionization efforts at Gimlet Media dragged on for two years, and were further complicated in February 2021 after Eric Eddings who, a former colleague of the producers of one of Gimlet's hit podcasts, *Reply All*, accused the co-hosts of creating a toxic work environment for non-white producers within the company and for working to thwart unionization efforts there (Rosman and Ugwu 2021). The employees of Gimlet Media, along with The Ringer, finally ratified three-year agreements with Spotify in April of 2021 with the Writers Guild of America East (WGAE). The agreement set minimum salary levels at both companies, placed restrictions on the use of outside contractors, and provided for a minimum 2 percent annual raise for covered employees (Kilkenny 2021). In December 2021, employees of iHeartMedia's podcasts—including hosts, producers, editors, researchers, and writers—also joined the WGAE over shared concerns about compensation, transparency in employment decisions, and commitments to diversity, equity, and inclusion (Chan 2021). In an interview with journalist Nicholas Quah (2020), a representative of the WGAE indicated that employees from at least a dozen podcast production companies were in talks with the organization about potential unionization efforts.

Conclusion

Podcasting has seen rapid and significant changes in the past several years. This chapter has outlined the processes of formalization that are reshaping the medium in its second decade. Leveraging the conceptual tools of power roles and media industry analysis, I've outlined the production and distribution processes for podcasting today. Established media companies such as iHeartMedia, SiriusXM, and Spotify have made aggressive moves into podcasting post-2014 by either acquiring or starting their own podcasting divisions (or both). This has injected hundreds of millions of dollars into the market and created the conditions for swift and wide-ranging formalization among producers, distributors, and exhibitors. While podcast advertising is still in its infancy compared to other media (something explored in greater detail in a later chapter), the expansion of podcast-oriented advertising and audience measurement firms has contributed to the "top-down" formalization of the medium. Spotify, for example, has injected over $1 billion into the medium since 2019 through its deluge of acquisitions and exclusive content partnerships. These moves, along with countering acquisitions by iHeartMedia, Amazon, and SiriusXM, have reshaped the medium. As a result, podcasting today looks more similar to other media industries in its structure and practices, particularly via cross-media intellectual property deals (or linking pins) for podcast content.

As Lobato and Thomas' (2015) analysis suggests, however, formalization is complex and involves the interaction of a number of different factors. Most podcasters are not employed by publishers like Gimlet, The Ringer, or Wondery, working instead on their own as amateurs or freelancers. As I have outlined in this chapter, formalization processes are occurring from the bottom up as well, with creators forming professional organizations, joining labor collectives, and even unionizing to control their own creative destinies. One key aspect of the formalization process—platformization—is perhaps the most consequential for an industry that was developed on top of the open technical ecosystem of RSS, and it is the subject of the next chapter.

CHAPTER THREE

Distribution and Exhibition Shifts—The Platformization of Podcasting

Kevin Goldberg's (2018) blog post read like a "whodunnit" detective novel. Following up on a *New York Times* exposé of the underground market for buying Twitter followers through shadow companies controlling tens of thousands of online bots (Confessore 2018), Goldberg wondered, could the list of top or trending podcasts on the Apple Podcasts charts be gamed in the same way? Similar to these shady companies buying their way into social media fame by artificially inflating their follower numbers, could someone launching a new podcast essentially hack their way into the top of the podcasts chart? How does the Apple Podcasts chart work? Apple has jealously guarded the weighting of factors that comprise its algorithm for the top podcasts charts, but Libsyn Senior VP Rob Walch has noted that the top podcasts list essentially reflects "the total number of new subscribers in the past 7 days, with a weighted average for the last 24, 48, and 72 hours" (Goldberg 2018). In this way, the list of top podcasts therefore remains fresh with new podcasts while also acknowledging the most consistently popular podcasts in its rankings.

A version of this chapter was published previously in Sullivan, J. L. (2019). The Platforms of Podcasting: Past and Present. *Social Media + Society*, 5(4). https://doi.org/10.1177/2056305119880002.

Looking at the top podcasts in the Apple Podcast rankings over several weeks in late 2017 and early 2018, Goldberg noted the "near unprecedented" rise of a little known podcast called *Kickass News*, which rocketed to the top of the Apple Podcasts list after acquiring new management in August 2017. He first looked at the official Twitter account and noted some early suspicions: about 71 percent of its 90,000 followers were likely fake according to Twitter Audit. He then compared the podcast's place on Apple's "top podcasts" chart with the top 200 episodes chart, reasoning that one of the top overall podcasts should have at least one episode in the top 200 list. He found none there. Like the manufacture of Twitter followers, Goldberg strongly suspected that the frequent appearance of the *Kickass News* podcast in the top Apple Podcasts list was being manufactured by a click farm service or online bots to continually unsubscribe and re-subscribe to the podcast. In other words, the sudden and strangely consistent popularity of *Kickass News* demonstrated that the Apple Podcasts top podcasts chart can be gamed. More evidence for this kind of manipulation was reported by prominent podcast journalist James Cridland (2018a), who reported being contacted multiple times by a shadowy company called Podcast Influencer that offered to get his podcast into the Apple Podcasts top 50 for $5,000 a month. A later follow-up investigation by Cridland himself seemed to confirm that Apple's "top podcasts" chart was rife with manipulation (Cridland 2018b). Why would a podcaster want to game Apple's "top podcasts" chart and even consider paying a princely sum in order to secure a top spot? The expectation is that listeners exploring podcasts via Apple's desktop or mobile app will be more likely to click on one of the podcasts in the "top podcasts" list due to its visual prominence in the app, thereby leading to more downloads and, consequently, the potential for more advertising revenue. However, Cridland (2018a) notes, Apple's podcast charts only measures popularity within Apple's ecosystem which (only) represents about 60 percent of all podcast listens. These podcast popularity charts are also "unrelated to downloads" and therefore "not a reflection of a podcast's total audience, and is not an advertising planning tool" (Cridland 2018a). So, why was there such an outcry among podcasters about this manipulation of Apple's discovery algorithm?

Clearly, the *Kickass News* podcast was "gaming" Apple's "top podcasts" chart by divining the components of the algorithm and cleverly exploiting that information to ensure that it appeared in rarefied company alongside much more well-known podcasts with large followings. This matters because major online platforms like Apple Podcasts, iHeartRadio, SiriusXM, Google Podcasts, and Spotify have come to play dominant roles in the podcast ecosystem. Not only have these platforms gobbled up other companies in a massive wave of consolidation, as explored in earlier chapters, but they have also become the most important gateways for many listeners to discover new content, including books, music, and podcasts. Thus, being "visible" on these platforms is often one of the major hurdles for new podcasters. Additionally, since many of these platform services have become content producers themselves (either through the acquisition of podcast networks like Spotify's purchase of Gimlet Media or through the launch of content exclusive to one of these platforms), they are likely to privilege their own content ahead of those of independents or competing platform services. The furor surrounding this incident of "gaming" discoverability on the Apple Podcasts charts demonstrates that platforms are becoming ever more important to the consumption of media content, including podcasts (see also Quah 2018c).

While podcasters were indignant at this incident of manipulation, this incident nevertheless demonstrated an important aspect of platformization: Media users and creators have not only been forced to comply with the artificial structures and requirements of platforms, but they have also discovered methods of *optimizing* their actions on these platforms to better meet their own goals. This optimization takes on many forms, such as "search engine optimization" (SEO) to maximize visibility on search platforms like Google and Yahoo! (Zhang and Cabage 2017), algorithmic visibility on social media platforms like Facebook (Bucher 2012), or "cloning" successful artists and spamming metadata to ensure discovery on music platforms like Spotify (Morris 2020). Indeed, the power of algorithmic discovery on a major online platform like Spotify is even having recursive effects on record labels, who are aiming to produce new music that is more likely to be featured on streaming platforms (Prey 2020). Is this cheating or simply rational optimization behavior in the context of the power of online platforms? The line between "gaming" and "optimizing" is blurry, and where specific behaviors fall on that line may depend upon whether the agent doing the optimization is an individual or a corporate entity (Petre, Duffy, and Hund 2019). As this example demonstrates, podcasters are increasingly adjusting their production and distribution strategies to accommodate the structural and algorithmic logics of online platforms.

This chapter explores the shifting landscape of podcast distribution and exhibition in the second decade of the twenty-first century. I focus my attention on the role of digital platforms in podcasting (both past and present) and their impacts on the emergent podcast industry structure as well as its content and form. Distribution is essential to the operation of any media industry, and it looms even larger in podcasting due to the centrality of RSS for the medium's very identity. Braun (2021, 32) notes that the concept of distribution is "concerned with the actions and infrastructures whose decisions impact to whom media messages go." Distribution structures in media industries are particularly key, Braun argues, because they not only serve as connection points for audiences to access all forms of information and entertainment, but because they have the power to essentially create publics. As such "reliable distribution networks create a central conceit of democratic life—that, through our media, we are speaking to the same assembled audience day in and day out" (Braun 2021, 38). Distribution systems demand our scrutiny, therefore, because of their ability to both enable and curtail forms of public discourse.

The distribution of podcasting has seen tectonic shifts since 2018, mainly due to the emergence of platforms as key intermediaries between creators and listeners. Platform services offered by tech giants such as Apple, Amazon, Google, Spotify, iHeartRadio, and now even YouTube are beginning to reshape how podcasts are discovered and consumed by listeners. Indeed, the importance of these platforms for directing the attention of audiences is having recursive effects on the process of podcast creation and marketing. As the example at the beginning of this chapter illustrates, podcasting success is increasingly linked to forms of platform optimization, as podcasters grapple with the shifting structures and terms of platforms as they seek to reach audiences with their content. As suggested by Srnicek (2016, 43), the key leverage provided by platforms stem from the ability of these services to "monopolize, extract, analyze, and use the increasingly large amounts of data that [are] being recorded." In the case of podcasting, the market imperative for audience consumption data is fueling industry consolidation among these competing platforms, though Apple's early dominance makes it the most likely beneficiary of podcast platformization. As I note in the conclusion, even though podcasting is built upon the open architecture of RSS, commercial pressures and the desire of market players to capitalize on the "winner-take-all" features of platforms are shaping the trajectory of the medium's current development.

Platforms and Cultural Production

Platforms can be understood at their most basic level as "digital infrastructures that enable two or more groups to interact" (Srnicek 2016, 43). These infrastructures act as intermediaries between different types of users, including customers, suppliers, producers, service providers, suppliers, and advertisers. Gillespie (2018, 254) offers a similar definition, noting that platforms can be understood as "sites and services that host public expression, store it on and serve it up from the cloud, organize access to it through search and recommendation, or install it onto mobile devices." The centralized organization of platforms allows for a shared space that affords users the "opportunity to communicate, interact or sell" (Gillespie 2010, 351). Widely utilized digital media such as social media (e.g., Facebook, Twitter, Snapchat), online shopping (e.g., Amazon, Overstock.com), and video sharing sites (e.g., YouTube, Vimeo) are some of the most common examples.

Platforms consist of both the technical infrastructures that allow for sharing of information and a set of rules (governance) that enable and constrain particular types of user activity. The shared technical infrastructure and open nature of these platforms often provide them with the aura of neutrality, much like a utility or common carrier service. Platforms are much more than neutral arbiters of interactions and transactions, however. By shaping the types of interactions among their participants in differential ways, platforms can also shape "how modularity and power are negotiated between a core unit with low variability and heterogeneous components of high variability" (Plantin et al. 2018, 298). In this way, platforms can serve differential functions and provide varying types of services for different users. In his exploration of YouTube, for example, Gillespie (2010) notes that the site presents itself strategically to different groups of users. To content providers, YouTube is a new television service, while to end users it is presented as an emancipatory tool for distributing user-generated content (Burgess and Green 2009; Green and Jenkins 2011). Thanks to their "privileged access" to monitor and record user data, platforms also typically offer their services for free to end users (as an economic "loss leader") in order to monetize user data (Srnicek 2016, 44). Facebook's profits, for example, arise chiefly from its ability to monetize users' private data that are generated and exchanged.

In a Web 2.0 era, platforms have become a focal point for scholarly inquiry due to their increased centrality in the creation and distribution of media. The financial success of major sites like YouTube, Facebook, and iTunes has encouraged the proliferation of new platforms in the marketplace. Nieborg and Poell (2018, 2) have identified these changes as *platformization,* or "the penetration of economic, governmental, and infrastructural extensions of digital platforms into the web and app ecosystems, fundamentally affecting the operations of the cultural industries." Nieborg and Poell note that a deeper understanding of platformization processes, including a more historically informed perspective on their evolving nature, can help scholars to "untangle the mutual articulation of market arrangements, infrastructures, and governance of content production, distribution, and advertising" (2018, 7). Their model emphasizes three specific aspects of platformization: how platforms shift larger market structures, how cultural production is *governed* through platforms, and how platformization transforms the infrastructure of cultural production (via data-oriented practices such as algorithms, data structures, SDKs, and APIs, among others). This last element, they note, refocuses attention on the "actual production and circulation practices" that are both enabled and constrained by platforms (Nieborg and Poell 2018, 8). Nieborg and Poell's theoretical framework is particularly useful for understanding the impacts of platformization on culture, and is leveraged here to better understand the changes that have occurred in podcasting. Like other forms of media, podcasting has also been re-shaped by platformization, though these transformations are distinct from other types of media largely due to the openness of its technical infrastructure.

Apple's iTunes and Early Podcast Platformization

Podcasting has been inextricably linked to tech giant Apple, which was chiefly responsible for popularizing it in the early 2000s. In the first few years of its existence, users were required to cut and paste RSS links into podcatching software in order to download audio files and syndicate (or "subscribe to") a podcast. In an era before social media giants like Facebook and Twitter, RSS feeds were popularized via individual websites, through blogs, traditional news websites, and via several new online directories that were launched in 2005. Two of the most popular directories of the time were PodcastAlley. com and PodcastPickle.com (Cochrane 2005). Thematic podcast networks also began to emerge, such as techpodcasts.com, which featured technology-themed podcasts. Users during this era were required to utilize a multi-step process to successfully listen to a podcast: first, locate the podcast via one of these small directories; second, copy the RSS feed address; third, paste it into podcatcher software; and finally, download the audio file to the computer for playback.

While RSS made it technically possible for users to subscribe via podcatcher software like iPodder, the process was cumbersome and not well understood outside communities of tech enthusiasts. When Apple CEO Steve Jobs announced the release of iTunes 4.9 at the Apple Worldwide Developers Conference on June 28, 2005, he trumpeted its ability to provide easy access to audio podcasts, calling podcasting "TiVO for radio." Unlike iTunes' music store, which sold music MP3 files direct to consumers, iTunes operated as a visually attractive and easily navigable podcatcher, allowing users to subscribe to RSS-enabled audio feeds via Apple's software. As one tech journalist recalled, "prior to the iTunes 4.9 update on June 28, 2005, podcasts were so clumsily arranged around the internet and so technologically challenging to use on any device other than a desktop or laptop computer that only the most tech-savvy even knew they existed" (Friess 2015). Apple's dominant market share in digital music sales (which reached 69 percent of the market by 2009) had the effect of instantly introducing podcasts to millions of potential listeners (Frommer 2009). In essence, "iTunes 4.9 effectively brought podcasting into the cultural mainstream" (Bottomley 2015a, 164).

The structure of Apple's initial podcatcher interface and governance structure shaped the development of podcasting distribution in several important ways. On the surface, the iTunes version 4.9 podcatcher software interface was virtually identical to that of iTunes' music store, with a search bar interface to facilitate keyword searches, a list of "Top Podcasts" indicating popular or most downloaded shows, and thematic categories of podcast content. To harmonize the podcasts section of iTunes with its music store counterpart (which featured music album covers), Apple introduced cover art for their podcasts. This encouraged producers to create visually stimulating identifiers for podcasts (all others were given a generic RSS icon), which, in turn, shaped consumers' expectations for podcasts. In his keynote address announcing iTunes Version 4.9, Steve Jobs' enthusiasm for podcasting was specifically linked to larger companies' content (including major radio broadcasters, network broadcasters, magazines, newspapers, and companies like Disney, Proctor & Gamble, Ford, and General Motors) rather than amateurs. Content from these institutional content providers was given prominent space on iTunes which allowed consumers to discover it more readily. This linkage created by Steve Jobs and Apple—between podcasting and professionalized, corporate media—bears more than a passing resemblance to David Sarnoff's RCA in the early days of radio. In the late 1920s, RCA effectively defined the practice of radio broadcasting as a corporate one-to-many experience, rather than an audio exchange among everyday citizens or creative amateurs (see Sterne et al. 2008a). Lastly, unlike its music store counterpart, Apple's pass-through of RSS feeds to its podcatcher terms meant that all podcasts be distributed for free on iTunes. Since Apple did not choose to host the audio data files for download (thereby essentially adopting the decentralization model of RSS), it also thereby rendered paywalls, pay-per-download, or other monetary exchanges for podcasting impossible via iTunes. This was one of the factors that pushed early podcasters to pursue advertiser-supported revenue models.

Podcasting's Post-2005 Platform Proliferation

The first element of Nieborg and Poell's (2018) model concerns the impacts of platform infrastructure on market structures. In the case of podcasting, the decentralized infrastructure of RSS is largely responsible for its fragmented structure today. Since 2005, there has been a proliferation of podcast platforms. While this level of fragmentation would seem to defy the centripetal pull of platformization, recent moves toward greater centralization are slowly altering the status quo. There are three primary functions of media-related platform services: *storage*, *discovery*, and *consumption*. Typical Web 2.0 platforms such as YouTube, Flickr, Netflix, or Amazon Prime encapsulate all three of these functions: they present content for users to discover or search through their interface; they serve as a data repository for the files to be delivered to the user (whether via download or streaming); and they offer embedded playing software to allow users to consume media. In the case of podcasting, these three functions have been often (though not always) separated into different services. As the primary distribution mechanism, RSS is simply a text file that points to content housed elsewhere on the web. Consequently, directory services like Apple Podcasts (Apple's new name for its iTunes podcatcher) point to the content rather than storing the audio or video files. Podcast data is typically stored on a traditional web host or on a dedicated podcast host site. Second, the content discovery function in podcasting is typically served by podcast directories that organize podcasts into categories along with keyword search capability. Third, listeners must rely upon software to consume digital audio content. On the one hand, this separation of functions into separate services has lowered barriers for market entrants, creating a rush of new competitive services specializing in one or more of these functions. On the other hand, the rush of companies and entrepreneurs to enter the podcasting market has created a somewhat confusing and chaotic landscape for both consumers and podcasters. The drive to streamline the process of podcast discovery and consumption in order to maximize audience size (in order to capture advertising revenue) is one of the major driving forces behind the increasing platformization of the medium today. These three functions and the current podcast platformization trends found in each are briefly considered below.

Storage Platforms and Consumption Metrics

Podcasting requires that audio data files are stored on servers and hosting services. There are a plethora companies hosting data files, many of which cater to the specific needs of podcasters. These services typically offer podcasters an array of features in addition to the storage of audio files and the management of the podcast RSS feed. Blubrry, for example, developed a plugin entitled PowerPress in 2008 to allow its customers to more easily create and maintain an RSS feed from their WordPress webpages and blogs. Other podcast hosts have developed similar WordPress plugins. As interest in podcasting has risen dramatically, there has been a rapid expansion in podcast hosting companies, all of them promising to streamline the process of storing podcast audio files, maintaining and validating podcast RSS feeds, and registering podcasts on the major directories (discussed below). These hosting companies include Podbean (launched 2006), Podomatic (launched 2008), BlogTalkRadio (launched 2008), Audioboom (launched 2009), Buzzsprout (launched 2009), Spreaker (launched 2009), Simplecast (launched 2013), Fireside.fm (launched 2015), and Castos (launched 2017), among many others. Like all forms of web hosting, there is a monthly subscription cost associated with podcast hosting (often graduated according to the number of downloads), so the distributed infrastructure of RSS ironically creates an initial financial barrier to new podcasters.[1] Podcast hosting companies are typically the first point of contact with independent podcasters, and they are the strongest podcast evangelists, since their business depends upon increasing the number of new content producers. With the rising

---

[1] This is not the case for two large storage platforms that offer free accounts, SoundCloud and Spotify for Podcasters (Anchor.fm).

commercial potential of the medium, some consolidation has begun to among podcast hosts. In 2017, for instance, BlogTalkRadio merged with Spreaker, and recently both companies were bought out by Voxnest.

Anchor.fm, the free amateur-focused podcasting platform launched to fanfare at South by Southwest festival in 2016 and subsequently purchased by Spotify in 2019 (and renamed "Spotify for Podcasters"), staked its business model on providing its users a free, "one stop" solution to podcasting (Shontell 2016). Anchor enabled users to record audio directly via a smartphone app, edit the file and add music via app, upload it to Anchor's servers, and distribute it directly to major directories like Apple Podcasts, Google Play Music, and Spotify, all for free. Anchor.fm generates income by embedding advertising across all of its user-produced podcast content. There has been exponential growth in the introduction of new podcasts, and much of that can be attributed to the success of Anchor in lowering the entry barrier to podcast production. As Figure 3.1 illustrates, despite its relatively late market entry, as of May 2023, Anchor hosted 24.2 percent of all new podcast episodes. For context, it's important to note that Anchor.fm's share of podcasts far eclipses long-established podcast hosts like Libsyn and Spreaker, and even outpaces SoundCloud, the other free podcast host.

Hosting companies are key players in the podcast market because their platforms allow them to gather valuable data on content consumption. Specifically, when content directories (like Apple Podcasts) reference the RSS feed to signal the transfer of an audio file, the podcast host registers the download from its server and notes the distribution source for the download as well as the operating system (desktop, iOS, or Android). Although podcast metrics are still in their infancy and there has been much debate among industry players about the appropriate consumption data, one key measure has been "downloads per episode" (DPE) as reported by the podcast host (podcast metrics are discussed in detail in Chapter 6). In 2017, hosting companies, along with advertisers, ad agencies, podcast networks, and representatives from public radio, collaborated under the auspices of the Interactive Advertising Bureau (IAB) to create a set of podcast measurement standards (Interactive Advertising Bureau 2017b) that were based largely on the DPE standard. This move placed podcast hosts as the central

Hosting Service	% of New Podcast Episodes
1. Spotify for Podcasters (Anchor.fm)	24.2%
2. Buzzsprout	9.3%
3. Spreaker	6.0%
4. Libsyn	4.6%
5. Omny Studio	4.6%
6. Megaphone	4.2%
7. Podbean	3.9%
8. Soundcloud	3.2%
9. RSS.com	2.2%
10. iVoox	2.0%
11. Acast	2.0%
12. Simplecast	1.8%
13. Transistor	1.5%
14. Triton Digital	1.0%

FIGURE 3.1 *Podcast media-hosting services by new episode share (May 2023).*
Source: Spurlock, J. (2023, June 1). Top Podcast Hosting Companies by Episode Share (May 2023). *Livewire Labs*. https://livewire.io/podcast-hosts-by-episode-share/.

platforms in the generation of an industry-wide standard for podcast consumption (Fleck 2018). The file storage platforms, then, act as a service provider to both podcasters and advertisers, though in distinct ways.

Discovery Platforms and the Threat of Podcast Enclosure

Since audio files are scattered around the internet and locatable via their RSS feeds, the second major function of podcast platforms is to facilitate the discovery of those podcasts and to allow listeners to "subscribe," which then provides them updates when new content is added for a particular show. Network externalities play an outsized role in podcast discovery, since listeners gravitate to directories that allow for greatest ease of discovery and that have the most comprehensive directories (network externalities are also key for search engines, and account for the huge market advantage of Google, for example). Discovery platforms typically do not store the audio files on their servers, and instead pass through the MP3 file that is accessed from the podcast host server. Like the MP3 file itself, the RSS feed acts as a "container technology" (Sterne 2006). The most dominant directory for the first decade of the medium was Apple Podcasts (formerly iTunes), which enjoyed a significant "first to market" advantage (Interactive Advertising Bureau 2017b). While there are over a hundred podcast directories online, there are only two other significant discovery platforms: YouTube (Google) and Spotify. US survey data from 2023 reveal that 33 percent of listeners discover podcasts on YouTube, followed by Spotify (24 percent) and Apple Podcasts (12 percent) (Götting 2023). Professional and indie podcasters are often bewildered at the panoply of distribution outlets. Most aim to include their shows in as many discovery platforms as possible to maximize audience traffic. This has fueled the growth in podcast hosting platforms that promise a "one stop" solution for distribution via the largest directories. Podcast hosting companies typically register their customers on all of the major discovery platforms.

Nieborg and Poell's (2018) model draws attention to the re-alignment of technical infrastructures thanks to the expanded reach of platforms via algorithms, SDKs, and APIs. In the case of podcasting, Apple's importance as a discovery platform is even greater thanks to its API, which extends its directory service beyond its own Apple Podcasts service. Popular mobile podcast consumption apps such as Overcast, Pocket Casts, Downcast, and Podcast Addict all utilize Apple's directory for listing podcasts by linking their apps to the Apple Podcasts API. Apple's terms of service also introduce a form of editorial control over the content and presentation of podcasts on its directory. At times podcast hosts receive complaints about their shows being "de-listed" from Apple Podcasts for violating its rules or terms of service. For example, Apple does not allow its name or the names of its products to be in any podcast title, it blocks long podcast titles, it prevents URL links from podcast show notes and even polices cover art images (Cochrane and Greenlee 2018). Apple Podcasts currently acts also as an archive for podcast shows, allowing listeners to discover shows that are no longer being actively produced (something that podcasters call "podfaded" shows). Some estimates are that perhaps only half of the more than 500 thousand podcasts listed on Apple Podcasts have posted new content in the past three months (Goldstein 2018). If Apple were to automatically "de-list" podcasts that had not recently updated their content, for example, Apple Podcasts would look quite different and much content would become almost impossible for listeners to find. Podcasting's dependence on platform APIs like Apple's is similar to trends in other social media such as Facebook and Twitter, wherein upstream decisions by the platform about information distribution can have profound consequences for downstream services, apps (Kastrenakes 2018), and even media scholars (Burgess and Bruns 2012).

Along with the power of discovery platforms to direct listeners' attention, they also have the potential to create artificial scarcities of content to maximize the potential for revenue. For example, the business press has been excitedly suggesting for some time that the "Netflix of podcasting" moment has arrived, whereby platforms serve up "premium" or "exclusive" audio content to listeners that requires a subscription fee (Nagy 2015; Porch 2018; Rowe 2017), although some are more circumspect about this potential (Quah 2018b; Rosenblatt 2018). Podcasters have largely approached the notion of "Netflix-ization" with scorn and derision (Fang 2018). In their eyes, podcasting will never transform into a subscription-based service due to the open architecture of RSS: How can you take something that is freely distributed via RSS and essentially lock it up behind a paywall?

The reality is, however, that *platform enclosure*—the creation of "walled gardens" of content available only to monthly subscribers—is slowly taking hold in podcasting. Ironically, indie podcasters themselves have paved the way for enclosure by adopting similar techniques for monetizing their own podcasts: that is, by offering "premium" content that is available only via a monthly subscription. Larger industry players are replicating these strategies to either lure more customers to their platform, or to "lock in" existing customers by encouraging them to access podcast content via their existing service. How can platform enclosure take hold in a medium that is built upon the open standard of RSS? The answer is that major audio content platforms are slowly steering listeners away from RSS-delivered audio content. For example, Spotify introduced three

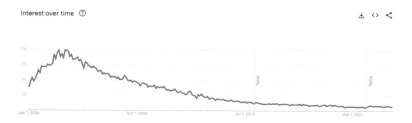

FIGURE 3.2 *Google search interest for "RSS" (2004–present).*

new podcasts in 2017, and these shows were only available on its streaming app, and not via RSS (Roettgers 2017). Spotify went a step further in 2018 and secured a deal to exclusively distribute the *Joe Budden Podcast*, a popular hip-hop music podcast (Saponara 2018). Spotify's deal with Joe Budden was noteworthy because it stipulated that new episodes of Budden's podcast would not be distributed via RSS, but would instead be found only on Spotify. Spotify's deal is the first that would essentially *remove* content that was previously distributed via RSS and lock its distribution into a proprietary platform. This move is not dissimilar to the recent strategic alliance between Facebook and *The New York Times*, where readers increasingly link to online news via the social media giant at the expense of the open framework of RSS (Plantin et al. 2018). As RSS recedes into the background as a major source of podcast distribution (see Figure 3.2), podcast directories and streaming platforms are aiming to shift distribution away from open infrastructures and toward their own services to maximize the "winner take all" functions of platforms.

Consumption Apps and Platform Alliances

The third important function of online media platforms is to allow users to consume the content. In the early years of podcasting prior to the introduction of the iPhone in 2007, most listeners consumed podcasts either on their computers or on dedicated digital audio devices such as iPods. In an increasingly mobile era, however, podcast consumption has shifted to mobile devices, mediated largely via the iOS and Android mobile operating systems. The Interactive Advertising Bureau (2017b) found that roughly 45–52 percent of all podcast consumption in the United States was achieved via the Apple Podcast app on iOS. The inclusion of a default, pre-installed podcast app in Apple's iOS Version 8.0 update in 2014 was a significant factor in expanding the audience for podcasting, resulting in 13.7 billion episode downloads on that platform in 2017 alone (Locker 2018). This dramatic increase in podcast listenership over such a short period of time demonstrates the power of apps—and the default software settings behind those apps—to drive discovery and consumption behaviors (for more on the power of software defaults, see Kitchin and Dodge 2011; Shah and Kesan 2008; Shah and Sandvig 2008). While Apple's iOS podcast app dominates, there are numerous competing apps that allow users to subscribe and consume podcasts such as Stitcher, Pocket Casts, Overcast, Podcast Addict, BeyondPod, DoggCatcher and Downcast, and Castbox, among many others. Adding to the fragmentation in consumption apps, some podcast hosting companies (like Podbean, for example) have launched a dedicated podcasting app. Lastly, the app-ification of podcasting is also well underway, with a number of popular podcasts such as *This American Life* and *The Dave Ramsey Show* launching their own dedicated apps within the iOS and Android app stores. Podcast hosting companies like Libsyn and Spreaker have fueled app-ification by offering to launch a dedicated app for their customers' podcasts as part of their subscription fee.

Mobile consumption apps are critical to the infrastructure of podcasting because they provide dual functionality as both tools of content discovery and consumption. Many of these apps are aligning themselves strategically and financially with discovery platforms to monetize their users' data and to introduce artificial scarcities. Several mobile apps have been increasingly become the target of acquisitions by large media companies wishing to gain a foothold in the podcasting market. For example, E.W. Scripps, a traditional media company that owns a diverse portfolio of legacy media such as newspapers, broadcast radio and television stations, purchased podcast advertising firm Midroll in 2015 for $10 million and quickly followed with a $4.5 million purchase of podcasting app Stitcher in 2016 (Perlberg 2016). Sensing the importance of consumption apps, in May 2018, a consortium of public radio organizations including NPR, WNYC Studios, WBEZ Chicago, and *This American Life* purchased Pocket Casts (Mullin 2018), though this consortium later sold the app to Automattic, the organization behind the Wordpress and Tumblr online platforms (Carman 2021e).

Podcast mobile apps are also moving to make strategic alliances with large content providers. For instance, Castbox—a new podcast mobile app that raised over $13 million in venture capital funding—has a section of its free app designated as "premium" content that is available via an in-app subscription (Sawers 2018). Some of the content in this premium section is produced by Castbox itself, and the rest is produced by its content partner, Wondery (InsideRadio 2018). Similarly, the iHeartRadio app (which has a very small curated list of podcasts in its own directory of 20,000) has leveraged its ties to the broadcast radio industry to make aggressive moves into podcasting. iHeartRadio purchased the HowStuffWorks podcast network for $55 million on September 15, 2018, enabling it to exclusively feature those podcasts and paving the way for more "premium" content for its mobile app (Jarvey 2018). While Apple has yet to move its own podcasting directory in the direction of platform enclosure, it is aggressively pursuing this strategy in video, having invested US $1 billion in acquiring and commissioning original content for a new streaming service that will compete directly with other video platform giants such as Netflix, Amazon Prime, and Hulu (D'Alessandro 2018; Mickle 2017). These platform alliances indicate that the fragmentation in podcasting is slowly giving way to platform consolidation in the service of monetization and audience maximization.

Platform Governance in a Fragmented Ecosystem

Nieborg and Poell's (2018) model also draws attention to the means by which platform governance shapes the means of cultural production. As noted above, podcasting has seen a proliferation of storage, discovery, and consumption platforms since 2005, making governance a patchwork affair. Each of the storage and discovery platforms includes their own terms of service (TOS) and editorial guidelines. As Gillespie (2018) has noted, the rules established by platforms exist primarily to protect the platform's public brand and profitability, though these goals are often intertwined with a "deeply felt commitment of the platform operators for nurturing a healthy community." Apple Podcasts' TOS outlines content parameters that are similar to those of other online platforms. For example, Apple's terms of service prohibit the following from podcasts listed on their iTunes services:

- Irrelevant content or spam.
- Explicit language without setting the <explicit> tag.
- Content that could be construed as racist, misogynist, or homophobic.
- Explicit or self-censored explicit language in titles, subtitles, or descriptions.
- References to illegal drugs, profanity, or violence in the title, description, artwork, or episodes.
- Content depicting graphic sex, violence, gore, illegal drugs, or hate themes.
- Third-party content or trademarks without legal authorization or usage rights.

    Source: Apple Media Services Terms and Conditions (https://www.apple.com/legal/internet-services/itunes/us/terms.html)

Apple's governance structure goes beyond the above editorial guidelines to include the protection of its brand identity. For instance, Apple prohibits the words Apple Music, iTunes Store, iTunes, Apple Podcasts, or Apple Inc. in podcast titles or descriptions, and prohibits pictures of its corporate logos, or of its technology (such as iPhone, iPad, or iPod) in any cover art image in its podcast directory. Podcast hosting companies have similar, but distinct, TOS agreements listed on their services, but given the increase in podcast launches post-2014 and their relatively small staffs, these services do not closely monitor the content of the podcasts they host.

Early in its existence and prior to its acquisition by Spotify, Anchor caused controversy within the podcasting community over its TOS. Flush with $10 million in venture capital funds (Roof 2017), Anchor has offered itself to would-be podcasters as a free service. Veteran podcasters and podcast hosting companies immediately began scrutinizing Anchor's TOS and found that the users of the site "grant [them] a worldwide, non-exclusive, royalty-free, sublicensable and transferable license to use, edit, modify, aggregate, reproduce, distribute, prepare derivative works of, display, and perform the User Content in connection with the operation of the Services." Veteran podcaster Dave Jackson (2018) noted at the time that Anchor's claim of ownership of user-generated content was much more restrictive than comparative social media platforms, including those of Twitter and Facebook. Anchor's move to centralize the control of the rights to podcast content points to the power of platforms to offer universal access as a "loss leader" in order to monetize user-generated content, in much the same way as Google leverages its content to sell advertising on YouTube.

The fragmented nature of podcast platforms also makes for a patchwork enforcement of editorial guidelines. In 2018, controversy surrounding the content of radio host and conspiracy theorist Alex Jones' *Infowars* program epitomized the challenges in policing content across podcasting's many platforms. On his *Infowars* radio program, which is also released as a podcast, along with several other *Infowars*-branded podcasts, right-wing host Jones was well-known for trafficking in conspiracy theories, including one that the Sandy Hook shooting was staged by "crisis actors." On August 5, 2018, after complaints from Sandy Hook victims' families and listeners, Spotify removed several episodes of Jones' podcast for violating its "hate speech" policy, followed swiftly by Apple, which completely removed (de-listed) five of its six *Infowars*-branded podcasts from its service (Vernon 2018). Podcast host Spreaker, which stored the audio files for *The Alex Jones Show* podcast, found itself suddenly thrust into the midst of a public controversy. Citing its own terms of service which prohibited the publication of "any content that promotes, either directly or indirectly, hate, racism, discrimination, pornography, or violence," Spreaker removed Jones' content from its own servers following the moves by Spotify and Apple (Schneider 2018). Many podcasters took note, however, that the main *Infowars* RSS feed was self-hosted on Jones' own website, and that listeners who wanted to access the content could simply subscribe manually to the feed (as they had done in the early days of podcasting) and continue to receive new episodes. Additionally, Apple faced mounting criticism for allowing the *Infowars* app (which contained much if not all of the same content) to remain in its App Store, arguing that it had not violated its App Store TOS, which did not feature the same language explicitly banning forms of hate speech. After a month of heavy criticism, on September 7, 2018 Apple relented and removed the *Infowars* app as well (Nicas 2018). Apple's choice to de-list *Infowars* also laid bare the symbiotic entanglements between their podcast directory and other apps, since all consumption apps that relied on Apple's directory API saw Alex Jones' content immediately removed from their directories as well, effectively ceding editorial control to Apple. The *Infowars* debacle served as an important inflection point in podcasting because it demonstrated the difficulties in managing a fractured governance structure from a multi-platform ecosystem.

Conclusion

Platformization has altered the landscape of podcast distribution in important ways. Online platforms have begun making major investments in the medium, hoping to attract listeners, advertisers, and new podcasters. Thanks to the decentralized architecture of RSS, the process of platformization outlined by Nieborg and Poell (2018) is progressing somewhat differently than for other large content-sharing services. Since the three functions of content platforms—storage, discovery, and consumption—are dispersed among podcast hosting companies, directories like Apple Podcasts, and mobile apps, respectively, podcasting initially appears less susceptible to the forces of platformization. However, as this discussion has outlined, the podcast market is undergoing rapid transformation, spurred largely by the interest of large tech giants like Apple, Spotify, and Google. Strategic alliances among discovery and consumption platforms, in particular, are moving podcasting in the direction of fully integrated content platforms like YouTube, Facebook, and Twitter. As Srnicek (2016, 98) has noted, the "tendencies" that emerge from the competitive dynamics of large platforms include the "expansion of extraction, positioning as a gatekeeper, and enclosure of ecosystems." Each of these tendencies can be observed in podcasting today, at least in the United States.

The network effects associated with platformization have differential benefits for listeners, content producers, podcast platforms, and advertisers. As podcasting becomes more popular, the number of podcasts in production has vastly expanded, creating an increasingly crowded content landscape. This presents a challenge for listeners hoping to discover new shows that may appeal to their particular interests. For listeners, then, centralized repositories like Apple Podcasts, Spotify, or Google Podcasts carry positive network effects thanks to the ease of discovery and the crowdsourced curation of podcasts (much like the Rotten Tomatoes ratings for films or Amazon's user-generated product reviews). Podcast networks, distributors, and advertisers, on the other hand, derive much different benefits from the network effects of platform centralization. For these players, the major value of platformization comes from their ability to glean more accurate consumption data from a large audience for the purposes of monetization. Current audience consumption data are based chiefly on server-side measures (downloads per episode) and platform-side measures such as subscriptions via podcatchers like Apple Podcasts, Spotify, Castbox, and Overcast, among others. What centralized platforms like Apple Podcasts and Spotify offer to distributors and advertisers is a glimpse into actual audience listening consumption. How much of that podcast episode, for example, was actually heard by audiences, and at what point did large numbers of listeners abandon the episode? Moreover, who is actually listening to what podcast? Thanks to their centrality as a destination for content consumption, online platforms such as Apple Podcasts and Spotify have access to a vast trove of personal data, including valuable information such as names, addresses, age, race, gender, credit card numbers, and more. This privileged access to listener data is directly contributing to the datafication of the podcast audience.

The implications of platform consolidation for independent podcasters are potentially more negative. On the one hand, the proliferation of storage and discovery platforms today works to the benefit of independent podcasters and amateurs because the ecosystem is still in considerable flux. Competing services and new technologies are launching almost daily, which lowers barriers to entry for new producers, particularly in the case of free services like Anchor.fm and SoundCloud. Once this industry churn has settled and the pace of consolidation quickens, distribution options for podcasters may begin to dwindle, leaving them with less autonomy to transform their hobby into full-time work on their own terms. Once large market players like Apple, Google, Amazon, and Spotify begin leveraging the power of network externalities to expand the podcast audience by offering paid subscription-based podcast content to their large existing customer bases, professional-quality podcasting (which some call "procasting") will become inextricably linked to platform services. As Nieborg and Poell (2018, 3) note, "as cultural production is becoming increasingly platform dependent, the autonomy and economic sustainability of particular forms of cultural production is increasingly compromised." Content producers wishing to reach audiences will naturally gravitate to such services because of their large listener base and the promotional advantages they provide. Independent podcasters have publicly scoffed at the idea that these platforms will ever dominate the medium because of its reliance on an open web standard, but content exclusivity deals and the increasing consolidation among discovery and consumption platforms may point to a platform-centric future, leaving RSS as a "second-class" distribution mechanism reserved for amateurs. In this sense, the oligopolization of podcast discovery stands to reshape the medium in the future.

CHAPTER FOUR

Professionalism and the Myth of Meritocracy

In *Gigged*, Sarah Kessler (2018) explores the explosion in Silicon Valley startups beginning in 2013, all of them hoping to reproduce the success of the ride-sharing service Uber. Describing themselves as "Uber for X," these entrepreneurs offered a vision of profitable companies built atop legions of contingent workers, providing what Kuehn and Corrigan (2013) have termed "hope labor." Following the runaway success of *Serial* in 2014, podcasting attracted similar entrepreneurial fervor. These new corporate players have also altered the expectations for podcasting by grafting commercial-style production values, audio quality, content genres, methods, and monetization structures onto the medium.

While podcasting was once synonymous with an informal, amateur ethos, it is increasingly being identified as a potential career for amateur cultural producers. Underlying these shifts in labor practice is the notion of *professionalism* (Evetts 2003). Professionalism provides a set of principles that allow a subset of individuals to organize and understand their labor and to distinguish their labor from amateurs (often by creating skill barriers to entry).

Copyright (2021) From "Uber for Radio? Professionalism and Production Cultures in Podcasting" by John L. Sullivan. Reproduced by permission of Taylor and Francis Group, LLC, a division of Informa plc. An earlier version of this chapter has been previously published and is used with permission.

While the professionalization of amateurs has been celebrated by some as a democratization of cultural production (Bruns 2008; Jenkins, Ford, and Green 2013; Shirky 2008), critical scholars have scrutinized a new regime that commodifies volunteer labor while offering few opportunities for those individuals to become part of the professional class (Andrejevic 2009; Duffy 2017; Kuehn and Corrigan 2013; Ross 2009; Scholz 2016; Terranova 2000).

In this chapter I explore labor shifts in online cultural production by examining emerging production cultures in podcasting. Specifically, I analyze the discourses of professionalism in two influential, well-known "how to" podcasts, *School of Podcasting* with Dave Jackson and *The Audacity to Podcast* with Daniel J. Lewis. These two podcasts are well-known to the podcasting community and have each won the People's Choice Award for "Best Technology Podcast": *The Audacity to Podcast* in 2012, and *School of Podcasting* in 2017 (The People's Choice Podcast Awards 2018). These podcasts are often recommended to new podcasters who are looking for advice on how to start and manage a podcast.

In these podcasts, Jackson and Lewis act as ersatz mentors to aspiring podcasters, offering advice about technology, show preparation, interviewing style, and audience maximization. The advice in these podcasts goes beyond a simple "how to," however. Embedded within these podcasts is a professional work ethos that guides cultural labor in a gig economy. This ethos is one of self-actualization and self-fulfillment, both of which can be achieved through freelance work. In situating podcasting as a viable alternative career, however, these "how to" programs also traffic in myths about the power of authenticity and meritocracy in a media landscape that is being reshaped by commercial and corporate interests. The gig economy relies on the bedrock principle of delayed gratification when it comes to cultural labor; that the long hours and tedious unpaid work required to cultivate skills will ultimately be recognized and financially rewarded by corporate producers. In other words, the gig economy is built upon the ethos of *meritocracy*, or the belief that market forces—often assessed and expressed via algorithmic formulas—will properly recognize and incentivize online and offline labor. These "how to" podcasts demonstrate the inherent contradictions underlying the boom in digital cultural labor.

Podcasting and the Formalization of User-Generated Content

As outlined in Chapter 1, scholars excitedly cataloged the cultural shift enabled by new content-sharing platforms online, arguing that online digital distribution had effectively leveled the playing field between media corporations and everyday citizens, allowing for a more democratic, "grass roots" economy (Freedman 2012). Shirky (2008), for example, has argued that we are witnessing the "mass amateurization" of cultural production. Benkler (2006) pushed this claim even further, arguing that human beings are experiencing a historical tipping point of engaged, democratic information access thanks to networked computing.

This utopian enthusiasm surrounding user-generated content, along with the surge in gig economy freelancing, has begun shifting the terms of labor for amateur podcasters. Amateur, online media producers are developing professional practices found in traditional media, and some are even abandoning their existing occupations to rely on their online activities for financial support. The movement of amateurs to actively pursue podcast production as a potential career can be understood as a form of "bottom up" formalization (see Chapter 2) as production practices become shared, routinized, and institutionalized via informal socialization practices. Indeed, podcasting has become not just a hobby activity, but a potential career for millions of disaffected creative professionals in the gig economy.

My focus in this chapter is specifically on the emergence of production cultures most commonly found in legacy forms of commercial media. What was once a bastion of "do-it-yourself" production ethos has now diversified into a constellation of new professional roles, including editors, advertisers, networks, technology companies, support software vendors, and a host of other ancillary services. Podcaster personalities like Leo Laporte, Marc Maron, Alex Blumberg, and others have served as role models for commercial success in the medium. This is having some recursive effects on independent, or "indie" podcasters by informing their own production practices.

The process underlying these shifts in labor practice is *professionalism* (or professionalization, which indicates the ongoing, emergent process of introducing professionalism into a given community of workers or creators). Sociologists have long been fascinated by professions and their role in organizing labor. One early and influential conceptualization of professionalism characterized it as a means for social communities to maintain a normative social order within capitalist economies (Parsons 1951). This view came under criticism in the 1970s and 1980s, with scholars arguing that professionalism represented an ideology that protected "powerful, privileged, self-interested monopolies" (Evetts 2003, 401). Either as normative value system or ideological system, it is clear that professionalism provides a set of principles that allow a subset of individuals to organize and understand their labor in particular way. Professionalism can also serve to create a "monopoly of competence legitimized by officially sanctioned 'expertise', and a monopoly of credibility with the public" (Larson 1977, 37). In this way, professions can be understood broadly as "the knowledge-based category of occupations which usually follow a period of tertiary education and vocational training and experience" (Evetts 2003, 397).

The rise of the gig economy—whereby amateur labor is decoupled from traditional institutional structures and managed remotely via apps or algorithms—has challenged traditional notions of professions. This shift has called into question traditional notions of "consumer" and "laborer." Media scholars have sought to understand the particular nature of online cultural production work and the unique collaborative affordances offered by online technologies. Bruns (2006; 2008) coined the term "produser" to describe this form of user-led content production and collaborative engagement, suggesting that it could provide a meaningful alternative to commercial media. Leadbeater and Miller (2004, 20) have described some of these amateur media creators as "pro-ams," or media creators who "pursue an activity as an amateur, mainly for the love of it, but [who] set a professional standard. Pro-Ams are unlikely to earn more than a small portion of their income from their pastime but they pursue it with the dedication and commitment associated with a professional." While the professionalization of amateurs has been celebrated as a form of democratization of cultural production, other scholars have critically scrutinized a new cultural production system that commodifies the volunteer labor with few opportunities for those individuals to become part of the professional class (Andrejevic 2009; Duffy 2015; Duffy and Pruchniewska 2017a; Kuehn and Corrigan 2013; Ross 2009; Terranova 2000).

Studying Production Cultures and Professionalism in Podcasting

Podcasting has traditionally attracted a small but dedicated cadre of amateur (mostly white male) producers (Markman 2012), but the explosion of its popularization since 2014 has brought a larger and more diverse group of producers into medium (Florini 2015). As the formalization of podcasting has progressed, cultures of podcast production have begun to flourish online. Indie podcasters congregate on Facebook groups, via Twitter handles, and at conferences dedicated to the medium such as PodFest, Third Coast International Audio Festival, and Podcast Movement (Sullivan 2018). Podcasters monitor each other's work as well, particularly those shows, like the "how to" podcasts investigated in this essay, to exchange tips on audio equipment, show management, marketing, and monetization. This type of "self-theorizing" talk about production practices to the types of professional talk among legacy media workers.

Examining the discourse between and among these production cultures can illuminate some of the concerns, struggles, and values that shape individuals' understanding of the medium and their own labor. What types of production practices are most valued among these production communities, and what practices are to be avoided? How is the concept of "professionalism" understood by Pro-Ams and amateur podcast producers? Toward what goals should indie podcasters strive in the rapidly formalizing landscape of podcasting? Lastly, what value systems or ethos should guide the production of podcasts?

As a medium freely distributed online, podcasting does not have an institutionalized structure for establishing social and professional norms as do other legacy industries like broadcast radio or television. The trade press typically fulfills this function in those industries (Corrigan 2018). In contrast, podcasting mobilizes online forums such as Facebook groups and podcasts themselves, where amateur and self-employed podcasters exchange narratives about their production practices. On the one hand, these discourses constitute a collection of "best practices" for podcasters, helping them to navigate the logistics of recording, editing, distributing, marketing, and monetizing podcasting. On the other hand, these discourses also work to socialize podcasters by employing assumptions about work ethics, expectations for success, and developing standards for audio quality, among other things. Thus, these discourses play a constitutive role in building a professional ethos around the cultural practice of podcasting.

To explore production discourses in podcasting, I look specifically at two popular, long-running weekly podcasts *School of Podcasting*, hosted by Dave Jackson (launched in 2005), and *The Audacity to Podcast* hosted by Daniel J. Lewis (launched in 2010). To obtain a representative sample from across the history of each show (*School of Podcasting* has recorded 630 episodes, and *The Audacity to Podcast* has 333 episodes), twenty episodes of each podcast were selected randomly for analysis. Each show's first episode was also included in the analysis, as well as an episode of *School of Podcasting* when Dave Jackson interviewed Daniel J. Lewis. Every show in the sample was downloaded and transcribed for analysis using Quirkos qualitative data software.

The Discourse of Entrepreneurism and Professional Standards

The ostensible aim of both *School of Podcasting* and *The Audacity to Podcast* is to provide training for amateurs to assist them creating, recording, and distributing, marketing, and monetizing their podcasts. Although blogging and podcasting have similar roots as a vibrant source for amateur, alternative media, the complexities of recording and editing sound, including the extra equipment (and associated costs) required to do this work, create technical barriers to entry for new podcasters. This creates a niche for shows like *School of Podcasting* and *The Audacity to Podcast*, both of which advertise themselves as new user-friendly guides to the world of podcasting. One of the chief aspects of professionalism is "the creation of a training credential that becomes a prerequisite for entering a labor market and performing a defined set of tasks" (Freidson 2001, 84). Jackson and Lewis position themselves as guardians of the complex world of podcasting by offering practical advice in the form of self-referential narratives about their own podcasting successes and failures. There were three main modes of professional discourse throughout the programs in this sample: (1) technical advice about production and distribution practices, including monetization strategies; (2) community building as a form of audience maximization; and (3) self-actualization, authenticity, and passion as the drivers to gig labor success.

Production and Marketing Advice: Professionalizing Audio Quality and Perfecting Sound

Throughout the episodes included in this sample, the primary topic of conversation was on the "best practices" for some of the technical aspects of launching a podcast, including recording and editing audio files, locating a web hosting service to store the audio files, managing the RSS feed, and making sure that the podcast was correctly listed in large directories such as Apple Podcasts, Google Podcasts, and Spotify, among others.

Although each podcast featured hundreds of episodes about specific tips, tricks, and "don'ts" regarding podcasting, Jackson and Lewis both argued consistently that the skill barriers to the medium were low. In one episode where Lewis describes the type of microphone and recording equipment he uses to record his show, for example, he made it clear that "If you want to start out podcasting, please don't let all of this high tech expensive equipment and all of these dollar signs intimidate you." When it came to questions of audio quality in the recording and editing process, Lewis eschewed the kind of perfectionism that defines commercial radio, noting:

> I'm not that worried about audio. I think your audio quality should be as good as you can get, but I've always realized that I'm the kind of person that can just never be happy with my audio, so I don't go that crazy with it.
>
> (Daniel J. Lewis, January 10, 2010)

Similarly, Jackson's podcast emphasized the conversational breeziness of podcast audio, noting that it required little in the way of extra time or effort, making it ideal as a hobby or "side hustle" in addition to a full-time job. When talking about the time necessary to launch and maintain a weekly podcast, Dave Jackson scoffed when reading one listener's email about how much time it takes to prepare for their podcast: "Here's somebody that's saying, 'Look, it takes me 14 hours to do two shows.' And again, for me, that's insane ....To me you shouldn't be spending more than six hours [per week] to actually put out the podcast, record it, things like that."

Despite the assurances from Jackson and Lewis that podcasting did not require a good deal of money or upfront time commitment to succeed, their recommendations for podcasters about best practices—couched in narratives about their own failure or those of others—offered up a conflicting set of precepts for a "quality" podcast. For example, both hosts spoke disparagingly about free web hosting services. Web hosting is necessary for podcasters to create a webpage for the show and is necessary to store the audio files and to maintain the RSS feed (which allows the podcast to be distributed). Dave Jackson remarked in a 2012 episode that "I would never do something [like that] for *The School of Podcasting*." The clear implication here is, of course, that free web hosting is inadequate and reflects poorly on the podcaster. Similarly, in an episode of *The Audacity to Podcast* in which Daniel J. Lewis reflects on some of his own early mistakes as a podcaster, noting:

> I also wasn't willing to invest money and maybe you can answer this question because I can't. What is it with podcasting that many people approached podcasting as a hobby? ... This is one of my mistakes. I wasn't willing to invest money in my podcast. I wanted to do everything for free.
> (Daniel J. Lewis, November 11, 2013)

In a 2010 episode Lewis links non-free web hosting to a sense of professionalism for podcasters. Exhorting his listeners to spend money on their own unique domain name (like "lewis.com"), he stated, "What's important about this is it just sounds so much more professional. Again, going back to branding, going back to having your own domain in the first place, is would you trust someone more if they say, 'Visit my podcast dot com.' Or if they say, 'Visit my podcast dot podbeam dot freepodcast dot com slash user?'" Similar to Jackson, the "mistake" of early podcasting is to find free services to host and distribute audio content. Both hosts also dispensed advice on techniques for interviewing and speaking on air. For example, Jackson critiqued several podcasts for featuring dull interviews with guests, including one of his early podcasts. He noted that there's "nothing more fun than interviewing somebody with a bunch of 'yup' and 'nope' answers." Citing his own mistakes as an amateur podcaster in 2013, Lewis noted that "another mistake I made was I didn't schedule my time for my podcast …. I started in 2007 and by 2009 I had only released nine complete episodes. Two years, nine episodes: That's fewer than one episode per month! I had a problem and that was, I was procrastinating." Here Lewis argues that scheduled regularity and a strong work ethic are necessary for podcasts to be successful. Jackson offered similar recommendations for the regularization of output, noting that audiences are expecting content on a regular basis.

This level of commitment extends to the crafting of each episode as well. Speaking in his debut episode, Lewis remarked, "You need to be professional. You need to have your thoughts organized." Similar to the social media entrepreneurs discussed by Duffy (2017), these podcast mentors emphasized the necessity of being consistent with creative output in order to regularize content production and cultivate an audience base. There is a contradiction at the heart of these podcasts, however: while they celebrate the openness of the medium and the freedom of amateurs to create new cultural content, they caution listeners against seeming "unprofessional" by eschewing time commitments, money, organization, and specific interview styles.

Additionally, Jackson and Lewis outlined specific strategies for monetizing podcast content, often offering their own shows as exemplars for successful monetization. Jackson, for example, offered "premium content" on a password-protected segment of his website for listeners who paid a monthly subscription fee. Lewis noted that this was a potentially successful model for monetization, but that the "model of premium stuff is a bit difficult because you have to have content that's in high enough demand … Someone else said it to me today, is that 'content wants to be free', and we want content for free. So, it's very difficult if you're going to charge for content." Lewis noted that some podcasters also rely on listener donations as well. Both hosts suggested that advertising sponsorships or affiliate links—whereby listeners could use a special code with an online retailer to obtain a discount—were more likely to be effective for amateur podcasters. Jackson noted that advertisers would expect to see metrics in order to "prove to the advertiser that that traffic came from you so that when it comes time to renew that advertiser, you can say, 'Well look, in a month time I brought you 120 clicks. You said that 30 people bought our product' et cetera." Monetizing podcast content through branded merchandise such as T-shirts and cups was also mentioned as a possible method of monetization.

This production and marketing advice dispensed by Lewis and Jackson thus emphasized several key points: First, that podcasts had relatively low barriers to entry, but for those wanting to produce "professional" quality shows, upfront investment was a necessity. Second, both hosts outlined specific production strategies, such as purchasing specific equipment, speaking technique, interview styles, and regularizing of new production as a means for success. Third, these hosts introduced monetization as a key goal for podcasters and outlined several strategies to extract value from listeners, either through subscriptions, donations, advertising sponsorship, or merchandising.

Building Communities, Not Audiences: Podcasting as Affective Labor

The podcasting advice outlined above often contrasted with other discourses that emphasized the unique aspects of podcasting labor as an engaging, interactive experience for both hosts and audiences. Both Lewis and Jackson mobilized terms often associated with non-profit media, such as "providing a service" for the audience or fostering a sense of "community" via podcast production. Part of the "service" that is expected of podcasters, they noted, is to create a *personal and emotional connection* with listeners while simultaneously commodifying those listeners by connecting them to advertisers via personal "host read" ad copy. As mentioned above, both hosts identified monetization as a central goal of successful podcasting. David Jackson framed this need rather baldly in a 2006 episode, stating, "What does the podcaster want? He wants listeners. Okay?" The key to this, however, was identified as building "relationships" with audiences and creating forms of organic "community" around the podcast. Both hosts argued that successful podcasters were able to expand their audience base by connecting to their listeners on a personal and emotional level. On top of the technical and entrepreneurial savvy, then, podcasting was associated with a type of affective labor that defines other types of Web 2.0 production as well (Andrejevic 2011; Duffy 2015; Gregg 2009).

Notwithstanding the professional advice about audio quality and monetization, both Jackson and Lewis argued that podcasting labor should be motivated by the desire to give something to others rather than crass, commercial imperatives. The message here was that a podcaster should "be a giver, not a taker." As Jackson stated in an early episode, "Behind the scenes, I really just want to help people. I mean, it sounds kind of cheesy, but that's really a lot of the motivation behind it." This altruistic goal was echoed by Lewis, who argued podcasters should be motivated by a desire to help others and to create a lasting personal connection. Speaking about another podcast he hosts that features TV show reviews, Lewis expanded upon this theme of selfless giving:

> It's not about us telling our stories. It's about making people smile and laugh and lifting their moods during a rough day … It's about sharing passions together ….[audiences] can join our community, listen to our podcast, and they feel like they're one of us and they enjoy chatting with us.
>
> (Daniel J. Lewis, November 11, 2013)

Both Jackson and Lewis argued that the motivation for podcasting from this desire to provide support, entertainment, or respite to listeners. As Lewis notes above, the ethos of podcasting is about giving away labor for free out of a desire and commitment to change others' lives for the better. Given the urgings of both hosts to pursue professionalism in podcast production, this public service-oriented discourse rests uncomfortably alongside the goals of audience monetization. The two were linked in one important way, however: The putative reward for such efforts was a sense of personal satisfaction that would inevitably lead to more listeners and—by extension—expanded opportunities for monetization.

Both podcasts linked this notion of affective labor to the interactions between the podcaster and the audience by repeatedly invoking the concept of "community." Successful podcasters were able to expand their audience by creating and carefully nurturing a community of listeners and responding to their desires. While podcasting audiences are typically the ones who listen to media content, Jackson and Lewis urged podcasters to carefully listen to their audiences to show them that they "care" about those audiences and their needs. For example, in a 2013 episode, Jackson played a voicemail from another podcaster who had conducted a survey of her listeners in order to determine the types of topics she should cover in her show. Jackson was enthusiastic about this approach, noting approvingly that "She listened to her audience and in the same way that people trust you because you're the expert, you trust your audience, right, because you're pals, you're buds." Lewis was similarly enthusiastic about fortifying personal connections to listeners, describing the interaction between podcaster and audience as a "relationship" that required careful nurturing. Instead of pursuing large numbers of downloads necessary for successful monetization, Lewis stressed that quality was more important than quantity, noting:

> Make this about relationships, not just numbers ... All of the tips I'm going to present to you today are related to relationships, connecting with people, not just trying to make another notch in your belt for RSS subscribers, but connecting with people. A relationship is far more beneficial to both of you in the relationship than just an extra subscriber, because a relationship has potential to go a whole lot farther in life.
> (Daniel J. Lewis, October 24, 2011)

One way to develop those relationships, argued Lewis, was to live broadcast the recording of the podcast so that podcasters could engage with listeners simultaneously. Lewis noted in a 2010 episode he was familiar with several repeat listeners in his chat room and was used to "calling my listeners by name. In the chat room right now, we've got Chuck, we've got Kay, we've got Faye, we've got Kylie Mac, we've got Ray was in here earlier ... I love that I know things about my listeners, and know what they're doing, and even consider them friends."

The foregrounding of this type of intensive relationship-building labor is similar to what scholars have found in other forms of online gig labor. In interviews with self-employed female bloggers, for example, Duffy and Pruchniewska (2017a) found that these entrepreneurs felt compelled to present themselves continually on social media in ways that reinforced traditional notions of femininity. Specifically, their interviewees felt a need engage in "soft self-promotion" to brand themselves through constant online interactions with their audience. These social media entrepreneurs found it increasingly challenging maintain these relationships with their audience, leading to stress and burnout (Duffy 2017). Similarly, both Lewis and Jackson argue that podcasting is less about building audience size than it is about reaching listeners by creating deeply emotional attachments to them in order to share ideas and to build an online community. These podcasts make it clear, however, that it is the responsibility of the podcaster to expend this emotional labor in order to ensure continued audience growth.

The Passionate Podcaster: Narratives of Authenticity and Self-actualization through Podcasting Labor

There is a contradiction at the heart of these "how to" podcasts. On the one hand, as outlined above, much of the content of these podcasts consists of practical advice on both the technical and entrepreneurial aspects of podcasting. At the same time, however, woven throughout these narratives is an underlying ethos of self-actualization or self-fulfillment that is strongly linked to freelance online cultural labor. Throughout the episodes sampled for this project, Jackson and Lewis strongly emphasized the necessity for successful podcasters to approach their craft with "passion" and "dedication" rather than to achieve high download numbers or to earn money from advertising. The key to podcasting success, according to these "how to" gurus, was to display your authentic, true personality in order to capture the audience's attention, imagination, and trust.

For example, in his debut episode, Daniel J. Lewis outlined the three core ingredients to a successful podcast: "P-O-D. Passion, organization, and dialogue. Passion is what is the most important thing for you to have in podcasting. If you are not passionate about what you're podcasting, then why are you podcasting?" As Lewis makes clear throughout his show, the motivation to create new content must come from an individual's inner drive and inspiration, regardless of whether the amateur podcaster has the skill or the equipment. The end result of this enthusiasm for your podcast subject matter was essentially the same for both hosts: it was to generate enthusiasm and a larger audience because, according to Lewis, "that passion is what will make people want to listen to you." Jackson similarly extolled the virtues of honesty in podcasting as the means for connecting most powerfully with listeners. He emphasized the importance of "being honest with yourself in terms of, 'This is what I want to talk about; this is what I love,' and find your voice. Be your voice."

Notions of authenticity were closely connected to ideals about the self-actualization that can come from gig labor. Both hosts spoke enthusiastically about "achieving the dream" of pursuing podcasting as an alternative to waged labor. As Lewis remarked, "be intentional about the things that you do, then someday, podcasting can help you achieve your dream, too. Whether it's a dream job, a dream position, a dream whatever, podcasting can help you get there." At times ignoring his own advice, Jackson argued that podcasting allowed individuals to free themselves from commercial conventions of audio production. In a 2007 episode, for example, he expressed his delight at having the creative freedom to decide upon the length of his show from one episode to the next:

> I'm less anxious for material. Every week, I'm going, 'You know what? If you just do a half an hour, that's okay. No one is saying you have to do 45 minutes or 55 minutes or whatever.' There's no rule. That's what's so lovely about this format, is that if for some reason I only have, heck, even 20 minutes or a half hour of material, it's okay.
>
> (Dave Jackson, September 17, 2007)

Lewis also contrasted podcasting labor with the more regimented, more constricted confines of wage labor. Over the first several years of his program, Lewis produced his show on weekends and evenings, all the while expressing his desire to pursue podcasting as a full-time occupation. He noted in 2012: "I had always loved this idea of being a freelancer, and I was getting to know more entrepreneurs and self-employed people, and I thought this idea was really neat because of the flexibility, because of the ability to pursue the passions that these people have, and it was really what I wanted to do." While Lewis chronicles his transition to podcasting several years later in his show, he offers some cautions to would-be podcast entrepreneurs looking to make a similar transition:

> You want to quit your job, you want to podcast full time and make all of your money just podcasting. I'll tell you what, it's very hard to do and most of the podcasters who are making lots of money form podcasting aren't making that lots of money form just their podcast. Their podcast is a part, but their podcast is a springboard to something else making them money.
> (Daniel J. Lewis, July 1, 2013)

Jackson and Lewis' orientation to the professionalization of podcasting emerges is both complex and contradictory. On the one hand, both hosts emphasize the creative freedoms and enhanced autonomy that is enabled through gig labor. On the other hand, they argue that successful freelance podcasting is dependent on the willingness of amateurs to project an indelible sense of authenticity to their audience and to carefully nurture that audience through extensive outreach, relationship maintenance, and affective labor.

Podcasting, Professionalism, and the Contradictions of Professional Labor

Podcasting is undergoing rapid formalization thanks to the entry of corporate media interests and an increased desire to seek profit by regularizing and standardizing the media. One major consequence of formalization in podcasting is the introduction of professionalism, or the development of standardized rules and routines that are meant to distinguish labor that is informed by the development of specialized skills and a particular orientation toward cultural labor. As I have explored in this chapter, two prominent "how to" podcasts—*School of Podcasting* and *The Audacity to Podcast*—actively construct a particular view of podcasting as an emergent, commercially viable industry that can serve as a full-time occupation for entrepreneurial amateurs. In these podcasts, hosts Jackson and Lewis argue that specific professional practices are key to success, such as the purchase and use of specific types of audio recording equipment, regularized production schedules, and reliance on advertising sponsorship and other monetization strategies. The hosts of these podcasts develop a specific image of the successful podcaster as a profit-driven professional. These discourses are extended via Jackson and Lewis' own self-branding as experts in the field. These two podcasts construct the notion of professionalism in two key ways. First, they dispense forms of knowledge that are important for the professionalization process, including technical knowledge about audio production, editing, and web hosting, among many other topics. Second, these hosts create an ethos of professionalism by offering praise for adopting standardized production techniques and by offering self-deprecating critiques of their own failures in this regard.

Podcasting production sits at an important nexus point between low- and high-skilled digital labor. Unlike "clickworkers" who perform micro-tasks for large platform-based web services like ClickRabbit, Fiverr, Amazon Turk, and ClickWorker (Casilli 2017; Scholz 2016), amateur podcasting involves the development of technical skills in audio recording, editing, and distribution. It is also accompanied by more creative autonomy than other forms of gig labor (such as ridesharing or grocery delivery, for example) in the sense that amateur labor is not specifically driven by algorithmic requirements or time constraints. Indeed, as outlined in these two "how to" podcasts, the promise of labor autonomy associated with podcast freelancing emerges as the cornerstone of their evangelism about the merits of the medium for amateur cultural production. At the heart of this discourse of professionalism is a powerful and seductive message of meritocracy: that amateur podcasters can successfully compete with established industry players thanks to the absence of industry gatekeepers, if they have the will to learn the skills and make shrewd choices about forms of production and distribution.

Yet amidst all of the highly detailed, technical advice, Jackson and Lewis' consistent message is that skills acquisition is only one part of the recipe for success. Indeed, as they emphasize, the innate precarity of gig labor can only be surmounted by being one's authentic, passionate self with their audience. On this point, Jackson and Lewis invoke an "imagined audience" that requires a level of ongoing emotional engagement in order to build an economically sustainable business. The affective labor described here has two components. First, it involves a particular type of self-branding that portrays one's self as unique and authentic by effectively stage-managing one's online presence on social media to cultivate new audiences. This emphasis on affective investment and authenticity as cornerstones of online labor has been found among other forms of gig labor such as social media marketing (Duffy and Pooley 2017; Scolere, Pruchniewska, and Duffy 2018), blogging (Duffy 2017; Duffy and Pruchniewska 2017a), and even amateur online pornography (Paasonen 2010). The second aspect of this affective labor involves a constant maintenance of the podcaster-audience relationship by incorporating listener feedback, suggestions, and their voices into the podcast itself. This type of "relational labor," as Baym (2015) has noted, refers to these continued efforts to "build social relationships that foster paid work." These forms of relational labor are largely invisible, yet are cited as the key for entrepreneurial success. As Terranova (2000, 38) notes, unwaged digital labor involves both technical skills and self-taught "forms of labour we do not immediately recognise as such: chat, real-life stories, mailing lists, amateur newsletters, and so on." The internalization of this ethos of self-actualization through skills-based professionalism and relational labor are the two pillars supporting notions of meritocracy in amateur podcasting.

Conclusion

In conclusion, these two "how to" podcasts offer a glimpse into how the inherent contradictions of the gig economy—freedom from wage labor on the one hand and precarity on the other hand—are discursively maintained. While they differ greatly in style, both *School of Podcasting* and *The Audacity to Podcast* construct podcasting as a profession by emphasizing specific production and distribution practices, by emphasizing the goal of audience maximization and monetization, and by embracing an entrepreneurial ethos. At the same time, hosts Jackson and Lewis rely advance familiar tropes of online gig labor by exhorting their listeners to cultivate and actively manage their relationships with audiences via forms of affective labor. At the core of these podcasts is an implicit message of meritocracy: If amateurs are willing to learn the skills, follow the advice, and invest the necessary time and capital, they will achieve economic viability. Given the stiff headwinds of a rapidly formalizing podcasting market, this call to taken on "hope labor" (Kuehn and Corrigan 2013) ultimately obscures the more grim economic realities facing online digital workers.

CHAPTER FIVE

Podcast Conventions and the Entrepreneurial Dream

Alex Blumberg's podcast entitled *Start Up* tells the story of his halting and sometimes comically inept efforts to start his own fledgling podcast production company, Gimlet Media. A public radio producer and refugee from National Public Radio's (NPR) hit series *This American Life*, Blumberg struggles to grasp the basics of startups, such as drafting a business model, courting skeptical venture capitalists, finding a financial partner, and cultivating his own personal brand. Blumberg's experiences—packaged self-referentially as a podcast series produced by the very production company that is the subject of his show—offer a revealing window into some of the profound changes currently underway in the podcasting ecosystem. Blumberg's transformation from a veteran of public radio storytelling into a self-employed entrepreneur looking to create a new business model is also something of a metaphor for the broader podcasting industry. Suddenly adrift from the familiar confines (and steady paycheck) of public radio, Blumberg is faced with continual uncertainty about the viability of his then newly formed company, Gimlet Media, and much of his early efforts center around both creating a unique identity for the company

---

An earlier version of this chapter has been previously published as Sullivan, J. L. (2018). Podcast Movement: Aspirational Labour and the Formalisation of Podcasting as a Cultural Industry. In D. Llinares, N. Fox, & R. Berry (Eds.), *Podcasting: New Aural Cultures and Digital Media* (pp. 35–56). Palgrave Macmillan.

and courting would-be investors. Of course, Gimlet not only found those early investors, but it positioned itself as perhaps the premier boutique podcast production company responsible for a number of acclaimed podcasts such as *Reply All* and *Homecoming*, attracting the attention of Spotify, which acquired the company for $230 million in 2019.

When Alex Blumberg's Start Up podcast was released in 2014, it resonated with audiences not just because of the intimate storytelling and wry introspection of the host, but also because the experiences of a novice entrepreneur in the rough and tumble world of the media business closely tracked the experiences of many independent podcasters. Presented with the potential opportunity to pursue podcasting as form of gainful employment, many of these indie podcast producers and hosts can be increasingly identified as an "aspirational labor" force. Aspirational labor describes free labor done in the hope or expectation of future (monetary) benefits. Independent podcasters' dreams of future commercial success are not fleeting, either. Blumberg's podcasting company Gimlet Media, for example, recently raised $15 million from venture capital investors thanks in part to deals with traditional media companies to create new films and television series from some of its more popular podcasts (Abbruzzese 2017; Locke 2017). The success of podcasting networks like Gimlet Media demonstrates that the process of integrating podcasting into the commercial media ecosystem is well underway.

This chapter explores the discourses surrounding the formalization of podcasting through the lens of podcast conventions, especially Podcast Movement (PM). PM was the brainchild of veteran podcaster Gary Leland and CPA Dan Franks, and launched in 2014 as a result of a successful Kickstarter campaign (Corcoran 2014), it has since grown to become the largest annual convention of podcast producers, distributors, and technology providers with over 2,000 attendees. PM attendees represent a broad cross-section of the podcasting universe, from independent, amateur podcasters to radio station executives, advertisers, podcast hosting companies, equipment manufacturers, podcast network professionals, and crowdfunding companies, among others. Since PM attracts such a wide variety of players in the podcast ecosystem, it is an ideal venue to observe the process of formalization up close. Based upon my own participant observation of PM16 in Chicago, along with a review of trade press articles, this chapter explores some of the deep tensions that have resulted from podcasting's recent rise in popularity. As I outline below, discourses of podcast formalization at PM16 co-existed with more utopian discourses of self-expression, authenticity, democratization, and media diversity. The uneasy tension between these two discourses is indicative of the struggle for identity at the heart of the podcast ecosystem.

Digital Labor and Discourses of Entrepreneurism

New podcast creators can face a dizzying array of technical decisions and options about how to record, edit, store, and market their audio creations. How to websites and blogs, how to podcasts, and podcaster conventions and meetups are key sites for industry socialization and professionalization. As noted in Chapter 4, podcasters are not unlike much of the "digital labor" in the rest of the economy insofar as they operate largely on the margins of traditional forms of capital creation and are reliant on digital tools, internet distribution, and are often dependent upon the increasingly central role that platforms occupy within the digital economy. Jarrett (2022, 35) defines digital labor as "the work of users, platform-mediated workers, and formal employees that generates value within the digital media industries." Jarret identifies three specific types of digital labor, the first being "user labor," or the everyday forms of cultural production (such as posting a photo to Pinterest or authoring a tweet) that nevertheless generates economic value for online services. Podcasters typically fall into the second type of digital labor outlined by Jarrett, which she terms "platform-mediated workers." This term she leverages to describe a wide variety of digital-oriented labor including physical gig laborers (such those working for ride-sharing companies like Uber or food delivery services such as Grubhub) as well as creative and technical workers such as bloggers, social media influencers, cammers, and live-streamers. Her third category of digital laborers—"formal workers"—refers to freelancers or any other worker earning an hourly or salaried wage. In her recent critical overview, Jarrett points to the contradiction that lies at the heart of digital labor. On the one hand, one of the defining features of digital labor is its economic precarity and continual uncertainty. Creators put in long hours and may even find the need to acquire entire new sets of skills, all of which may be undertaken with the distant promise of steady paid work. As outlined in the previous chapter, this "aspirational labor" is a common feature of online digital creator communities. On the other hand, some workers may find greater career opportunities and upward economic mobility within the gig economy, particularly in developing economies. Additionally, one of the "great promises of the post-Fordist labor environment was the improved conditions in the workplace for work to become more meaningful" by "doing away with the emotional and creative constraints imposed upon industrialized worker" (Jarrett 2022, 100).

If there is a conceptual glue that binds together these two conflicting realities of digital labor, it is the discourse of *entrepreneurism*. Paraphrasing the influential Austrian economist Joseph Schumpeter, Lobato and Thomas (2015, 45) describe this historical figure of the entrepreneur as "a risk-taker, the harbinger of creative destruction, a visionary who creates value where it did not previously exist." Entrepreneurs, according to Schumpeter, are a "revolutionary force" in otherwise static and stagnant economic systems. The image of the modern entrepreneur has been heavily influenced by popular myths surrounding celebrity CEOs like Richard Branson of Virgin Group, Mark Zuckerberg of Facebook, and Steve Jobs of Apple: individuals who started small with a brilliant concept or prototype, who then went on to develop multi-billion dollar corporate powerhouses. The popular image of the prototypical entrepreneur is also closely intertwined with Silicon Valley tech startup culture. In her investigation of Silicon Valley startups, Marwick (2013, 257) notes that entrepreneurs "personify individualism, technological innovation, creativity, and intelligence—all characteristics that reinforce the myth of meritocracy." The entrepreneur "invests in their work and embraces risk; is the one brave enough to venture out of the 'iron cage' of waged labor and fling themselves wholly into the dangerous currents of capitalism. They are independent, self-reliant, and innovative, able to adapt themselves, their labor, and their products to changing circumstances as a matter of necessity" (Jarrett 2022, 107). Arvidsson (2019) argues that discourses about the freedom and self-fulfillment inherent in entrepreneurial labor have become a means to square with the shifts away from job security and stable wages brought about by neoliberal capitalism.

Podcasting Conferences, Conventions, and Communities of Practice

Podcasting conferences and conventions are ideal venues to observe the creation and maintenance of entrepreneurial myths about the medium. While providing a physical space where podcast professionals, amateurs, advertisers, and aspirants can meet and exchange knowledge and business cards, these conventions are powerful in fostering discourses of entrepreneurialism. In these spaces, creators and enthusiasts attend sessions dedicated to both the craft as well as the management and marketing of podcasting. They also swap stories, exchange tips, recommend equipment, and socialize one another into the industrial role of "podcaster." Much like the "how to" podcasts described in the previous chapter, then, podcasting conventions present scholars with unique opportunities to "listen in" to industrial discourses in order to better understand how podcast practitioners and professionals conceptualize both the industry and their own labor.

As interest in the medium has grown, so too has the number of conventions and meetups related to podcasting.[1] Indeed, there are likely numerous podcasting-related events on offer every single week of the year, but there are a few prominent events that take place around the globe. Perhaps one of the earliest and most prominent is Podcast Movement (PM),[2] launched in 2014 by Dan Franks, Jared Easley, Gary Leland, and Mitch Todd as the result of a Kickstarter campaign. Since the initial conference in Dallas, Texas, Podcast Movement has grown into a major annual event, with over 3,000 attendees, including independent podcast creators, audio vendors, radio and podcast professionals,

---

[1] For a helpful list of audio and podcasting festivals and events, see Siobhan McHugh's (2022) *The Power of Podcasting*, pp. 42–6.
[2] https://podcastmovement.com/

and advertisers. Podfest Multimedia Expo,[3] a competitor to Podcast Movement, was launched by independent podcaster Chris Krimitsos in 2015, features a similar lineup of speakers aimed at assisting podcast creators in their production practices. Some of the session tracks at PodFest Expo include topics such as "Creation & Launch," "Technology & Innovation," "Audience Growth," and "Monetization & Marketing" (Cutting Edge Events 2022). In 2021 during the height of the COVID-19 pandemic, Podfest Expo set a Guinness Book of World Record for the largest week-long virtual podcasting event ever, with 5,816 participants (Guinness World Records 2021). Other podcasting events such as Third Coast International Audio Festival[4] in Chicago or Hearsay Audio Festival[5] in Ireland focus on creative audio storytelling and feature awards for best podcasts. Even smaller events such as the Independent Podcast Convention[6] in Philadelphia, founded by Joe Pardo, offer both audio training, marketing strategies, and informal mentoring to independent podcasters.

In this chapter I focus attention on the Podcast Movement conference, since it is one of the largest and most heavily attended podcasting conferences in the world. It also serves as a microcosm of the formalization and professionalization forces that have reshaped the medium in the pas several years. I focus specifically on a participation observation of the 2016 Podcast Movement (PM16), which was held in Chicago with over 1,500 attendees and eighty-two different sessions across a week of events (Almo 2016). The conference featured a number of different event "tracks" or themes, such as "technical," "marketing," "creation," and "monetization" along with keynote presentations with well-known podcasting hosts and celebrities. The PM16 conference itself served as a kind of broader stage upon which discourses of entrepreneurism were exchanged.

---

[3]https://podfestexpo.com/
[4]https://thirdcoastfestival.org/
[5]https://hearsayhomefires.ie/
[6]https://www.indiepodcon.com/

Entrepreneurialism at PM16: Discourses of Artistry, Authenticity, and Autonomy

Upon descending the escalator into the cavernous basement conference center of the downtown Hyatt in Chicago, one notices the familiar trappings of a typical technology-related convention: a registration desk, a large main stage room for keynotes, smaller conference rooms for panels and breakout meeting sessions, and a large area with vendors selling technology-related products and services. Amidst the chino-clad professionals from traditional media companies were a motley collection of largely amateur podcasters milling about. Since the entry fee of several hundred dollars is prohibitive for most (though presenters were able to attend for free or at a reduced rate), amateur podcasters went to PM with the implicit promise of improving the reach and professionalism of their podcasts in order to gain an entree into the world of advertising support. These are the "pro-ams," or media creators who "pursue an activity as an amateur, mainly for the love of it, but [who] set a professional standard. Pro-Ams are unlikely to earn more than a small portion of their income from their pastime but they pursue it with the dedication and commitment associated with a professional" (Leadbeater and Miller 2004, 20).

If they are not already semi-professional in their orientation, the unstated goal of Podcast Movement was to encourage amateurs to become professionals: by giving "how to" seminars on the mechanics of high quality audio production and editing, by educating amateurs about the fledgling business of audience metrics, by introducing them to terminology in the advertising business, and by facilitating networking opportunities with key decision-makers working in media companies. While Leadbeater and Miller's definition was meant to describe a new class of media producers who have voluntarily adopted the content formats and production routines of commercial media, in the case of podcasting, it is more accurate to state that commercial media techniques and industry standards are being consciously grafted onto what was hitherto a largely amateur, user-generated media form.

Artistry and Authenticity

The entrepreneurial ethos was seen directly in the keynote speeches given at PM16. These sessions featured recognizable, successful podcasters offering up their own narratives about how they got started, how they developed content for their podcast, and how their own commitment to the medium had paid off for them in both figurative and literal ways. The keynote speakers were popular luminaries in the podcasting world, some of whom had spent a decade or more producing podcasts. Others had relatively recently stepped into the role of podcast hosts. The thread that tied all these speakers together, however, was the fact that they had cultivated large audiences for their podcasts (or, at least large enough to garner the conspicuous attention of major national advertisers).

The keynotes explored some key themes surrounding podcast production—namely, that podcasts are a form of deeply personal, intimate form of creative expression that has unique power to connect listeners to stories. For example, Glynn Washington, host of WNYC radio show and podcast *Snap Judgment*, roved the keynote stage with a kind of religious fervor, urging amateur podcasters in the audience to think about their productions as nothing less than the next frontier of narrative, noting:

> I don't care about podcasting! [audience laughter] I don't! I don't care … What I care about is storytelling, and passion, and energy, and magic [audience applause] and that's what you care about as well … There's not enough money here to make us care about anything else. We are here because of that magic, that storytelling, that passion. Because there are easier ways to get paid [audience laughter]. I'm feeling some things as a storyteller. This is a storytelling craft.

Throughout his keynote, Washington explicitly identified podcasting as an immediate, almost visceral form of narrative, something he noted that public media was sometimes lacking. Here podcasting was linked explicitly to other forms of narrative creativity: to novels, to poetry, and to music. Discourses of creativity and passion were paramount in Washington's keynote, and he generally eschewed mass media production models, noting that the best "inspiration is from amateurs."

Another common refrain among the keynote speakers was that podcasts were set apart from the typical constraints of commercial or mass-produced media, making them a uniquely *authentic* form of cultural expression. Authenticity is a cornerstone concept within the practice of entrepreneurialism. Among Silicon Valley entrepreneurs, one form of "authenticity" is being true to your own ideals and "following your passion." As podcaster Kevin Smith enthused in front of a crowd of podcasters at his keynote: "The medium belongs to you!" Another aspect of authenticity, as Marwick (2013, 251) discovered, involves the "creation and promotion of intimate knowledge." In other words, the way Silicon Valley entrepreneurs communicate to others about their efforts should convey not just a desire to start a business and get rich, but to reveal something deep about themselves and their own identity in the process. In the case of podcasting and other Web 2.0 media, the pursuit of authenticity has emerged as a possible remedy to the mass-produced, over-commercialized, cookie-cutter culture of commercial media.

The keynote presenters at PM16 described their own version of a "personal epiphany" moment when they realized that they wanted to pursue podcasting as either a full-time or part-time vocation. This epiphany was typically the result of listening to other podcasts (most if not all podcasters admitted to being heavy podcast listeners as well). Integral to these origin narratives was their inspiration to add their own unique voice and perspective to the cultural conversation. Tracy Clayton, co-host of the Buzzfeed podcast *Another Round with Heben and Tracy*, explained the transformative effects of podcasting's ability to channel unique, authentic voices and experiences:

> One of the benefits of podcasting is [that] you get to listen. And if you choose to listen to people who live a different life than you do, a different reality than you do, you can learn so much. And when you learn you can start admitting changes in the real world, and we need a lot of those. So, find some Black podcasts, shut up and listen to them. Tell your friends about them. It's a good start [audience applause].

Similarly, Anna Sale, host of the WYNC podcast *Death, Sex, and Money*, took the keynote stage to explain that her interest in podcasting sprung from her dissatisfaction with the types of stories that she was able to tell about the people she interviewed as a traditional NPR journalist. She pursued podcasting because she felt that the everyday Americans she covered on the radio had an "urge to feel heard, the urge to feel connected," and that their authentic stories could be completed told only through the long-form medium of podcasting.

The concept of authenticity was also deployed in other sessions in the PM16 schedule, mainly as a kind of rhetorical bulwark against the argument that podcasters who introduced advertising into their shows would be branded as "sell outs." For example, Farnoosh Torabi, host of the *So Money* podcast and a CNBC financial expert, outlined her initial anxiety about introducing an advertising sponsor on her podcast:

> I had been doing a daily show, literally Monday, Tuesday, Wednesday, Thursday, Friday, Saturday, Sunday—for over six months, seven months at this point and I felt like I'd given so much good content for free to my audience that I was worried. I thought, Will they disrespect me if I start having sponsors? Am I going to 'sell out'? And I thought, no, you know what. In fact, one listener said to me, 'Farnoosh, when are you going to have sponsors, because doesn't that legitimize you in some ways? You must not be doing that well if you don't have a sponsor.'

Here the potential anxiety over betraying the authenticity of the host's perspectives on personal finance is neatly dispatched by the deployment of a counter-narrative: that without some sort of commercial validation of her podcast, her content is perhaps less "legitimate." As I explore later, the notion of legitimation through monetization was a strong undercurrent at the largely industry-centered panel discussions.

Other panel sessions emphasized how specific word choices and vocal style of the individual podcast host should be preserved during "on air" advertising pitches in order to make the pitch request less forced or jarring to the listener. Being "authentic" in this context meant that podcasters should attempt to use their own words and, if necessary, to manufacture a more homespun enthusiasm for a sponsor's product instead of reading stale and stilted advertising copy. The mantra in these sessions was to "be true to yourself," all within the context of the commercialization of the podcast. These discourses of authenticity surrounding podcasting are similar to those uncovered by Duffy (2015) among female fashion bloggers in that any sign of overt commercialism threatens the perceived integrity and originality of amateur-produced media.

Autonomy

Integral to the entrepreneurial ethos of PM16 was the recurring theme of podcasting as a gateway to greater personal *autonomy* in media production careers. Autonomy here refers to the professional liberation of podcasters from the (largely commercial) forces that typically circumscribe creative labor in a market economy. Podcasters taking the stage across PM16 noted that they were fortunate to do this kind of work because they had finally found a career path that allowed them to pursue their passion while also "paying the bills." Even the logo for the conference itself (see Figure 5.1), a clenched fist with a microphone, served to underscore the ethos of personal empowerment that dominated the convention. The packed keynote by Hollywood actor, producer, and podcaster Kevin Smith encapsulated many of these claims. Smith argued that everyone now had access to technologies that allowed them to "self express," which allowed for podcasting to enjoy the status of a uniquely democratic medium. Given his previous experiences as a motion picture writer, producer, and actor, Smith focused heavily on the liberation of podcasting from traditional gatekeepers in commercial media. He noted:

> "[In] every other medium of self-expression in this world, if you want to say something, you can say it, but if you want to say it on a grand scale, or if you want to write large on a massive canvas that everyone can see, there *will* be a gatekeeper. You can make any TV show you want, but if you want to put it on a network, you're going to encounter someone who'll say, 'Let me see if this is good enough for us.' You can write any book you want and self-publish, but if you want to publish through a label or something like that, there *will* be a gatekeeper. You can make any movie you want, but if you want to put it in a movie theater, a legit movie house, sooner or later, someone will say, Let me see if this is good enough. Let me see if your self-expression counts." *This medium* had none of that. There's no gatekeeper, man.

FIGURE 5.1 *Podcast Movement 2016 logo.*

Underlying Smith's narrative about the absence of gatekeepers is the notion that online labor can act as liberation from the drudgery of traditional creative work.

Myths of autonomy via entrepreneurial online labor are a recurring theme in Silicon-Valley-style discourses. Indeed, the goal of tech entrepreneurs today has shifted somewhat away from becoming the next tech giant like Apple or Facebook, and instead toward "having pride in a small business that gives them autonomy" (Heller 2013). Yet, as others have found, the much-vaunted autonomy of Web 2.0 is often accompanied by under-compensated work, wage insecurity, copious amounts of overtime, and personal stress (Andrejevic 2013; Duffy 2015; Duffy and Pruchniewska 2017a; Scholz 2016; Terranova 2000).

Formalization of Production Practices: Self-Branding and the Politics of Aspirational Labor

While the keynotes at PM16 celebrated podcasting as an authentic, liberating, and uniquely creative practice, the numerous "how to" demonstrations problematized many of these claims. At these sessions, many of which were hosted by "solopreneur" podcasters, promised attendees a backstage look at specific production practices, covering both mundane topics such as the optimal types of podcasting equipment (microphones, sound mixers, editing software), the mechanics of cultivating advertising sponsors, and audience metrics, to more intangible topics such as how to harness one's personal experiences and creativity to create compelling audio content. These sessions featured provocative titles such as "Go From Podcaster to Media Superstar," "Brutally Honest Storytelling," and "How to Get Off the Plateau and Create a Hit Episode that will Skyrocket your Downloads." Podcast practitioners as well as representatives from podcast networks actively socialized attendees into professional production practices that were required to attract advertising support. These "how to" sessions, then, were the front lines of the broader formalization effort.

The most prevalent of these discourses was that podcasting was a uniquely meritocratic medium. Consistently, podcasters in the "how to" sessions emphasized that anyone who put in the hard work required to connect with their listening audience (and, incidentally, who subscribed the speaker's podcast or signed up for exclusive content on their website) would grow the size of their audience. For example, podcaster Daniel J. Lewis, host of *The Audacity to Podcast* (and one of the chief subjects of the earlier chapter), held sway with a large audience at his session entitled "How to make your podcast stand out." Lewis began his session with a series of questions: "Do you want more listeners? [Audience responds: Yes!] Do you want more money? [Audience responds: Yes!] ... Do you want more hard work? [Audience responds: No! Laughs] But here's the truth: You say you don't want more hard work, but it takes work. Don't believe the people who tell you it's super easy." Lewis went on to describe a number of labor-intensive steps he recommended for podcasters to grow their audience, including managing multiple social media accounts for their podcast (Facebook, Twitter, etc.), engaging in email marketing, producing "bonus" content in addition to the podcast to send out to email subscribers, and more. "The secret to getting more," noted Lewis, "is giving more." This was echoed by podcaster, newspaper columnist, radio host, and comedian Josh Elledge in his session called "Go from podcaster to media superstar." Elledge emphasized that high online visibility was the key to audience engagement:

> A lot of us, I think unfortunately, get into the trap where we end up spending so much time on the nuts and bolts of podcasting that we're not growing our business. And so, one thing I would recommend that you do is that you spend twice as much time—this is a good litmus test—*twice* as much time building the business of your podcast than actually working on your podcast.

Elledge noted that the key for independent podcasters was to find ways to market yourself on through other media (including more popular podcasts), since cross-promotion was the only way to get known by audiences. As these and other independents urged, podcasting success was found in a mixture of social media omnipresence and self-branding prowess.

The foregrounding of this type of intensive relationship-building labor as part of podcasting entrepreneurship is similar to what scholars have found in other forms of digital content production. PM16 speakers outlined a number of strategies to achieve podcasting success such as compulsory online visibility, the push to generate "extra" content in order to entice listeners to subscribe and developing a long-term relationship with listeners by addressing them directly and personally through multiple online media.

The ultimate goal, of course, was to attract a larger listener base so that podcasters could begin to attract sponsorship and begin to earn money. The "how to" sessions therefore encapsulated the notion of what Kuehn and Corrigan (2013) term "hope labor" in podcast production. Hope labor refers to "un- or under-compensated work carried out in the present, often for experience or exposure, in the hope that future employment opportunities may follow" (p. 10). Duffy (2015) refers to this intensive labor done in the belief that future economic benefits may follow as "aspirational labor." In the emerging commercial podcast ecosystem as discussed at PM16, amateurs were being enticed by the promise of autonomy and creative freedom, yet were also being encouraged to work for long hours with little realistic hope of achieving commercial success.

Podcast Metrics and Monetization: The Dynamics of Formalization

The looming, existential question that hung over every session and hallway conversation at PM16 was how to mold podcasting into a reliable revenue-generating medium. Even the conference's Wi-Fi password ("getmoney") pointed unequivocally to this goal. Away from the keynote stage, where optimism about the unique authenticity of podcasts held sway, almost all of the panel discussions revolved around the intricacies of attracting advertising revenue. The key sticking point for many industry representatives (and, by extension, for advertisers) was the lack of common metric for assessing audience size. Throughout these panels, the message to amateur podcasters was clear: without any data about the size and character of your listeners, or without the visibility and cross-promotion that came with carriage on one of the podcast networks, advertisers would likely pay little attention. Assuming that podcasters had compiled sufficient data, however, even the lowest bar for minimal advertiser support was still likely out of reach for most independent podcasters. As PM16 demonstrated, the stirring of interest by advertisers in the podcasting space has begun the process of regularizing the use of metrics as well as the adoption of other typical industry practices (such as "upfront" sales). In these discussions about advertising, the personal, unique nature of podcast production was eclipsed by the standardization and formalization of audience metrics.

Podcast Metrics

In my conversations with hosting service representatives and industry professionals at PM16, it became clear that the process of generating, interpreting, and touting data about podcast audiences was a paramount issue. Indeed, a number of panel sessions hosted by professionals working for networks and hosting companies were designed to educate independent podcasters about various measurement techniques and the necessity for quantifying their audience in order to pursue transactions with advertisers. While all PM16 presenters and panelists agreed on the importance of metrics to the development of podcasting as a viable media industry, the definition of those metrics was highly contested terrain. In one session, Edison Research CEO Larry Rosin outlined a positive outlook for podcasting based upon his company's survey research data. Rosin noted that 21 percent of a nationwide sample of respondents in 2016 (an estimated audience of 57 million) reported listening to a podcast in the previous month. While Edison's data were referenced often in basic "proof of concept" pitches from independent podcasters to potential investors, representatives of podcasting hosting firms (like Blubrry, Libsyn, and PodBean, among others) to whom I spoke on the convention floor were largely dismissive of Edison's survey data, arguing that only "hard" data such as subscriber counts and episode download totals (as measured by server log data, which the podcast hosting firms controlled) gave a truly accurate picture of the listening audience. Additionally, the ability to provide varying types of server-based measurements to their podcaster-users was one technique of hosting companies to differentiate themselves from one another in the competitive market for the business of individual podcasters.

At several industry-specific panels, representatives from podcast hosts, media-buying firms, NPR, and advertising agencies presented a somewhat united front, noting that the industry was moving in the direction of standardized audience metrics. Many cited the work of the Interactive Advertising Bureau (IAB), which had convened a large working group of companies to hammer out an agreed-upon set of standards (Interactive Advertising Bureau 2017a). Steve Mulder, Senior Director of Audience Insights at NPR, laid out this common interest in one panel discussion when he observed that "without deliberate and thoughtful measurement, without improvements in measurement, the podcast industry won't mature as fast as we want it to." Despite this mutually understood necessity for standardization, there is a considerable amount of jockeying among different industry players about which measurement standards should be adopted. At PM16, PodTrac CEO Mark McCrery explained that he and his fellow hosting companies had identified "unique downloads per episode [a]s the industry standard," noting that these numbers were "analogous to numbers that Nielsen and ComScore put out for other media types." Here the notion that podcast metrics should be roughly analogous to metrics utilized for other online media is an attempt to synchronize podcast measurement with these other forms, allowing advertisers to compare the efficiency of their buys across these forms. The intensity of the debates at PM16 over the establishment of a commercially viable system of audience measurement indicates its importance to the formalization of podcasting. These debates are explored much more extensively in Chapter 6.

Monetization and Advertising Support

There were many sessions at PM16 devoted to the monetization of podcasts, many with similar titles such as "Under the hood: How podcast monetization really works," "How to sell out while keeping it real: Taking the revenue step," "How to build an audience and revenue for your podcast," and "Podcast monetization: The economics of podcasting." While multiple modes of monetization were mentioned throughout the panel sessions, including crowdfunding and "in kind" sales (though t-shirts and other branded merchandise), the dominant model discussed was on-air advertising. The centrality of advertising as the "default" funding mechanism for podcasting has invited other structural shifts as well. For example, for the first time in 2015, the Interactive Advertising Bureau (IAB) began hosting an "upfront" session for advertisers to purchase time on upcoming shows and for podcasters to pitch new podcast series to advertisers (Johnson 2016).

The needs of advertisers for a systematic, predictable environment for pitching products have begun to shift the balance of power away from hosting services and toward podcast networks. Based upon their comments at PM16, advertisers have come to regard podcast networks (like Panoply, NPR, or Gimlet Media) as reliable "tastemakers" for quality podcasts. Advertising sales company executives at PM16 also noted that it was simpler to make deals for sponsorship with networks than with individual podcasters because networks offered them groups of listeners across a number of different podcasts for broader exposure and reach. Due to this new business reality in podcasting, Chris Yarusso, Associate Media Director Mediavest/Spark actively urged independent podcasters to seek carriage on networks, noting that "being part of a network is probably a smart thing to do so you can get access to brands that won't otherwise find you." One panel even discussed an emerging sub-genre of "sponsored" podcasts, wherein a sole-sponsored program (General Electric was one example) underwrites and assumes editorial control over the content of the podcast. These types of public relations-oriented podcasts become a kind of "native advertising" for their sponsor. It is important to note here that the increasing centrality of networks to the podcast ecosystem essentially formalizes these networks as distribution gatekeepers, in direct opposition to the kind of freedom and autonomy that Kevin Smith celebrated in his keynote. Likewise, the introduction of fully sponsored content formats challenges the very notion of authenticity that was so central to the utopian discourses about podcasting at PM16.

The industry-oriented panels at PM16 also underscored the instability and precarity of emerging advertising-supported revenue models in the podcasting ecosystem. This precarity was felt by independent podcasters and industry watchers alike. Solo podcasters remarked that their efforts to secure sponsors were stymied until they were able to demonstrate to advertisers that their shows received an average of fifty thousand downloads per episode. A representative from Libsyn noted that *less than one percent* of their hosted podcasts met this minimum episode download threshold. A number of attendees who posted reflections on their own blogs after PM16 expressed some skepticism about the viability of an advertiser-supported ecosystem for podcasting. For example, podcaster and entrepreneur Matt Cundil (2016) reflected after the conference that "no one has figured out how to monetize the medium; which leads to many shared ideas about marketing, promotion and revenue opportunities. A number of podcasters are resigned to not making any [revenue]; satisfied with the branding and exposure for themselves, guests and clients." Another post-mortem by sports broadcaster and sometime podcaster Jason Barrett noted the one statistic that stood out to him the most: that the broadcast radio industry is a $2 billion annual industry, while podcasting is currently a $100 million annual industry. He offered the following "reality check" for podcast enthusiasts:

> The world isn't all sunshine and rainbows, and the economic returns in the podcasting world are low compared to radio. If the financial numbers echoed throughout multiple sessions are accurate, that would make the radio industry 20x more profitable than the podcasting business. That's enormous.
>
> (Barrett 2016)

More recent digital advertising data has underscored the market difficulties facing digital content producers like podcasters. According to the recent Group M "Interaction 17" report, while 77 cents of each new advertising dollar in 2017 is expected to be spent on digital advertising, "more than two-thirds of global ad spend growth from 2012 to 2016" came from just two online services: Google and Facebook (Davies 2017). This type of "reality check" about the potentially murky future of podcast monetization was largely muted at PM16, however. Most industry presenters focused on podcasting's huge potential for growth instead of the rather slim chance that most podcasters would be able to eke a living wage out of their hobby.

Conclusion

The professional discourses at Podcast Movement 2016 were characterized by two contradictory impulses: one was a sunny entrepreneurial fervor, while the other was the hard-nosed realism of industry formalization. On the surface, Podcast Movement celebrated podcasting as an authentic medium that offered a welcome respite from the stale content and rigid professional structures of mainstream broadcast media. Through the keynotes and the on stage "how to" sessions, PM presenters largely ignored or downplayed the often conflicting aims of creativity and commerce. Instead, their presentations captured the entrepreneurial spirit by emphasizing the creative freedoms offered by podcasting, the sense of personal and professional autonomy it offered as opposed to a traditional "9-to-5" job, and the joys of creating original content that represented one's true, "authentic" self. There was a strong counter-narrative within PM16, however. This narrative was prominent on the stages of the panel discussions, most of which were peopled by media professionals working for radio broadcasters, podcast networks, technology companies, and advertisers. These panel sessions served to socialize amateur podcasters into the routines and structures of mass media production, to emphasize the importance of audience metrics, and to firmly establish the centrality of advertising sponsorship as the most viable form of revenue support. These efforts are part of a broader effort of formalization that is currently underway in podcasting.

As scholars of other forms of user-generated digital content have noted (Duffy and Pruchniewska 2017a; McChesney 2013; Terranova 2000), the net effect of the formalization of podcasting may be to effectively curtail many of the imagined freedoms of digital entrepreneurialism. While podcasting networks, hosts, and advertisers have brought an influx of capital into the ecosystem, they have also begun to establish themselves as professional gatekeepers for new content and curators of existing content. Some of these companies, like E.W. Scripps, have created synergies across different power roles. Podcasters working with SiriusXM, for example, have access to the following services all within the same corporate umbrella: an extensive network of other podcasts for revenue sharing and cross-promotion (Earwolf and Wolfpop), an in-house advertising firm specializing in podcasting (Midroll), and a mobile platform for distributing those podcasts (Stitcher, first purchased by E.W. Scripps in June 2016 and then sold to SiriusXM in 2020). These synergies work to concentrate the resources available to support podcasting into a few companies with deep pockets, creating scarcities that will make it more difficult for amateur, start up podcasters to be able to cultivate a large base of listeners (a prerequisite for advertising support). The effects of formalization will be felt not just in the economic structure of the industry, but in the content as well. For example, talent scouts for the larger networks will search for podcasts that are similar in style or content to other popular podcasts. This will encourage amateurs to adopt similar formats and content for their own podcasts in an effort to attract the attention and resources that these networks can provide.

Lurking in the background of PM16 were the shifts in conception of the audience. As the number of podcast listeners has expanded in the past several years, professionals and amateurs alike have grappled with techniques for reaching these audiences and expanding the reach of their shows. Likewise, the emergence of advertising as a more viable form of podcast monetization has suddenly occupied a central role in the conversations and presentations at podcast conventions and meetups like Podcast Movement. These transformations in both audience metrics and monetization are the focus of the next two chapters.

CHAPTER SIX

Market Information Regimes in Podcasting: Formalization and Audience Metrics

Big tech and media companies like Apple, Spotify, iHeartMedia, and SiruisXM have all made heavy investments in podcasting. Two major tech giants—Amazon and Google—arrived fashionably late to the platform party, but they too have launched podcast services that are connected to their existing platform offerings. Amazon, for example, added podcasts to its existing Amazon Music app in September 2020 in an attempt to directly compete with Spotify (Carman 2020b) along with an open submission system for independent podcasters to pitch new content for its Audible service (Evans and Boadi 2020). After years of watching standalone podcasting apps flourish on its Android mobile ecosystem, Google created its own podcasting app and directory in June 2018, vowing to leverage its substantial lead in search to provide personalized podcast recommendations to listeners (Newton 2018). While Google's podcast app was initially only available on its Android platform and via a web browser, Google took direct aim at Apple's dominance in podcasting by launching an iOS standalone app in March 2020 (Gartenberg 2020), followed by the rollout of a dedicated podcast service on its YouTube video platform in 2022 (Shapiro 2022). As the dominant player in web search and video sharing, Google's entry into podcasting may have significant consequences for podcasting because of the company's ability to "surface" individual podcast episodes and even clips within those episodes based upon a keyword search (Carman 2019c). The key to Google's approach is to have its servers transcribe all podcast audio to allow it to be searchable via its search algorithm (J. Wang 2019). The ability of a platform service like Google Podcasts to "surface" podcast episodes or individual audio clips based upon user keyword searches represents a sea change in the medium. The broadcast radio model of "shows" and "episodes" may give way to much more targeted, micro-content model found on social media platforms. When audiences can access specific moments of a podcast that arise out of a keyword search rather than subscribing to a specific podcast and hearing that moment embedded contextually within a discussion or conversation, the entire nature of podcast listening and discovery is reshaped. Platform services like Google Podcasts and Spotify are not simply tinkering with user-directed discovery of podcasting content, however. Instead, what is going on "underneath the hood" (e.g., in the underlying code) is a fundamental reshaping of how audiences themselves are imagined and understood.

That platform services like Google were beginning to change the rules of the game was plain enough to decision-makers within the British Broadcasting Corporation (BBC). The BBC, of course, is unique in its singular role as one of the most influential public service broadcasters in radio. It was the first British broadcaster to make one of its radio series, *In Our Time*, available as a podcast in 2004, followed up by a full launch of podcasts in 2007 (BBC News 2014). The BBC has made significant investments in podcasting ever since by allowing its audio programs and series to be time-shifted via podcasts, now distributed largely through its own mobile podcasting app called BBC Sounds in 2018 (BBC News 2018; Berry 2020). In 2020, the BBC announced that it would launch its own in-house production unit dedicated solely to the development of new audio content for podcasting (BBC News 2020). Given its aggressive (and early) expansion into podcasting, it was noteworthy that in 2019 the BBC blocked the new Google Podcasts service, along with Google search and the Google AI Assistant, from accessing its podcasts (Cridland 2019). In a post on the BBC website, Kieran Clifton, the Director of BBC Distribution & Business Development, explained this unorthodox move by noting that "Google has since begun to direct people who search for a BBC podcast into its own podcast service, rather than BBC Sounds or other third party services, which reduces people's choice" (Clifton 2019). Aside from the prospect of Google directing search queries to its own platform service, there was another issue lurking in the background that was a deal-breaker for the BBC. While the BBC's move was made to ostensibly ensure that their content was globally available through its BBC Sounds app, one reporter observed that "it really sounds like the disagreement here is over listener data" (Welch 2019). Indeed, the BBC's decision to remove its podcasts from Google was because Google refused to provide access to the kinds of audience metrics that they need in order to evaluate the consumption of their content.

This spat between Google and the BBC placed a spotlight on several important shifts in podcasting, particularly regarding the surveillance of audience media consumption. First, this episode revealed that detailed audience metrics are becoming increasingly important to podcasting as it has continued on the path to formalization. Providers and platforms like Google Podcasts, Apple Podcasts, and Spotify can maximize access to detailed consumption metrics that appeal to marketers and advertisers because of their "walled garden" environments wherein its users' every action is monitored and logged. Google is singularly well-positioned in this regard given its access to so much data about user search queries and specific listener habits through its Google Podcasts platform. Second, platforms have enormous advantages when it comes to the storage and sale of audience data because of the unique "all in one" architecture of their services (see Chapter 3 for more details on the nature of platforms). They can leverage their access to user account information to glean more detailed insights into audience behaviors. Google, for example, has the ability to reveal to podcasters what specific search query terms were used prior to playing a specific podcast on Google podcasts and how many times a particular podcast appeared in a Google search (Cridland 2020c). The BBC perhaps recognized the dangers associated with listing their content some of these giant platforms and the loss of control over their own content that came with that, opting to keep that control over their own content by releasing it on their own content platform, BBC Sounds.

This example demonstrates an important institutional shift that is being accelerated by platformization: the datafication of the audience. In short, datafication involves the quantification of human activity to enable surveillance, prediction, and mass customization of advertising. In an era of big data (Mayer-Schönberger and Cukier 2013), the concept of the audience is being reshaped via the mass collection, storage, and analysis of user-generated data. The process of audience datafication is being driven largely by platform providers like Google, Amazon, and Facebook, among many others. These services continually store and process information about their users in an effort to tailor their information services to specific users. This is the new age of "mobile personalization," argue Turow and Couldry (2018) wherein:

> individuals, wherever they are, are (a) continuous targets of personally-adapted messages and content; (b) potential producers of content and so, in some sense, personalizers of the media environment; and (c) the subjects of continuous tracking and profiling, with (a) and (b) generating the incentives that drive (c). It is (c), our subjection to continuous tracking and profiling via media platforms, which makes surveillance capitalism possible.
> (p. 421)

This drive to extract, sort, analyze, and commodify user-generated data fuels an ever-increasing drive by platforms to expand their access to even more specific data about audiences' media consumption habits, fueling a system of "surveillance capitalism" (Zuboff 2019). I will return to these arguments later in the chapter, but suffice to say that podcasting is not immune from the push toward audience datafication.

Platformization is not the only process that is pushing audience datafication, however. Because advertising is the engine that drives much of the revenues for platform services, a key ingredient to their success is granting detailed access to the behaviors of their users. As podcasting has pushed into the cultural and economic mainstream, advertisers have shown increased interest in leveraging its niche, highly dedicated audiences as an ideal venue for targeted appeals. Advertisers have not jumped into podcasting with blind faith in the commercial potential of the medium, however. Rather, they have insisted upon reliable audience metrics to protect their clients and investments. Until recently, however, there were no standardized measurements of audience exposure, nor was there validation of metrics provided by a third-party (such as Nielsen or Arbitron in broadcast radio). As journalist Nicholas Quah (2018d) observed, "Compared to the broader digital media environment—where audience behavior is measurable to the nanosecond and where close user targeting is table stakes for advertisers—the podcast analytics universe is virtually prehistoric." Audience metrics have evolved since 2017 thanks to the efforts of the Interactive Advertising Bureau (IAB), though global measures of podcast consumption are still elusive. Even with the influence of a major trade organization like the IAB, there is a spirited and sometimes contentious debate among different players within podcasting about which metrics should become the standard, or whether there is any prospect for standardization. These debates underscore the contested dynamics of industry formalization.

Formalization, Monetization, and Market Information Regimes

As noted in earlier chapters, the podcasting landscape has been reshaped in the past several years by acquisitions and mergers among players in the industry. Major platform services like Spotify, SiriusXM, iHeartMedia, Google, and Apple have all made moves to more closely bind consumers to their proprietary services, threatening the open architecture of distribution via RSS (Sullivan 2019). The formalization trends discussed in previous chapters are also driving increased interest among amateurs and professional podcasters in *monetization*, or the ability to translate listenership into revenue via advertising sponsorship. The introduction of monetization schemes for podcasting and other online cultural products is not new. Even in the early days of the medium in 2004–5, a few podcasters developed rudimentary mechanisms for underwriting their efforts, such as selling merchandise to their audience (t-shirts, mugs, and other paraphernalia with a show logo) and "direct response" advertising (whereby podcasts offer their listeners a reduced rate with a special promotional code for the services of an underwriting sponsor). The differences in today's podcast landscape reside in both the scope of monetization efforts and in the entry of larger corporate players into the market. Prominent podcast hosting companies such as Libsyn and Blubrry, for example, have touted their ability to track podcast audience consumption as key selling points.

Just like the decentralized nature of RSS, there are multiple strategies and services that provide data on podcast listenership. These range in methodology from telephone surveys, online surveys, server download logs, and RSS feed redirects. As I explore in this chapter, the chief metric for podcasters has been downloads, or "downloads per episode" (DPE). This has emerged as the standard proxy for listener consumption of podcasts. However, as I outline later in the chapter, the development of platform-based audience metrics for podcasting represents a fundamental shift in DPE as podcasting's extant *market information regime*. A market information regime, as conceptualized by Anand and Peterson (2000, 271), comprises "regularly updated information about market activity provided by an independent supplier, presented in a predictable format with consistent frequency, and available to all interested parties at a nominal cost." These regimes are socially constructed mechanisms that allow for players within a marketplace to gauge competition, benchmark their own performance, set goals, and engage in marketplace surveillance. As Kosterich and Napoli (2016, 255) note, the information that these market regimes provide to media creators and companies "becomes fundamental to how marketplace participants perceive the dynamics of their market, and thus affects organizational strategy and decision making. They are, essentially, the agreed upon lens through which marketplace participants perceive their world." Legacy media such as broadcast television and radio have firmly established market information regimes that stretch back for decades in the form of audience ratings (Buzzard 2015; J. G. Webster, Phalen, and Lichty 2014), although the introduction of social media analytics (D'heer and Verdegem 2015; Kosterich and Napoli 2016) and online distribution via streaming platforms (Alexander 2016; Steinberg 2017) have introduced some disruptions to the status quo.

Information regimes in media markets are not stagnant but evolve over time. Changes to information regimes are driven by several factors, including the emergence of new technologies, competitive pressures among existing market players, and the arrival of new market players. As Bermejo (2009, 137) noted,

> All participants in the trading of audiences are interested in measurement taking place, but they have conflicting interests over the results of the measurement—and industrial dynamics are shaped by the 'common-currency' logic, that is, "the demand for a single standard accepted by buyers and sellers as authoritative" (Meehan 1993, 387), which produces monopolistic tendencies.

In other words, intra-industry debates about audience metrics inevitably reveal the underlying power dynamics among industry players. As Bermejo's (2009) analysis of ratings history also makes clear, shifts in the development of audience metrics often move toward a single monopoly supplier model that is regarded as impartial. Information regimes also do not necessarily progress in a linear fashion toward ever more accurate metrics of audience media consumption, either. Indeed, audience techniques that have been historically prone to incomplete or highly particularized measures can nevertheless persist simply because they have garnered the institutional support from powerful market actors. These market players have learned to work with these existing information regimes despite their methodological shortcomings and this creates a kind of inertia that is often difficult for insurgents to overcome. As podcast audience measurement expert Tom Webster (2017) ruefully noted, "Any measurement/ratings system is a game, and the winners aren't the best operators—they are the ones that best play that game, even to the detriment of the medium." Webster calls this the "optimization trap," wherein market players put all their efforts toward maximizing their performance as represented by an existing and dominant market information regime, which ultimately works to depress innovation in developing new metrics.

Of course, there are many other less mechanistic and more anecdotal forms of audience consumption data as well. Other methods of monetization can provide something of a glimpse into the audience for a particular podcast. Like other forms of online media (including vidcasting and social media marketing), podcasting typically features high levels of engagement between podcaster and listeners. Podcast hosts may engage with their audience via email, social media, or even online community forums. Email lists or email-driven newsletters or other marketing efforts can yield some important information about the size and character of the listening audience, for example. Many podcasters also sell branded merchandise and other items, so sales figures can become a somewhat indirect indicator of audience size and engagement. While podcasts are distributed for free via RSS, some podcasts feature "premium" content that is available to monthly subscribers, and the subscriber base here can offer some clues about consumption. Lastly, online crowdfunding campaigns via Patreon, Indiegogo, or Kickstarter can also provide some insight into the size and dedication of a podcast listener base.

While all of these monetization methods provide some data, they are much more valuable to individual podcasters than they are to advertisers. Third party advertisers routinely demand more precise measures of audience consumption in order to validate their investment in media content. Additionally, consumption data allow advertisers to compute the precise cost of their buy in terms of dollars per thousand listeners (abbreviated as CPM), which is necessary to be able to compare the efficiency of one medium versus another in reaching a particular target audience (something discussed in more detail in the next chapter). Since precise and independently verified consumption data are the necessary elements for the creation of advertising markets, and thus the formalization of the medium, I will consider here these specific types of consumption metrics for podcasting.

Shifting Market Information Regimes in Podcasting

In this chapter I trace the development of market information regimes in podcasting by first outlining the contested audience metrics in the mid-2000s. Beginning as early as 2005, prominent podcast hosting companies competed for podcasters (their customers) by offering information about the number of downloads for each audio file—or episode—that was hosted on their servers. The "download per episode" (DPE) number became something of an industry standard for measuring audience size, though podcasts hosts developed their own proprietary means for measuring this number. Early attempts to standardize measurements of DPE were met with controversy. Companies like Podtrac and Chartable have added some details to basic download stats through RSS re-directs, but the goal of these services has been primarily to provide a more globally accurate count of downloads. Key market players in podcasting formed a technical working group under the auspices of the IAB to create the podcast measurement guidelines in late 2017 (Interactive Advertising Bureau 2017b). With the IAB agreeing to "certify" podcast hosting companies for compliance with these guidelines, the stage was set for a full formalization of podcast consumption metrics via the DPE standard.

The second stage in the formalization of podcast metrics was initially brought about in part by Apple, which began to offer anonymized download metrics to individual podcasters for free in 2017 (Kafka 2017c). Apple's move to provide download stats was significant due to Apple's central role as one of oldest and largest podcast distributors. The download statistics offered by Apple gave podcasters a glimpse into their audience, though it was limited to listeners accessing their podcasts on Apple devices or via the Apple Podcasts API. The recent entry of Spotify, Google, and other platforms into podcasting has complicated podcast audience measurement by introducing new and much more expansive means of capturing audience data due to the greatly expanded surveillance capabilities of these platform services. This threatens to upend the existing market information regime in favor of a much more data-rich profile of listeners, which includes demographics, location data, and other media and consumer variables. This more platform-centric, data-intensive emerging market information regime will likely have recursive impacts on the production and distribution of podcasts. Additionally, this shift toward data-driven metrics also plays into the hands of platforms by necessitating the kind of access to audience behaviors that only platforms can provide. The new era of podcast metrics also moves away from the decentralized, largely anonymous architecture of RSS toward more instrusive forms of surveillance. This poses a direct challenge to podcast listener privacy as well.

Custom Audience Studies: Demonstrating the Market Viability of Podcasting

As a relatively new medium, podcasting does not have a dominant third-party provider of audience consumption data, such as the role that Nielsen plays for the broadcast television and radio market, for example. Instead, podcasting operates much like an emerging media market with a cacophony of different companies and services providing glimpses into how podcasts are listened to and by whom. The primary culprit for all of this disparate audience information is the decentralized nature of RSS. With many different industry players—podcast hosting companies, platform providers, and mobile apps—tracking and reporting consumption, the field is awash in competing numbers. This reality, coupled with Apple's decision to block subscription-based podcasting in 2005, may have depressed the early development of advertising for the medium. As one early overview of podcast advertising in 2007 commented, "advertising practices on podcasts are not yet established and best practices not yet identified" due to the lack of consistent information about podcast consumption habits (Haygood 2007, 518). Even as late as 2018, trade magazine *AdWeek* declared that the podcasting metrics landscape continued to be the "Wild West," lamenting that "there is currently no uniform system for accurately gauging a podcast's listenership" which is "counterproductive for advertisers because it prevents them from optimally targeting what is otherwise a highly engaged and captive audience" (Fleck 2018). While many podcasting insiders greeted this *AdWeek* article with skepticism bordering on disdain (Quah 2018a), the perception that podcasting metrics are rudimentary is common among advertisers and media buyers who have become accustomed to making highly targeted buys on social media and other online media platforms like YouTube and Facebook.

Despite the fact that podcasting has been a mainstream medium for over fifteen years, the markets surrounding it are in their nascent stages. The audience information environment in emerging media markets like podcasting is typically quite chaotic. These markets are awash in different types of information about the audience from different sources, often leading to conflicting metrics about how media are being consumed. It is in these types of market environments, notes audience research scholar Peter Miller (1994), that "custom" audience studies are prevalent. These types of research studies are marked by a "specifically tailored inquiry" into a specific medium or audience group and are often—though not always—commissioned by a specific media client. As Miller explains, these studies are typically "one off" interventions, aimed at capturing the media consumption behavior of a specific audience group that is of interest to the commissioning client. These types of custom studies are "most effective when they are introduced in an information void" where there is little to no existing information about consumption for that medium (Miller 1994, 61). Custom studies are typically utilized as market research to demonstrate a "proof of concept" to potential advertisers that a specific medium has either sufficient audience size or quality to warrant investment. The problem with custom studies is that their results often pertain only to a small group of audiences which, along with inevitable questions about methodology, face issues of credibility.

As follow-ups to these initial custom studies (or contemporaneously), existing audience research measurement companies may begin to offer what Miller (1994, 63) terms "syndicated studies." The syndicated study "offers comparative, longitudinal information about audiences that can be used to see advertising space or time." Syndicated studies utilize standardized methodologies to study a wide range of audiences across different types of media to establish an "apples-to-apples" comparison of those audiences for the purpose of media buying and selling. The process of establishing such a system of audience measurement is typically logistically difficult and quite costly, argues Miller, so substantial capital investment from multiple clients is needed to support these syndicated studies. The goal of syndicated audience research studies service is to establish "a social convention" or market standard for measurement which not only ensures that its results are mutually accepted by all market players. The successful development of a syndicated audience research services establishes the kind of market information regime imagined by Anand and Peterson (2000). It also ensures a market path dependency on that syndicated study to make it difficult if not impossible for new or competing measurement standards to emerge. This is similar to how the Nielsen television ratings system operates in the United States, for instance.

The early development of podcasting markets during the first decade of the twenty-first century was marked by a number of custom audience research studies that were designed to demonstrate the viability of podcasting as an advertising medium. These were primarily survey-based audience research to ascertain the size and character of the podcast audience. The Pew Research Center, for example, released one such early podcast user study in April 2005, noting that 29 percent of the 22 million iPod or MP3 player owners in the United States had downloaded a podcast, representing an estimate of 6 million podcast users (Rainie and Madden 2005). The Pew Research Center conducted an annual nationwide survey of US podcast audiences for several years thereafter before they switched to rely on an annual survey of podcast listening provided by audience research companies Edison Research and Triton Digital.

Edison Research, a large audience measurement company founded in 1994, is one of the most visible providers of online audio data for the podcasting industry. Known primarily for its exit polling during US elections that provides the majority of data for the National Election Poll, Edison also serves as major market research provider for both broadcast and new media companies such as Disney, Apple, Amazon, Google, and Spotify (Edison Research 2021). Edison Research, along with another market research firm Triton Digital, publishes an annual report entitled *The Infinite Dial* each March that provides a global snapshot of digital audio consumption in the United States. The report utilizes a nationwide telephone survey methodology to track consumer attitudes, listening behaviors, and purchasing decisions. Of importance for podcasting, this annual report tracks the relative size of the US audience for podcasts, the average amount of time spent with the medium, as well as the demographic makeup of US podcast listeners. The survey-based audience research provided by Edison and Triton Digital provides a broad overview of the podcast audience, which is seen in the industry as more of an expression of overall market viability than as an indicator of the consumption for any particular podcast. As Figure 6.1 illustrates, the size of the podcast audience has been expanding significantly since 2008, with much of the growth occurring post-2014 to an estimated 120 million US monthly podcast listeners in 2023 (or 42 percent of the US population twelve years of age and older) (Edison Research 2023).

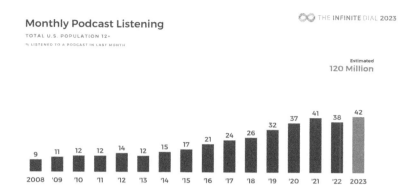

FIGURE 6.1 *Monthly podcast listening (2008–23).*
Source: Edison Research (2023, March 2). *The Infinite Dial 2023.* https://www.edisonresearch.com/infinite-dial-2023-from-edison-research-with-amazon-music-wondery-and-art19/.

The 2023 *Infinite Dial* report also revealed that regular podcast consumers listened to an average of nine podcasts in the last week, an encouraging sign of the dedication to the medium among these listeners. While the numbers provided by Edison Research and Triton Digital do not drive the buying and selling of advertising, they are nevertheless critical for the health of the podcasting industry because of their clear demonstration of consistent audience growth. These numbers act, therefore, as a "proof of concept" of podcasting's market viability.

The Emergence of the Download Standard

The survey data provided by *The Infinite Dial* are useful in the sense that they provide a global view of the size and nature of the (US) podcasting audience. This longitudinal, survey-based research provided by Edison and Triton Digital has also demonstrated that podcasting is a rapidly expanding medium, adding millions of regular listeners each year. Numbers like these have served to bolster the claims that podcasting is emerging as an important medium worthy of attention (and investment) from media companies.

However, large-scale survey data does not necessarily help individual podcasters understand the audience for their particular show, nor does it allow advertisers to compare one podcast against another to determine the best fit for their campaign. Podcast consumption metrics, therefore, are needed for this purpose.

The push for consistent, comparable, and verifiable audience consumption metrics in podcasting has been a longtime effort in podcasting. The problem has not necessarily been a lack of data, but instead the absence of an agreed-upon standard for what types of data should be counted as evidence of podcasting listening. Podcasting as a technology is awash in different types of data, all of which can be potentially useful as barometers of audience consumption. One key problem for podcasting is that there are, in fact, multiple potential sources of consumption data, each of which emerges from a different stage in the distribution process. The open nature of the RSS protocol—which was built around bandwidth efficiency rather than user surveillance—also complicates the process of obtaining precise consumption metrics. In many ways, consumption metrics have been part of the DNA of podcasting almost from its inception. The medium was built around the legacy media model of subscriptions, whereby listeners interested in a particular podcast would add a podcast's RSS feed to their RSS reader or podcatcher and would be automatically informed when new content was available. This accounted for the medium's notions of seriality (Sterne et al. 2008b). This model was tailor made for the technology era of the early 2000s, when bandwidth limits were of greater concern and mobile devices required a connection to a computer in order to access downloaded content (Bottomley 2020). Once Apple added podcast subscriptions to its iTunes software in 2005, the size of a podcast's subscriber base (via iTunes) became a metrics that could be useful for generating hit lists of "top" podcasts in a particular genre. Thus, the RSS feed acted as a mechanism for facilitating both the discovery of new content and the physical distribution of that content to an end user.

RSS subscriptions were, at best, vaguely proximate measures of actual podcast listening. A (slightly) more precise metric was the actual download of the audio file. Every time an audio file was downloaded by podcatcher software, the content delivery network (CDN) service that hosts the audio file (usually in MP3 format) makes a record of every "call" or request to access a specific file on their server. This generally takes place whenever a digital device downloads one or more episodes of a specific show. Because the podcast host is the beginning point of the distribution process because they store and provide access to the digital audio file for anyone wishing to access it, these companies have the longest track record of providing download metrics to their customers. These metrics can include not just the specific audio file and when it was downloaded, but also information about the podcatcher software used as well as the type of computer operating system or mobile operating system (Android, iOS) that requested the file from the server. Because IP addresses are also logged by the CDN, the podcast host can also track location data of the request.

The download of the audio file, therefore—as measured by the web server that is storing the content—represented the closest approximate metric of podcast consumption (listening) available in a pre-mobile era. The download metric is, of course, rudimentary in comparison to some of the very sophisticated metrics offered by contemporary platform services such as Facebook, YouTube, and Spotify. A single download also does not necessarily translate to one unique listener, since a listener can theoretically request the same audio file from multiple devices, thereby artificially inflating the number of downloads. In the early maturation years of podcasting circa 2004–6, individual podcasters relied on download numbers provided by their podcast host (of which there were only a few at the time) or by server logs provided by their web hosting company. This marked the emergence of the first standard in podcasting, the DPE. However, advertisers who may have been interested in podcasting as an "up and coming" medium faced a highly fractured audience metrics environment. Each podcast hosting company gathered their own download data, with estimates. The chief concern for advertisers at the time was that there was little to no transparency about how podcasts hosts were obtaining these download numbers. Consequently, there was a great deal of variation in these download figures, which complicated the process of comparing one podcast to another to evaluate the best choice for a particular advertising buy. As reported in *Adweek* at the time, "media planners don't always know what they are getting, and find buying dozens of small podcasts far too labor-intensive"

(Shields 2005). Like the open, fragmented nature of the RSS-standard, podcast download data was offered by many different players in the distribution process—the CDN, the podcast host, the podcatcher, and later, the mobile podcast app—often resulting in varying estimates due to measurement differences.

Podtrac and the Move toward Standardization

Formalization requires some degree of standardization. Due to the open nature of RSS and a somewhat fragmented market structure, audience metrics standardization has traditionally been the Achille's Heel of the medium. While RSS subscriptions and download numbers were regularly referenced as rough estimates of podcast listening in the early years of the century, differences in measurement between podcast hosting company resulted in a complex and somewhat muddled metrics landscape. In order to effectively compare the downloads of one podcast with another, a more standardized measure was needed.

An early step toward some standardization in podcast metrics was the launch of the company Podtrac in November of 2005. Podtrac, headed by CEO Mark McCrery, a former advertising executive, promised to achieve two key measurement goals: (1) a single, comparable global measure of all podcast downloads regardless of CDN or hosting platform and (2) the ability to create consumer profiles of the listener base for particular podcasts in order to appeal to potential advertisers. The first goal was to allow for podcasts to be measured by a third-party service, which would essentially standardize the DPE metrics, allowing for the first time an "apples to apples" comparison of consumption (as measured by downloads) between specific podcasts. Podtrac achieved this via a small change in the episode "enclosure" URL of the RSS feed. Once podcasters include a Podtrac-specific URL in the RSS feed, this URL acts as a redirect that registers the download request with Podtrac. Podtrac also uses "proprietary algorithms" to analyze these raw server request logs to try to "eliminate redundant requests, bots, and fraudulent traffic" to essentially track "unique" downloads of a particular podcast episode (Podtrac 2020). Once podcasters opt in to Podtrac's RSS redirect service, the following information is gathered for each podcast episode download request:

- the date and time of the request
- the IP address of the client making the request
- the URL of the target media file
- the source of the request (software and device)
- various other parameters in the HTTP request headers.

Another important goal was for podcasters to create demographic and behavioral data about their listeners in order to match those listeners to potential advertisers (Shields 2005). Podtrac essentially offered themselves as a middle man to facilitate these transactions. In order to maximize the institutional legitimacy of their efforts, Podtrac partnered with established media research firms Mediamark Research Inc. (MRI) and Taylor Nelson Sofres (TNS) to generate an online survey questionnaire for podcasters to complete about their listeners.

Podtrac's introduction of what is known as "prefix analytics," or the use of a prefix in front of the download URL for a specific audio file (Barletta 2021), is also used by a number of companies such as Blubrry, a hosting company, along with podcast advertising and measurement companies such as Chartable (launched in 2019) and Podsights (launched in 2018).[1] Chartable and Podsights, in particular, have gone even further with URL prefix analytics to better capture "attribution," or measuring the success of a specific advertising campaign. Chartable, for example, uses URL prefixes to track whether individuals who click links on social media to a specific podcast episode actually listen to the show itself once they get to the show's website (Carman 2019b). Despite its potential to assist individual podcasters in their financial transactions with advertisers, prefix analytics still has not provided kind of standardization that is common in broadcast radio and television: a monopoly provider of data that covers all programming. The push to formalize podcast listening remained therefore largely fragmented and incomplete.

---

[1] Both Chartable and Podsights were acquired by Spotify in February 2022.

Standardization Skirmishes and the Role of the IAB

Toward the end of the first decade of the 2000s, then, the DPE metric emerged as an industry standard, mainly because it represented something that could be directly measured and quantified. While this was a significant step toward the formalization of the medium, differences in download measurements between hosting companies, coupled with the challenges of identifying unique downloads (as opposed to raw download data), complicated the ability of podcasters to precisely identify the size of their listening audience. Podtrac's emergence in 2005 promised to provide a standard "apples to apples" comparison of downloads from one podcast to another, but the opt-in requirement for podcasters meant that only those podcasts who registered with Podtrac would have their downloads measured via its service.[2] The introduction of Apple's iPhone in 2007 complicated the metrics environment still further heralding a shift in consumption away from the desktop and toward a mobile-centric ecosystem, which is discussed in detail later in the chapter.

On the heels of the blockbuster success of *Serial* in 2014, efforts to standardize the measurement of podcast downloads from podcast hosts and CDNs began in earnest. Under the auspices of the IAB, a major online industry trade association, a "Podcast Technical Working Group," was created with representatives from podcasting hosting companies, major podcast and radio distributors and networks including NPR, and measurement firms such as Nielsen and Podtrac. The goal of the working group was to establish a uniform set of criteria for measuring unique downloads, which would serve as a rough and nebulous approximation of consumption. Version 1.0 of these IAB standards was released in September, 2016 (Interactive Advertising Bureau 2016), though National Public Radio (NPR) pre-emptively distributed its own "working document" on podcast measurement in February of 2016, hoping to be the first to influence future discussions about podcast metrics (S. Wang 2016). NPR's effort was angrily denounced days later by Todd

---

[2] For example, currently the number one podcast in terms of popularity, *The Joe Rogan Experience*, is not measured by Podtrac and therefore does not appear on their regular rankings of most popular shows.

Cochrane (2016), CEO of RawVoice/Blubrry, one of the members of the IAB Working Group, who labeled NPR's document "fraught with measurement shortfalls and an inflammatory statement that threatens to undermine the credibility of podcasting and podcast measurement." Despite these intra-industry skirmishes, members of NPR's audience measurement staff were among the members of the IAB Working Group and contributed to the draft document that was released in September.

For the first time, the 2016 IAB Report actually defined the podcasting medium itself as "an on-demand media format that listeners either download to listen to later or consume online" (Interactive Advertising Bureau 2016, 3). The report also added certain types of "streaming" to this definition insofar as streamed podcast files are essentially "downloaded via the standard HTTP protocol." The definition of what counts as a podcast, therefore, included both the traditional download of an entire audio file to a podcatcher and the instantaneous streaming of content— or "progressive downloading"—featured on music streaming platforms like Spotify. The revised working document, released in 2017, specified several types of user data captured by the download server outlined by the IAB that would provide insights into the consumption of podcasts. Some of those data include the IP address of the request (which can identify the specific server location through which the user is accessing the internet, and can roughly be associated with geolocation), the date and time of the download, the bytes served by the download (to assess whether the file was completely downloaded or not), and the user agent (the app, desktop website, or other means of accessing the file) (Interactive Advertising Bureau 2017b, 9). Similar to the methodology adopted by Podtrac in 2005, the working report also recommended that podcast companies employ filtering algorithms to eliminate duplicate downloads, bots, bogus requests, and spam requests to arrive at a unique download number. Interestingly, the 2017 revised document also applied a "threshold level" criterion whereby at least one minute of the podcast would need to be downloaded from the server to "count" as a valid download.

The initial IAB working report was careful to note that information about true podcast consumption was incomplete due to the lack of information about actual listening behaviors. It noted that "The native players that operate on iOS systems, namely the

Apple Podcasts App and iTunes offer no technology for confirming that a podcast file was played. This lack of client-side response prevents podcast distributors from measuring ad plays at the level expected in other digital media" (Interactive Advertising Bureau 2016, 3). Instead, the IAB suggested that unique listeners could be identified "by a combination of IP address and User Agent" along with specific data about the time frame when particular audio file was accessed (Interactive Advertising Bureau 2017b, 16). More specific client-side metrics would appear later in 2017.

The IAB specifications, now in version 2.1, have become the industry standard for measuring podcast consumption. Indeed, the IAB has begun acting as a kind of third-party compliance organization by certifying hosting companies and podcast advertisers as being compliant with the IAB audience measurement specifications. In December, 2018, podcast host Blubrry, along with NPR, were the first podcast-related companies to receive certification as being IAB-compliant after rigorous review by a team from the IAB (Cridland 2018d). Since that time, the number of IAB-certified podcast companies has grown to twenty-one, including major podcast hosting companies such as Libsyn, Anchor, Simplecast, Buzzsprout, and Spreaker (Interactive Advertising Bureau 2021a). Notably, the largest podcasting platforms, Apple and Spotify, are not among those on this list. Remarking at the Podcast Movement convention in 2016, PodTrac CEO Mark McCrery explained that regarded "unique downloads per episode [a]s the industry standard," noting that these numbers were "analogous to numbers that Nielsen and ComScore put out for other media types."

Even with the stamp of approval from IAB, however, server-side podcast metrics can still be subject to manipulation. One programmer utilized a cheap Raspberry Pi computer, 4G USB modem, and a user-agent spoof service to automate multiple download requests for a single podcast episode from what appeared to be different users from different user agents and IP addresses (Gourraud 2020). All of these "fake" download requests were registered by multiple third-party services such as Podtrac and Chartable as legitimate requests. Even with the stringent requirements of the IAB on podcast hosts and measurement services, server-side metrics are not always foolproof.

Platformization, Mobile Apps, and the Era of Client-Side Metrics

Measuring downloads via server-side techniques that are officially certified by the IAB is the current industry standard for obtaining some insights into the size and nature of the audience for a specific podcast. Despite these metrics, some important questions linger, most importantly: How many of those downloaded podcast episodes are being heard by listeners? Many of the most popular services for podcast listening such as Apple Podcasts regularly download several episodes in advance for users who "subscribe" or "follow" a particular podcast. Those episodes are counted as a "download" for the purposes of server-side audience metrics, but the question of whether those cached episodes are actually consumed by the listener is a murky one. To truly measure consumption of podcasts, more specific data from the software managing the download—the podcatcher or, more likely, the mobile app—are needed. The software that actually plays the digital audio file is, in fact, the only point in the distribution chain where true listening consumption can be precisely measured. Since podcast consumption has shifted to take place largely on mobile devices such as smartphones and tablets, mobile apps and major online platforms that dominate mobile app audio listening such as Apple Podcasts and Spotify have become key players in the new economy of audience data. Because these "client" apps are the end points in the distribution of podcasts in the sense that they queue and play the content for the listener, these client services are able to precisely track when an episode is heard, how much of that episode is listened to, and, perhaps most importantly, who is doing the listening.

Apple's Consumption Metrics

Perhaps the most important player in the podcasting ecosystem has been Apple, due in large part to its early integration of podcasting into iTunes and its mobile operating system, iOS. While Apple's inclusion of podcasts within its iTunes software provided an early boost for the medium by dramatically expanding its reach to mainstream audiences, it did not fundamentally alter the existing status quo for measuring audiences. Apple's iTunes functioned primarily as an easy-to-navigate directory, allowing for audiences to more easily locate, subscribe, and listen to podcasts via their Apple media devices. Apple gathers a great deal of information about individual consumers thanks to their online purchasing ecosystem for music tracks and, after the release of the first iPhone in 2007, iOS apps. This information includes demographic data, credit card information, and detailed information about the usage of Apple products (such as apps downloaded, etc.). After the launch of its cloud storage service iCloud in 2011 (Apple 2011), Apple dramatically expanded its ability to gather and store information about its uses. However, Apple has shown itself to be either a careful steward of this extremely valuable information or an absentee landlord, depending upon your point of view. Apple prevents or has not provided the means for third parties to access data about how its customers consume media across their various devices, nor has it allowed third party media metrics providers such as Nielsen access to its consumption data. As Erik Diehn, VP of business development at Midroll Media explained, "Podcasts are the only part of the store where Apple doesn't host the content and doesn't monetize in any way, so it doesn't have the same incentive to track them as closely" (Blattberg 2015). Because Apple indexes about 70 percent of all available podcasts and almost 80 percent of all of podcast listening still occurs on Apple media devices like the iPhone (Willens 2017), podcasters wishing to gain insights into the consumption of their shows had to rely upon the typical (though rough and incomplete) metrics: podcast downloads as reported by podcast hosting companies or by third party services like Podtrac.

This began to change in June of 2017, when Apple announced at its Worldwide Developer Conference that it would begin allowing individuals to gain access to anonymized consumption data for individual podcasts (Kafka 2017a). As Gimlet Media CEO Matt Lieber tweeted at the time, "It may look obscure, but this is the biggest thing to happen to the podcast business since *Serial* first went nuclear" (Quah 2017). The sea change offered by Apple at their 2017 annual software developers conference was that, for the first time, the company would be offering outside access to one of the company's most jealously guarded assets—actual media consumption data of millions of iPhone users. Apple began releasing this information to individual podcasters via an interface on their website rather than passing through the data to the podcast hosting companies (where the audio files are hosted and downloaded). This had the net effect of making Apple's consumption data available only to individual podcast creators. Apple's announcement that it would begin providing podcast consumption data as registered via the Apple Podcasts mobile app (Kafka 2017c; Quah 2017; Willens 2017) was something of a welcome bombshell for podcast analytics for two key reasons. First, because podcast listening at the time was dominated by Apple Podcasts, at least in the United States, obtaining access to consumption data via this app offered an important window onto a large portion of a podcast's listening universe. Second, Apple was providing podcast creators with detailed statistics about their iOS mobile client application, Apple Podcasts. Because the Apple Podcasts mobile app allowed users both to subscribe to podcasts and to play the downloaded audio file, for the first time podcasters could gain insights into actual real-world consumption of their content.

Client-side metrics via the Apple Podcasts app opened up new vistas for actual listener consumption of podcast content. For example, podcasters could see how much of their episodes were actually listened to by audiences, including a detailed timeline of each episode that could demonstrate when listening dropped off (Buzzsprout 2018). Other important metrics such as the number of unique listeners, the number of devices listening to a specific episode, and the country of origin listeners were also available to podcasters. In December of 2018, after twelve months of being able to access these consumption metrics on Apple's podcasting platform, journalist Nicholas Quah (2018d) posed the question: "Did Apple's new analytics fundamentally change *anything* for publishers and the podcast business? After checking in with over a dozen sources throughout various corners of the podcast ecosystem, there seems to be a general consensus around the answer: No, not really. But it has brought some positives." After interviewing a number of industry insiders, Quah found that the expected downward re-alignment of audience size as a result of switching from downloads to actual podcast consumption was less dire than originally imagined. In fact, twelve months after the introduction of Apple's podcast analytics dashboard, most advertisers still reported a reliance on server-based download data for their deals with podcasters, demonstrating some of the inherent institutional challenges in the adoption of a new information regime built upon client-side metrics (Quah 2018d). Most reported to Quah that the introduction of the IAB's download measurement standardization had proven more influential than Apple's podcast analytics, though Apple's data was reportedly helpful in demonstrating to advertisers that podcast listeners were listening consistently to their episodes and not skipping ads: something of initial concern to advertisers. Some podcasters reported an ability to sell "post-roll" ads (advertisements that occurred at the end of a podcast episode) thanks to Apple's consumption data, which showed that audiences were consistently listening to an entire episode through to the end.

Apps and the Future of Podcast Consumption Metrics

Apple was one of the first, but certainly not the last, to offer anonymized listening data to individual podcasters. Music streaming platform Spotify began offering a similar "dashboard" of user data in 2019. Like Apple, other platform services like Spotify and Google Podcasts offered dashboards with data about the number of podcast subscribers, unique plays, geographic region of the listener, as well as starts and stops of actual episode plays. Spotify also offered more specifics on each individual user than Apple Podcasts, however, by allowing podcasters access to aggregated demographic data about their listeners, such as age and gender (Spotify 2019). Demographic data are key for advertisers, since they allow for specific targeting of smaller niche markets for products and services. Thanks to Spotify's purchase of Anchor, the fastest growing podcasting service, these statistics are also available to creators who host their podcasts for free through their service. Along with access to listener demographic data such as age and gender, Spotify's podcaster analytics informs podcasters what music artists are also streamed most often their listeners (Heater 2019). Spotify's move to match Apple's dashboard-style audience analytics has thus brought the notion of podcast consumption analytics into the mainstream. Google Podcasts introduced its own "Google Podcasts Manager" in May 2020, which mimicked many of the same features as Apple's listener dashboard, offering anonymized data on the number of plays of each podcast episode through its platform, subscriber counts, and the device that was used to play the audio file, such as a mobile phone, tablet, or desktop computer (Ciancutti 2020). In October 2020, Google launched a new feature of its dashboard which enabled podcasters to see search impressions and clicks from Google search queries that surfaced an episode of their podcast (Schwartz 2020). This move enabled podcasters to essentially track their traffic from Google's powerful search engine to their content.

The consumption-based podcast metrics offered by major tech companies like Apple, Google, and Spotify point to the increased importance of client-side data gathering and processing of audio consumption. The main targets of this often-invisible user data collection come in the form of apps, or mobile applications. Apps are the primary means for consumers to interact with internet-delivered content and services via their mobile devices, and constitute a largely under-researched area of media studies (see Morris and Murray 2018; Morris and Patterson 2015; Nieborg 2016; Nieborg, young, and Joseph 2019; Sophus Lai and Flensburg 2020 for some examples). As mobile podcast apps proliferate across the Android and iOS ecosystems, the ability of those mobile apps to monitor and report on the podcast consumption habits of listeners is increasing. Seeking to capitalize on the enhanced ability of client-centered apps to measure podcast consumption more accurately, a number of podcast hosting companies are launching their own apps in the hopes that listeners will use the app to listen to shows hosted on their service. Companies like Podbean, Spreaker, Stitcher, and Wondery, for example, all offer their own free mobile apps to capture listening behaviors. Larger music and audio platform providers like NPR, iHeartRadio, SiriusXM, Amazon, the BBC (Berry 2020), and Spotify have all launched robust mobile apps that aim to canalize audience consumption into these more measurable formats.

NPR and Remote Audio Data (RAD)

As noted in this chapter, there are two primary means of gathering data on podcast consumption. The first relies upon server-side measures of file downloads and has been mostly standardized under the auspices of the IAB since 2016. The second is the more recent turn toward client-side mobile apps and platforms, which can record actual audience listening behaviors, including starts, stops, skips, as well as more details about the demographics of those audiences. There is a third audience metric that was developed by National Public Radio (NPR) in the United States which functions as a kind of hybrid between the server-based and client-based metric models. After more than a year of active in-house development, NPR announced the launch of a technology called Remote Audio Data (RAD) in November 2018. RAD aimed to provide podcast consumption metrics by embedding specific URL tags within the audio file (Carman 2018). When those tags were reached by a listener, a ping would be sent to a file server indicating that a unique listener had reached that particular point in the audio file. This would be particularly important for advertisers, for example, because it would allow podcasters to count precisely how many times an audio advertisement embedded within the podcast had been heard by listeners. Importantly, NPR offered this technology for free to all players in the podcasting ecosystem, including podcast companies, platforms, and app developers. At the launch in 2018, a number of podcasting advertisers and hosting companies pledged to integrate RAD into their systems, including Acast, AdsWizz, Blubrry, Podtrac, RadioPublic, Triton Digital, and PRX, among others (Inside Radio 2018).

NPR's RAD technology was important because it offered something of an amalgam of server-side and client-side audience metrics. RAD operated like prefix analytics providers like Podtrac by implementing URL tags—though embedded within the audio file as opposed to the RSS feed—to count listens as registered by a web server. At the same time, RAD offered more specific data on listening by going beyond download metrics to associate these tags at multiple points within an audio file, essentially making it a more precise client-side measure of actual listening. Because RAD has the potential to be widely implemented across podcast hosts, platforms, and CDNs, it held out the potential to become a universal measure of podcast consumption that was not tied specifically to the internal mechanics of a particular device, platform, or podcatcher app. Crucially, however, RAD relied upon these podcasting clients, apps, and platforms to implement it in their systems in order for the tags to function. During the several years following its launch, the largest platform providers such as Apple, Spotify, and Google have largely ignored RAD in favor of their own individual metric dashboards. This has essentially all but guaranteed the continued fragmentation of podcast consumption measurement. Without the adoption of the largest podcast directories and platforms through which the majority of audiences access podcast content, the future of RAD is uncertain at best.

Conclusion

Podcasting metrics continues to be a somewhat fluid and contested realm within the broader formalization of the medium. Due to the open nature of the RSS standard, early efforts to create an audience metrics standard revolved around server-side download measures, or the DPE standard. The emergence of a set of working guidelines for the measurement of podcast downloads under the auspices of the IAB has furthered the formalization of the medium by providing an agreed-upon set of standards for measuring these server-side downloads. This current information regime—built upon the DPE standard—places podcast hosting firms, CDNs, and measurement companies like Podtrac as central players in the monetization process since these companies are positioned to provide standardized podcast download data to creators and advertisers alike. While measures of unique downloads and RSS subscriptions have been key performance metrics since the emergence of the medium, these metrics lack the ability to discern whether an audio file was actually played by a listener, nor do they provide any detailed identifying information about those listeners.

In the past several years, however, this existing DPE information regime is being challenged by platform services like Spotify, Google, and Apple. These platforms have access to actual consumption data largely through their mobile apps, and are able to provide creators and advertisers with much more detailed information about the nature of podcast listeners, including their age, gender, and other demographic information. As podcast listening becomes increasingly mobile centric, the medium will become inextricably intertwined with the mobile platform and podcatching apps that have come to dominate our experience with the medium. This "app-ification" of podcasting comes with its own set of challenges. For example, as

Morris and Patterson have convincingly argued (2015), while apps have dramatically expanded access to podcasting for casual listeners, the function of these apps as sophisticated surveillance technologies may work to narrow range of freedom and creative potential of the medium as well, all in the service of making audiences economically viable for advertisers.

Indeed, some longtime industry insiders and observers are beginning to sound the alarm about the potential privacy pitfalls of the new frontier in podcast consumption tracking. Following the announcement of NPR's RAD technology in 2018, for example, Marco Arment, the software developer behind the popular iOS podcatcher app Overcast, announced that he would not be integrating RAD into his app because there was no opt-out mechanism for listeners (Ingram 2018). In December 2019, longtime podcast hosting company Libsyn banned podcast advertising company Podsights from its URL tracking in order "to protect listener privacy" (Jeffries 2020). In February 2020, radio giant PRX hosted a privacy-focused symposium of industry professionals to address "emerging threats" to the open ecosystem of podcasting due to invisible podcast audience tracking (Eskin 2020). Because consumption metrics that rely on prefix analytics gather user IP addresses, which can be matched to other types of location-specific demographic data, some in the industry have raised concerns that the gathering of these data without user consent runs afoul both of the General Data Protection Regulation (GDPR) in Europe as well as the California Consumer Privacy Act (CCPA) in the United States (Passy 2020a). The black box nature of platform analytics services will likely continue to push the medium further into the realm of more sophisticated listener surveillance in order to meet the demands of advertisers.

The increasing datafication of podcasting also promises to reshape the relationship between creators and audiences by reconceptualizing listeners as an amalgam of specific data points that are represented by numbers and graphs. As I will explore in the next chapter, advertisers have become increasingly accustomed to a cast array of detailed information about online audiences that are routinely available for online media platforms like Facebook, Instagram and YouTube. Rather than focusing on content genres as the driver for advertising buys, detailed podcast consumption profiles shift the focus only the purchase of specific audience demographics as in other forms of media. Coupled with the expansion of "drop in" promotional messages to podcasts—known as digital advertising insertion (DAI)—the business of podcast advertising is becoming aligned more closely with the types of audience markets found on YouTube, Facebook, and other forms of social media. Podcasters who wish to monetize their content via advertising will have to reckon with these new realities of audience datafication. The major platform providers are best positioned to take advantage of podcast audience datafication thanks to their detailed, proprietary podcast consumption metrics.

This focus on audience maximization is folding back on content creators as well, as the goal of producing content slowly gives way to the goal of producing *audiences* (Caraway 2011; Fisher 2015; Fuchs 2012). With so much detailed information available to podcasters about their audiences, including when they stopped, skipped, and dropped off their listening, the process of creating content can be affected by the constant audience feedback loop, particularly for those working at private podcast networks like Gimlet and Wondery. As Petre (2015) has outlined in her exploration of digital newsroom dynamics, the introduction of metric-driven performance standards has dramatically changed labor practices for journalists by driving them toward audience maximization and away from traditional journalistic standards. Similarly, Tandoc (2019, 5) noted that, along with threats to their autonomy from both internal and external pressures, journalists "are also now routinely exposed to the influence of their audiences who, through analytics, tell them what kinds of articles they like clicking on and spending time in." The pressure to command audience attention over content quality is another potential pitfall for a podcasting ecosystem that is driven by audience metrics.

CHAPTER SEVEN

"This Episode Is Brought to You by …": Advertising and Podcast Monetization

From its beginnings, podcasting has been identified by its roots as a hobbyist form, whereby amateurs leverage podcasting "to express something they're passionate about," as scholar and podcast expert Siobhan McHugh (2022, 12) explains. In her book about the power of audio storytelling (McHugh 2022), she writes that the main validation and motivation that podcasting offers for creators is the ability to tell dynamic stories and to make connections to an audience. Indeed, podcasting undoubtedly offers amateurs and hobbyists a unique opportunity to create compelling audio without the imposition of institutional gatekeepers (as explored in Chapter 2), and it is certainly true that only a small percentage of creators earn money via their podcasts, and fewer still can earn enough to turn their podcasting hobby into a viable career. Nevertheless, amateur podcast creators have sought to financially subsidize their productions from the earliest days of podcasting, and a great deal of informal chatter among practitioners today— amateur and professional alike—revolves around strategies for effectively monetizing podcast content. Indeed, early podcast hosting companies that emerged in the mid-2000s like Libsyn and Blubrry/Rawvoice regularly touted their ability to streamline the process of podcast monetization as a means of attracting new podcasters to their services.

One of the key drivers of industry formalization is the capacity to monetize forms of cultural production. In its first decade, podcasters approached the medium mainly as a creative outlet that allowed them the freedom to reach and interact with an audience. Early research by Markman (2012), for instance, found that interpersonal and personal goals were key in explaining the motivations of regular podcasters, with "content and financial reasons" being secondary. Despite this desire to explore the creative freedoms of audio production and to connect to a listening public, the desire to monetize podcast content as a means of financial support has been a feature of the medium from its earliest incarnations. One early survey of 1,084 independent podcasters from around the world (Mocigemba and Riechmann 2007) found that roughly 42 percent of respondents in North America had commercial ambitions for their podcast, with similar percentages from respondents in Asia and Latin America. These early podcasters confronted a landscape of relatively small, hyperniche audiences with little in the way of direct financial support for their creative labor.

As the production and distribution of podcasting has been radically transformed in the past several years due to the rapid influx of capital and the emergence of online platform services like Spotify, SiriusXM, and others as key intermediaries, the monetary value of podcasting as an industry has risen dramatically as well. In particular, the creation of new monetization models, especially via the development of advertising markets within podcasting, has opened the door to potential revenues that would have seemed impossible a decade ago. In fact, as I will explore in this chapter, since 2018 large amounts of capital have been infused into podcasting via advertising revenues. According to figures published by the Interactive Advertising Bureau (IAB), for instance, US podcast advertising revenue topped $1 billion in 2021, a 72 percent increase from the previous year (2022). The IAB further predicted that the size of the advertising market would exceed $2 billion in 2022, and $4 billion by the end of 2024 (Forristal 2022). Advertising, therefore, has emerged as the central driver in podcast industry revenue, which has had carry over effects into other aspects of the medium. For example, podcast-specific ad agencies have entered the market to capitalize on the growth in listeners (especially among the podcasts with a significant audience size such as *The Joe Rogan Experience*, *Smartless*, and *Call Her Daddy*). Companies that specialize in ad targeting, audience measurement, and monitoring the effectiveness of podcast-specific ad campaigns such as Chartable and Podsights, which were both purchased by Spotify in 2022, have become key intermediaries in this rapidly expanding marketplace. Finally, platform providers such as Spotify, SiriusXM, and iHeartMedia have all made moves to position themselves strategically to take advantage of the boom in podcast advertising revenue by pioneering new metrics and promising advertisers ever more detailed profiles of podcast listeners.

This chapter will consider the types of podcast monetization that have become part of the expanding industrialization of the medium in the past several years. First, I turn to a brief discussion of informal media economies and forms of monetization that have captured the recent attention of scholars, though this literature is almost exclusively focused on the role of platforms in shaping the ability of amateur creators to monetize their labor. Next, I consider several types of micro-monetization that were commonly found among early podcasters and are still viable today for shows with smaller or niche audiences. Then, I consider the transformations that have occurred in the industry thanks to the maturation of advertising markets. As with other aspects of the industry, the picture of monetization tells a story of two different types of podcasting on two ends of the Long Tail spectrum: The first is the Tail, identified by independent, hobbyist-driven content that relies primarily on its listeners for direct financial support, generally in the form of small donations or monthly subscriptions. The second is the Head, which operates as an advertiser-driven medium similar to broadcast radio wherein sponsors seek specific audience demographics and gravitate toward shows with large audiences, many of which are now distributed exclusively via platforms services. Finally, I explore some of the ways in which the content of podcasting itself is become part of "branded" experiences for companies and individuals. Major retailers such as Trader Joe's and McDonalds, for example, are creating original podcast content in order to draw attention to their brands. The chapter utilizes an analysis of trade press, podcasting content, and background interviews with industry professionals to outline the formalization of advertising markets within podcasting and the effects on content, as well as the privacy of podcast listeners.

Monetization of Online Cultural Production

As explored earlier in the book, podcasting is part of a broader shift occurring within the digital economy toward forms of independent cultural production with lower costs and few institutional gatekeepers. This lack of institutional constraints on creativity comes at the cost of institutional support for independent podcasters, however. Consequently, independent digital creators such as bloggers, social media influencers, vidders, and podcasters are often confronted with high levels of economic precarity, since all of their labor is essentially up front before any kind of financial compensation is earned, if at all. Thus, as explored in Chapter 4, the creative efforts of independent podcasters can be understood as a form of "aspirational labor" (Duffy 2017; Sullivan 2018), or "hope labor" (Kuehn and Corrigan 2013). Of course, some regular podcasters produce their shows as part of their salaried jobs. Some examples might be on-air hosts, producers, or editors employed by a major production company like Gimlet Media or WNYC or perhaps for a specialized company that produces podcasts for corporate clients wishing to generate positive public relations for themselves via branded podcast content (something discussed later in this chapter). My main focus here, however, will be on the forms of podcast monetization pursued by independent podcasters.

As explored in Chapter 2, early independent podcasters can be understood as part of the what Lobato and Thomas (2015) have called the "informal media economy." Whereas formal media economies are understood within the analytical frameworks of corporate institutions with regularized practices and skilled employees, and subject to forms of state regulation (Havens and Lotz 2011; Turow 1997), the informal economy encompasses "the sum of economic activity occurring beyond the view of the state," and can include activities such as "unregistered employment, domestic housework, street trade, non-market production, and backyard tinkering" (Lobato and Thomas 2015, 26). The key to informal economies of production is that they are not necessarily separate from more formal economies, but are instead "connected and co-dependent" because they have the capacity to affect one another (2015, 45). So, for example, innovations in the informal sector may become more formalized when they become adopted or co-opted by larger more established institutional players. Conversely, these informal markets and practices may themselves evolve into more formal markets, such as with video sharing site YouTube following its purchase by Google. Informal economies therefore fall into something of a "grey area" when it comes to media economics. Independent podcasters, particularly the early adopters of the medium beginning in 2004–5, utilized several strategies for obtaining financial support for their labor, though only a relatively small percentage of them actually sought to gain financial compensation for their creative labor.

Perhaps the most extensive scholarly treatment of these new informal yet professionalized creative economies has been Cunningham and Craig's *Social Media Entertainment* (2019). Cunningham and Craig (2019, 5) have outlined what they call "social media entertainment (SME)," which refers broadly to "an emerging proto-industry fueled by the professionalization of amateur content creators using new entertainment and communicative formats, including vlogging, gameplay, and do-it-yourself (DIY), to develop potentially sustainable businesses based on significant followings that can extend across multiple platforms." The aim to theorize a new brand of online entrepreneurs called "creators," or "commercializing and professionalizing native social media users who generate and circulate original content to incubate, promote, and monetize their own media brand on the major social media platforms as well as offline" (2019, 70). These new online creators, they argue, are categorically distinct from radio amateurs in the early twentieth century, they argue, because these independents have crafted viable careers from their online cultural productions. These creators occupy many different roles that had previously been the provenance of professionalized careers, such as producer, actor, writer, and director. Additionally, "through the entrepreneurial agency afforded by [online] platforms, a content creator can operate as his or her own ad sales representative, securing partnerships with the platforms for split revenue" (Cunningham and Craig 2019, 12). Creators are also a somewhat different breed from traditional media professionals due to the continual need to perform "relational labor" (Baym 2015) with their audience to maintain a sense of connection and community, which also serves a major source of stress and pressure.

Cunningham and Craig framed this new approach to grasping this murky continuum between amateur and professional productions as "creator studies." These new content entrepreneurs were creating cultural products with commercial value, yet "they did not own their platforms. Rather, what most distinguished creators was their ability to harness platforms to aggregate and engage online communities of interest, which they convert into varying forms of cultural and commercial value" (Craig 2022, 62–3). This new breed of entrepreneurial online creators has been found in various places around the internet, among YouTube vidders (Bishop 2018a; Burgess and Green 2018), Instagram influencers (Abidin 2016; Arriagada and Ibáñez 2020), fashion bloggers and influencers (Arriagada and Bishop 2021; Duffy 2017; Duffy and Pruchniewska 2017a) among others. The key to social media entertainment (SME) is that these forms of online cultural production are almost totally dependent upon the affordances provided by specific online social media platforms. They are also, by extension, bounded by the technical infrastructures and constraints of these platforms as well. For example, in response to widespread criticism about advertising monetization of extremist content in 2017, video streaming site YouTube instituted rather strict and draconian rules about what types of "sensitive" content was allowed on the site (Kumar 2019). Dubbed the YouTube "adpocalypse," these new rules were algorithmically enforced with no notice, causing millions of YouTube videos and channels to be "de-monetized" with little to no recourse for vidders. This is just one example of many in which platform algorithms work autonomously behind the scenes to promote certain types of online content while rendering other content effectively invisible (see, for example Bishop 2018b; Bucher 2012).

Can creator studies offer some theoretical guideposts for understanding the podcasting industry? The answer is somewhat complicated. Cunningham and Craig's embrace of informal media economies and the blurred lines between professional and amateur certainly applies to the communities of practice surrounding podcasting today. As these examples illustrate, online platforms have taken center stage as the key intermediaries that shape the terms of content monetization. Most if not all of these platforms have monetization functions built into the platform itself. Indeed, recouping a percentage of each financial exchange transacted on the platform is the primary business model for these platforms. On the other hand, due to the decentralized nature of RSS, there are few if any built-in tools available to independent podcasters for monetizing their content. As noted in previous chapters, the rapid expansion of platform services into podcasting has made a much wider array of built-in tools available for podcasters to monetize, although the affordances of these tools, along with the legal, financial, and privacy terms governing their use, are determined entirely by the platform. Similar to other social media platforms that have seen an explosion in independent cultural production, therefore, these platforms are now key intermediaries between podcasters and their audiences, sitting at the center of each transaction, setting rates of exchange, and in some cases taking a percentage of the revenues. While many successful strategies for monetizing podcasting exist outside the boundaries of one particular platform or mobile app, the increasing centralization of platforms in podcasting aims to recreate business models found in social media.

Monetization Strategies within Podcasting

There are several monetization strategies that have been adopted by podcasters as a means of financial support. Many of these revenue streams were identified by Vanessa Quirk's (2015) *Guide to Podcasting*, though the rapid expansion in the number of podcasts as well as the size of the global audience has begun to create something of an industry bifurcation between listener-driven and advertising-driven revenue models. It's important to recognize that only a very small percentage of all independent podcasters make a sustainable living income from their creative content. Most creators instead turn to podcasting as a hobby or second job (what some call a "side hustle") or as a means to extend their own personal brand or influence with a target audience. One of the chief barriers to financial sustainability in podcasting is found in the Long Tail nature of the medium: there is a concentration of listeners at the head among the largest and most well-known podcasts, and this is where advertisers have focused their buys for their campaigns. As such, monetization via advertising is typically reserved for podcasts that are professionally produced and feature recognizable talent, such as celebrities, actors, or recognized subject experts (such as *The Ramsey Show* (1992–) featuring Dave Ramsey, a well-known personal finance guru). In short, consistent with the Long Tail structure of the industry, the landscape of podcast monetization is essentially bifurcated. Most podcasters who have much smaller or hyper niche audiences and who seek financial support for their creative efforts chiefly rely on their listeners to provide this support. This is a form of what I will call "micro-monetization," or *first party monetization*, since podcast creators must rely upon their community of listeners for financial support, typically in the form of small amounts, even mico-transactions. Much larger podcasts can take advantage of *"third party monetization"* wherein the attention of listeners is essentially sold to third parties—typically advertisers—who then provide pay to the podcast creator directly on a per listener basis. As I explore below, most of the revenue growth within the industry has been a direct result of third-party monetization via advertising. Platform providers such as Spotify, SiriusXM, and iHeartMedia, among others, have played a central role in the development of third-party monetization, positioning themselves as key intermediaries in these transactions between advertisers and podcasters. Some, like Spotify, have taken over a central role in podcast monetization by inserting advertisements across hundreds of thousands of podcasts streamed over their service, especially those shows hosted for free on Anchor (now Spotify for Podcasters). The dramatic increase in advertiser interest in podcasting has also galvanized a new push for ever more detailed data about listeners and their podcast consumption, raising important privacy issues in the process.

"The Riches Are in the Niches": Strategies for Micro-monetization

One of the defining features of podcasting is the close relationship between the host and listener, which is an outgrowth of both the informal, conversational style of podcasts as well as the intimacy associated with headphone listening. The nature of podcasting's parasocial relationship between host and audience is integral to the medium's monetization, since most independent podcasters rely upon their audience for any kind of financial support. There are two main reasons for this "first party" monetization among smaller podcasts: First, podcasts with fewer than 10,000 downloads per episode—which represent most podcasts being released today—are generally too small to attract the attention of brand advertisers. Second, since podcasters typically interact regularly with their listeners via email, social media, or even community chat rooms, the podcast audience represents the most straightforward method for obtaining financial support for a podcast. In the case of a new podcast or one with a small but dedicated listener base—perhaps because the podcast is on a niche topic—monetizing one's audience represents the only viable strategy for obtaining financial support. As Rob Walch, VP of Podcaster Relations at Libsyn, calls this first party strategy "the riches are in the niches." He cautions that "if your number one reason you're going to get started podcasting, is if you think you're going to monetize it with advertising, you're going to be disappointed, 95–96 percent chance of disappointment … People that make the most money from podcasting don't make it from advertising. They make it from promoting a product promoting their brand, promoting themselves as a speaker" (Grimson 2020). In fact, selling one's services or expertise is just one of a number of first-party monetization strategies that have been leveraged by creators to obtain financial support for their podcast. The reality is that smaller, independent podcasters who wish to monetize will typically deploy multiple strategies to help underwrite the production costs of their shows. Each of these strategies is outlined briefly below.

Crowdfunding/Direct Support

Perhaps the most direct method of podcast monetization is simply asking listeners for donations on a one time or recurring basis. The emergence of crowdfunding platforms such as Kickstarter, Indiegogo, and more recently services such as Patreon (designed primarily to support artistic and creative endeavors via recurring payments from an individual "patron" to a creator) and Buy Me A Coffee have greatly eased the process for podcasters to essentially monetize their listening base. Crowdfunding essentially involves individual creators making an "open call" for the "provision of financial resources either in form of donation or in exchange for some form of reward and/or voting rights" (Lambert and Schwienbacher 2010). Larger podcasts and those looking to launch may opt for "all or nothing" crowdfunding services like Kickstarter or Indiegogo, which require creators to set a specific funding target which must be met through individual donations to receive any funding. PRX podcast network Radiotopia, for example, leveraged Kickstarter to raise over $600,000 on a $25,000 funding goal in 2015 to help support the production of existing podcasts such as *99% Invisible* (2010–) and *Benjamin Walker's Radio Diaries* (2013–) and to support the creation of a "pilot development fund" to seek out new podcasts and podcast talent for the network.[1] Other popular podcasts such as Glynn Washington's *Snap Judgment* (2010–) have also leveraged crowdfunding via Kickstarter to underwrite the production costs of specific seasons of the podcast.[2] Washington raised over $200,000 to support the production of Season 6 of the podcast in 2016.

This type of big budget fundraising is exceedingly rare for smaller independent podcasters, however. Instead, most of these independents who choose to monetize their work rely upon small, regular donations from listeners. This is a form of patronage related to a long history of arts patronage from wealthy elites going back to Medieval Europe. Patronage refers to the action of a patron (in this case, a podcast listener) "supporting, encouraging, or countenancing a person, institution, work, or art" (Wohn et al. 2019, 99). "Digital patronage" refers to "the act of singular and sustained financial support to a content creator as a form of appreciation for their work and occurs within unique sociotechnical systems that support financial exchange in addition to creative expression" (Bonifacio and Wohn 2020, 1). Unlike the wealthy patrons of old, however, today's digital patrons are typically the economic peers of the creator(s) who contribute small amounts in order to subsidize the production or labor costs associated with a particular creative activity, or to simply demonstrate appreciation (as a form of "tipping"). This form of monetization relies on a

---

[1] https://www.kickstarter.com/projects/1748303376/radiotopia-a-storytelling-revolution
[2] See, for example: https://www.kickstarter.com/projects/214975253/keep-snap-snappin-the-biggest-baddest-season-ever

strong relationship and connection between creator and listener, and requires a great deal of emotional and relational labor from the creator in order to maintain the relationship (see, for example, Baym 2018; Duffy 2017; Duffy and Pruchniewska 2017b). Digital patronage is a particular type of crowdfunding in that "formalizes and monetizes these long-term creator-fan relationships through recurrent subscriptions" (Bonifacio, Hair, and Wohn 2023, 5). This type of crowdfunding is found in many forms of online cultural production today, including vidcasting via YouTube (which has built in tools for channel memberships), video game streaming via Twitch, online sex work via OnlyFans, for example.

These digital patronage practices are most often associated with online digital platforms, which have built micro-payment systems in and subscription-based funding tiers into their infrastructure. Podcasting, as noted throughout the book, is decentralized by nature thanks to RSS distribution, and therefore cannot rely upon a single platform to provide monetization features. Instead, podcast crowdfunding has typically relied upon dedicated crowdfunding platforms such as Patreon and Buy Me A Coffee. Patreon launched in 2013 and is one of the largest and most lucrative artist-oriented platforms, valued at over $4 billion (Silberling 2021). Patreon subscribers earned a combined $2 billion in 2021 (Dean 2022). Patreon is heavily used by podcast creators as a source of monetization. According to Patreon data aggregator Graphtreon (2023), podcasters were collectively paid over $3.64 million in the month of May 2023, a 46 percent increase from May 2020. During the month of May 2023, 15,784 podcasters utilized the platform, yielding an average monthly payout of $229.36 per podcaster (see Figure 7.1). The potential earnings from digital patronage can be quite large. For example, comedian Tim Dillon, host of *The Tim Dillon Show*, offers bonus content and increased interaction with the host via two different membership tiers ($5 and $20 a month) on Patreon. Dillon has over 40,000 patrons on Patreon and receives a payout of $214,052 per month. This staggering sum is far outside the norm for most podcasters, however.

As noted above, podcasters have generally relied upon external platforms like Patreon to manage regular subscriptions and donations for their shows due to the decentralized nature of RSS. However, recent additions to the namespaces in the RSS specification

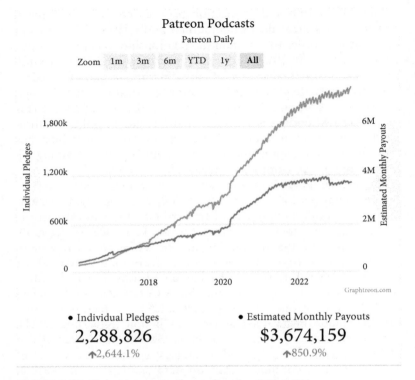

FIGURE 7.1 *Patreon payouts for podcasting (2016–23).*
Source: Graphtreon (2023). Patreon podcast statistics. https://graphtreon.com/patreon-stats/podcasts.

by the Podcasting 2.0 team have allowed listeners to make microcontributions via cryptocurrency to individual podcasters via mobile apps that support and recognize these new namespaces. These payments are made via the Bitcoin Lightning Network (leveraging a cryptocurrency platform service), allowing listeners to "boost" a show by making instant small monetary transfers in satoshis or "sats" (where 4,420 sats is equal to one dollar, as of August 2022) either at whim or on a recurring basis (Chambers 2022). The development of this new framework for leveraging small donations directly to podcasters via cryptocurrency is the brainchild of podcasting pioneer Adam Curry, who has proposed a "Value4Value" system for podcast monetization whereby listeners are encouraged to give back to a podcaster the value that they perceive they have gained from listening (van Rooden 2020). While Curry has been an outspoken advocate for the Value4Value monetization framework on his podcasts, only a small handful of podcast apps and services have made the necessary software changes to allow for these micro-donations within their own listening apps (see Cridland 2022 for a list of these apps).

Paywalls, Subscriptions, and Bonus Content

Podcasting is distributed freely via RSS, so listeners can easily download the content to a device and app of their choosing. As noted in Chapter 3, Apple's decision to essentially prevent creators from monetizing spoken word content in the same way they did with recorded music on their iTunes service in 2005 meant that podcasters were left to seek out other methods of monetizing their content outside of iTunes. One natural method of monetizing content is to create an artificial scarcity by placing that content, or extra "bonus" content, behind a digital paywall and ask listeners to pay for accessing that content. Placing previously free content or bonus content behind a digital paywall is not a new idea, of course, as major news services like *The New York Times* have adopted this strategy. Streaming services like Netflix, Disney+, and Amazon Prime rely upon paywalls and monthly subscriptions, and even YouTube launched its YouTube Red premium subscription service in 2015 as a means to underwrite the cost of more expensive original programming (Ha 2018). Before the rise of platforms in the industry, podcasters could create a separate, private RSS feed to distribute bonus content to paid subscribers. The comedy podcast network Maximum Fun, for instance, provides a private RSS feed with extra content from their podcasts for users who purchase a $5 monthly membership.[3] Creating a separate, private RSS feed for paid subscribers was one way for early podcasters to create something of an artificial paywall without an actual digital fence blocking access to content.

Even in podcasting—a form known for freely distributed content—as big media companies made substantial investments

---

[3] https://maximum-fun-faq.groovehq.com/help/i-cant-find-the-bonus-content-email-with-the-new-password-how-do-i-listen

starting in 2014, some in the industry wondered what type of service would step into the void and become the "Netflix of podcasts" by offering a subscription-based podcast distribution model. Online business website *Fast Company* returned to this question repeatedly, first when Midroll launched the Howl premium network in 2015 with a dedicated app and $4.99 per month subscription fee (Nagy 2015). When Stitcher was purchased by Midroll's parent company in 2016, it wrapped Howl into the new Stitcher Premium service which carried the same $4.99 per month fee (Thorpe 2016). Several years later, when podcast app CastBox launched its own premium tier within the app, another round of prognostication about the end of free distribution made the rounds (Porch 2018). While several different companies have launched subscription-based, paywalled services for podcasting, they have faced challenges that are not necessarily found on other purely platform-based streaming services. As podcast journalist Nicholas Quah (2015) astutely observed:

> Unlike Netflix and television/movies or Tidal and music, podcast audiences have little-to-no experience with paying for shows in the past, and the hurdle of convincing users to go from an entire experiential history of enduring host-read ads, which they can skip fairly easily, to paying for an ad-free experience is tremendous.

Perhaps the most expensive and controversial foray into paywalled podcasting content was the 2019 launch of Luminary, a company with $100 million in venture capital backing (Rottgers 2019). Luminary's business model was to offer a $7.99 per month subscription-only service for podcasts, managed by its own mobile app. The company aimed to lure in new paying listeners by promising them an advertising-free listening environment along with exclusive content. Its cavalier attitude toward ad-supported podcasting and re-posting of existing free podcast content without prior permission quickly garnered the ire of existing podcast creators, some of whom demanded that Luminary remove their podcasts from its service (Carman 2019a). The service has also struggled to attract paying subscribers and returned to investors to raise another $30 million in 2020 in the midst of strong competition with Spotify (Shaw and Anand 2020).

In spite of Luminary's missteps, monetizing podcasts via paid subscriptions have entered the mainstream of the industry. Within a month of each other in 2021, both Apple Podcasts (Axon 2021) and Spotify (Carman 2021c) launched their own in-app paywalls for creators to use in order to manage listener subscriptions. These platform-based subscription services are not free for podcasters, however. Apple's subscription service came under criticism due to its proposed cut of 30 percent of subscription revenue, dropping to 15 percent in the second year (Trew 2021). Spotify's announced that its subscription service would take a much more modest 5 percent cut of podcast subscription revenue starting in 2023 (Carman 2021c). Spotify also set three tiers of monetary rates for subscriptions: $2.99, $4.99, or $7.99 per month. Six months after the launch of Apple's subscription service, the largest channels of subscribed users on the service were largely centered around the big, professionalized podcast networks such as Wondery (number one), Luminary, and Pushkin Industries (Peterson 2021).

Merchandising

Early podcasters also turned to merchandising of branded products as another method for small-scale monetization. Whether it was T-shirts, magnets, stickers, mugs, or other types of small consumables, merchandise (or "merch," as it colloquially known) can provide creators with some income, either as direct sales or as giveaway gifts to encourage the type of one-time or recurring contributions outlined above. The popularity of creating merchandise for independents and small businesses has resulted in the emergence of online retailers such as Printful, Printify, Redbubble, and Threadless, among others, that offer on-demand printing and design for small businesses. One enterprising online retailer based in New York even secured the URL "podcastmerch.com" to sell custom branded merchandise to independent podcasters. Merchandise can also serve to more closely connect listeners to the podcast content. For example, Critical Role,[4] a podcast and YouTube vidding network centered around fantasy role playing games such as Dungeons and

---

[4]https://critrole.com/

Dragons, sells custom dice in a branded leather bag to listeners who want to support their shows (Dennis 2021).

Live Events

A number of podcasters have been able to effectively monetize from their audiences via tickets sold for live events or recordings. Some podcasters have been able to leverage their content to draw in local audiences to live events. The surrealist, fictional podcast *Welcome to Night Vale*, for example, leveraged its enthusiastic audience to sell tickets to live recordings and performances of its podcast (Bottomley 2015b), and even created a live production based upon the podcast called "The Haunting of Night Vale" which toured theaters in the United States in 2022 with original content not available on the podcast (Manley 2021). Similarly, UK comedian Richard Herring subsidizes the production of his comedy podcast *Richard Herring's Leicester Square Theatre Podcast* (RHLSTP) in part by selling tickets to the live recording of the podcast (Spinelli and Dann 2019). An Axios report from 2019 (Fischer 2019) found that the number of live events based upon podcasts had increased 2,000 percent since 2013, though many of the most profitable events were essentially personality-driven podcasts such as *Pod Save America* and *Armchair Expert with Dax Shepard*. For popular podcasts like true crime show *My Favorite Murder* or NPR's *Wait Wait … Don't Tell Me*, average ticket prices were over $100 (Fischer 2019).

In an interview with one podcast producer, Quirk (2015) found that the revenue from live performances wasn't necessarily a steady or incredibly lucrative form of monetization due to the extensive logistics and costs associated with renting local theaters (if they are not donated) and arranging for concessions. Instead, these events were "a great way to engage audiences" in the podcast and potentially grow the show's listenership (Quirk 2015). Other podcasts such as *The Moth* are essentially recordings of live storytelling events that are then packaged as a regular podcast. Other types of local events such as podcasting workshops, conferences, and conventions are also potential revenue streams for podcasters, though these events are typically larger in scope and more formal organizations have evolved to facilitate and fundraise for these types of events.

Indirect Monetization via Intermediary Services

For many independent content creators, their podcast is essentially a "loss leader," acting primarily as a kind of public stage to establish one's credibility in a particular subject area or to obtain "leads" from the listening audience for another business venture. For example, many of the most well-known podcast hosting companies such as Libsyn, Buzzsprout, and Blubrry, among many others, have created podcast series using their own employees as talent to draw in new would-be podcasters for their services. These podcasts, such as *The Feed* (Libsyn), *How to Start a Podcast* (Buzzsprout), *Buzzcast* (Buzzsprout), *Podcasting Smarter* (Podbean), Blubrry Podcasting (Blubrry), and *Captivate Insider* (Captivate Audio, now owned by Global media group), are all educational in nature, featuring content on best practices for producing and marketing podcasts. There are tens of thousands of podcasts covering other educational topics as well, such as cooking, financial planning, legal advice, comic book collecting, car shopping, and even real estate investing. The goal of many of these podcasts is to build a small but loyal base of regular listeners who then may visit the podcaster's website, open a paid account with the podcaster's company, or engage in some other kind of financial transaction outside of the podcast itself.

This type of indirect monetization is also common for book authors who have either self-published or are hoping to expand sales through the awareness generated by their podcast. Many self-help books written about podcasting, in fact, have either been created as an outgrowth of a successful podcast or have been accompanied by a podcast in order to create interest in the book itself. Some are longtime industry experts, like Evo Terra, who until 2023 hosted his own show about the industry called *Podcast Pontifications* and may have generated leads for his podcast consulting company Simpler Media. Perhaps the quintessential example of this type of "loss leader" monetization is the *Entrepreneurs on Fire* (EOF) podcast (2012–), created and hosted by entrepreneur John Lee Dumas. Dumas' concept was to interview business entrepreneurs on a weekly basis, figuring that his listeners would be largely would-be entrepreneurs themselves. His podcast is freely distributed via RSS, but Dumas' main source of income is from a private membership community he created called "Podcasters Paradise," which aims to assist budding creators create their own financially sustainable podcasts. Dumas' podcast is particularly noteworthy not necessarily because he reportedly earns a six figure monthly income from his podcast, but because he publishes his monthly income reports[5] as a "proof of concept" that podcasting can be a viable career option. Several independent creators I interviewed cited Dumas as one of their inspirations for starting their own podcast.

Third-Party Podcast Monetization: Advertising

With first party monetization, the market exchange occurs between the creator or podcast producer and the audience, in what Napoli (2003) terms the "content market." The introduction of advertising introduces a new type of product exchange into the market whereby advertisers purchase the attention of the audience from content producers, also known as the "audience market." Due to the open nature of RSS and Apple's initial decision in 2005 to keep podcasting content free and not monetized like the rest of its iTunes music service, advertising has always been part of the DNA of the medium. As I explore below, direct response advertising has been a monetization option for independent creators, and it still comprises a substantial portion of the podcast advertising market. However, the post-*Serial* emergence of blockbuster podcasts with large audiences—many of them celebrity-driven—has convinced brand advertisers to add podcasts to their portfolios. Here I consider four different types of podcast advertising: direct response, brand advertising, programmatic advertising, and branded content.

Podcasting's audience is still relatively tiny in comparison to other forms of media, especially broadcast radio, which still dominates the audio landscape. For example, US radio advertising revenue in 2021 was roughly $11 billion (Guttman 2022), while podcast advertising revenues topped out at $1.4 billion during the same year, representing a 72 percent growth from the previous year (Interactive Advertising Bureau 2022). So, what can possibly account for this surge of interest in podcast monetization? Part of the answer has to do with podcasting's sense of intimacy,

---

[5]Found at https://www.eofire.com/income/

which is one of its most distinguishing characteristics. While this deep emotional connection between the voice of the podcaster and the listener has been largely celebrated by critics and audio scholars, this defining feature of podcasting has also attracted the intense interest of advertisers. Digital advertisers are keen to leverage podcasting's sense of intimacy to enhance their own ability to connect with consumers. In short, podcasts offer in abundance what advertisers call *engagement*. Audience research has discovered that podcast listeners are more committed to their favorite programs by listening to multiple episodes and regularly consuming most if not all the content, which may include embedded advertising. For example, a recent study of podcast "Super Listeners," defined as audiences who listen to more than 5 hours of podcast content per week, discovered that 51 percent of them pay more attention to advertisements than they do on other media, and 56 percent of them stated that hearing a podcast advertisement made them more likely to purchase a product or service (Edison Research 2022a).

Podcasting's unique draw for listeners is the intimacy of their connection to a show and host. There is a genuine relationship and connection there between podcaster and listener, despite that relationship being largely para-social in nature. Some podcasters worry that they will alienate their audience by turning to advertising as a means of financial support. Not only will their listeners have to potentially endure multiple advertisements within a single episode, but they may find that the entire flow of the program is disrupted, something previously distinguished podcasting from commercial radio. One survey of over 1,000 podcast listeners commissioned by voiceover marketplace Voices, for example, found that a majority thought advertising "interrupted the podcast's flow" and that podcast adverts were "too repetitive" and "too excessive" (Inside Radio 2022a). Listeners may also experience a sense of resentment toward the podcaster, that she is potentially taking advantage of the intimacy of that podcaster-audience relationship in order to line their own pockets. The intimacy of the podcasting experience and its distinctiveness from commercial radio, therefore, creates a dilemma for podcasting. There are three primary modes of advertising on podcasts, direct response, brand advertising, and branded content. Each of these is explored briefly below.

Direct Response Advertising

Thanks to the open architecture of RSS as a distribution technique, podcasting remains a relatively decentralized medium. This decentralization was an early boon for innovation and exploration, but the associated difficulties in measuring audience size, demographic makeup, and content consumption (as discussed in the previous chapter), along with the relatively small and niche audiences, meant that advertisers largely ignored podcasting in its early formative years. For early podcast creators, therefore, options for third party sponsorship via advertising were comparatively limited. While brand advertisers were often loathe to take a chance on an upstart medium, *direct response advertising* offered opportunities for podcasters to earn small amounts from their shows.

Direct response advertising is a long-standing technique for brands to market their products and services directly to specific consumers instead of creating generalized pitches for a broad general audience. Direct response forms of advertising have a long history, going back to the 1980s when marketers predicted that broad-based advertising broadsides would give way to much more targeted campaigns aimed at specific consumers who would be more likely to respond to these appeals (Schultz 2020). For example, marketers focused on enticements such as coupons, promotional codes, toll-free telephone numbers, and special membership programs (like record clubs) to sell directly to customers without purchasing time for advertising spots in the mass media. As Brian Kurtz describes in his 2019 book *OverDeliver: Build a Business for a Lifetime Playing the Long Game in Direct Response Marketing*, direct response is different from traditional advertising in the sense that the advertiser always knows whether or not an impression has been made on the customer because they initiate an action that is immediately recognized. He notes that "with most general advertising, you can't measure how effective the ad was because there's no way to measure whether the customer takes an action as a result of the ad. Direct marketing, on the other hand, is all about measurability and therefore accountability" (Kurtz 2019, 6). When consumers purchase a product or service with a specialized coupon or code that is associated with a particular form of media outreach, therefore, advertisers can ascertain the precise message seen and acted upon by those consumers. In this sense, every customer who uses a coupon or promotional code is counted as a definite ad impression. Direct response approaches to reaching customers are typically much cheaper than spot or brand advertising because the advertiser only pays for those customers who respond by using the coupon or product code.

Since direct response advertising is something of a heavier lift for consumers because it asks them to act because of hearing a pitch, it is typically more effective with a highly selective or targeted audience that will be more likely to respond to these appeals. With its hyper-niche content and engaged listening audiences, podcasting is something of a natural fit for this type of advertising. Some early podcast creators developed relationships with individual brands or products, announcing unique promotional codes on their shows and encouraging listeners to use the codes for a discount with the company or brand being advertised. Companies that sell products or services online, Casper Mattress, email marketing service Mailchimp, web content company Squarespace, and even Amazon's Audible audio book service all rely heavily on direct response advertising. Podcast advertising executive Heather Osgood (2020) noted in 2020 that "somewhere between 60 and 70 percent of all the campaigns being run on advertisements in podcasts right now are direct response." Indeed, the IAB has tracked the types of advertising used in podcasting and found that just over half of all podcast adverts (51 percent in 2021) were direct response (2022). Independent podcast creators often pursue financial relationships with direct response advertisers because they are relatively easy to arrange. Some brands even provide tools on their website to help podcasters create their own unique promotional codes for a product and then track the usage of that code on the advertiser's website. The podcaster receives a small commission every time the promotional code is used by a listener.

Brand Advertising
While direct response advertising pitches have been the most common form of third-party advertising in podcasting, the dramatic expansion of the podcast audience in the past several years has attracted the attention of traditional brand advertisers. Unlike direct response appeals that are perfectly "accountable" due to the use of coupons and promotional codes, brand advertisers create

broad-based messages about products and services in hopes that consumers will hear those appeals and act on them. For media like broadcast radio, there has been decades of research and agreed-upon ratings metrics to evaluate the reach and effectiveness of radio advertisements. Podcasting, on the other hand, represented an uncharted and largely unknown medium with uncertain prospects for profitability. Even as late as 2015, after the unparalleled success of *Serial*, one podcast advertising professional with whom I spoke described the difficulty in trying to sell podcasts to advertising, noting that: "We were evangelizing it to the advertising industry ... Folks were like, I don't understand podcasting, never mind podcast ads. And so we had a mission to try and explain it to the industry ... There was no playbook." In part due to the influx of capital into the industry by major platforms and media companies like Spotify, Amazon, and SiriusXM, advertisers have since begun to add podcasting to their brand campaigns with more regularity. In fact, major consumer brands are spending millions of dollars monthly on audio advertising spots across many podcasts, particularly those featuring sports-related content (see Figure 7.2).

Rank	Advertiser	September Spend	Top Genre	Number of shows detected
1	BetterHelp	$7,334,000	Comedy	796
2	Amazon	$3,163,000	Sports	339
3	HelloFresh	$2,850,000	Comedy	205
4	DraftKings	$2,724,000	Sports	273
5	Samsung	$2,201,000	Sports	370
6	Shopify	$2,065,000	Sports	500
7	Simplisafe	$1,976,000	Sports	94
8	Geico	$1,822,000	Sports	268
9	Athletic Greens	$1,798,000	Sports	228
10	ZipRecruiter	$1,739,000	Sports	129
11	Progressive	$1,703,000	Society & Culture	415
12	Google	$1,644,000	News	99
13	Capital One	$1,638,000	Sports	106
14	Indeed	$1,606,000	Sports	151
15	FanDuel	$1,536,000	Sports	78

FIGURE 7.2 *Top 15 podcast advertisers in September 2022.*
Source: Magellan AI, "Top 15 advertisers in September 2022," Located at: https://www.magellan.ai/pages/archive/2022/top-15-podcast-advertisers-september-2022.

Brand advertising in podcasting is similar to audio advertising found on commercial radio. It is typically 15–30 seconds long and can appear at multiple places throughout a podcast. *Pre-roll* advertisements are run in the first 25 percent of a podcast, though most often occur before or after the introduction to a show. These advertisements are the most likely to be heard by listeners who are waiting for the show to begin, making this somewhat premium advertising space. However, *mid-roll* advertisements are even more premium than pre-roll ads, simply because listeners may choose to skip over these ad messages to get to the beginning of the podcast. As the name suggests, mid-roll advertisements are placed halfway during the podcast during a break in the content. Finally, *post-roll* ads are placed at the end of the podcast, though there are few incentives for audiences to continue to listen to advertising after the podcast content is complete.

While broadcast radio advertising is usually identified with spot advertising, whereby a separate audio message is recorded and inserted in between radio content (sometimes with jarring differences in volume and audio character), podcasting is more commonly associated with *host-read* advertising. Host-read advertising is sometimes termed "native advertising" simply because it is read aloud by the host in the podcast itself, thus creating a seamless listening experience for the audience. Advertisers who sponsor podcasts will typically send a script or talking points about their product to podcast creators and ask for them to either read or "ad lib" a promotional endorsement into their content. As one podcaster I interviewed described, some advertisers included specific requirements to these loose scripts, including directions regarding content, tone, and length. This podcaster described the process:

> Advertisers pay for ads of a certain length. So they pay for a 30-second ad or a 60-second ad, but they give us required talking points that take twice as long. And then they want you to ad lib. They're like, "Have fun with it! Share some personal experience!" And most podcasters are giving them all that extra time.

Podcast industry executives refer to host-read advertising as "baked in" because the audio is added to the podcast at the time of recording and cannot be altered after the episode is released via the RSS feed unless the original audio file itself is changed and swapped out. The advertising message is thus frozen within the podcast episode and cannot be changed later if, for instance, a new brand message is adopted or if a product or service being advertised on the podcast is no longer being sold. For this reason, advertisers have argued that baked in podcast advertising does not "scale," meaning that they cannot be adapted to fit into new and developing campaigns (Rosenblatt 2019). However, research from Nielsen (2020) has indicated that host-read advertising is more acceptable to listeners, and that audiences experience better brand recall for this type of advertising than for traditional spot advertising.

The price of podcast advertising varies widely according to the specific show and audience size. In comparison to other forms of media, podcasting has been known for relatively low CPM (cost per mil) rates, which indicates the cost for reaching 1,000 listeners with an advertising message. According to AdvertiseCast (2022), an advertising platform acquired by hosting company Libsyn in 2021, the average CPM for a 30-second podcast advertisement is $18, while that rate increases to $25 for a 60-second spot. Podcast CPM rates are rising, however, in part thanks to the acquisition of podcast networks and publishers by large tech platforms like Spotify and Amazon. Journalist Ashley Carman (2021f) found, for instance, that smaller advertisers saw the price for a 60-second advertisement on some podcasts as much as doubled in price. One ad buyer noted that Spotify had as much as tripled the CPM rates for shows that it had either acquired or licensed to an exclusive carriage deal, with *The Joe Rogan Experience* now requiring a minimum $1 million spend for any advertisement and upwards to a $60 CPM for that show alone. The upshot is that smaller advertisers are now contending with national brands with large budgets for advertising, creating a "rush to the top" for advertising rates, squeezing many smaller advertisers out.

Programmatic Advertising, DAI, and Algorithmic Surveillance

Platformization and AI-driven algorithms are beginning to play a larger role in the sale and distribution of brand advertising, allowing advertisements to "scale" across many different podcasts and podcast genres. Podcast advertising has developed significantly since 2015, with companies developing platforms and services to automate the process of buying and selling advertising across a huge array of shows, often directed by AI-driven algorithms with little direct human intervention. The key innovation in podcast advertising has been the emergence of *programmatic advertising*. Programmatic advertising involves "the automated serving of digital ads in real time based on individual ad impression opportunities" (Busch 2016, 8). In essence, programmatic approaches automate the process of buying and selling digital advertising by creating ad "exchanges," or digital marketplaces that allow publishers and advertisers "buy and sell advertising space, often through real-time bidding, most often display, video and mobile ad inventory. Agencies use Demand-Side Platforms (or DSPs), software programs used to purchase advertising in an automated fashion, to track money spent, ad prices and placement, audience data and metrics, and targeted audiences" (Watkins 2019, 13). Programmatic advertising offers a number of advantages over traditional advertising in the sense that it is *targeted* to specific consumers at a granular level, it can be *deployed in real time* (e.g., dynamically delivered to a consumer when they access a particular type of digital content), and *automated* via algorithms (Busch 2016). Both Facebook and Google were early adopters of programmatic advertising by creating their own "supply-side platforms" (SSPs) of user-generated content, which were then matched with "demand-side platforms" (DSPs) that allowed advertisers to upload their ad messages intended for specific consumer targets. Algorithms then place ads in front of specific consumers in real time, either as the result of specific text or keyword markers (called "prospecting") or when a specific consumer demographic is identified by the SSP (called "retargeting") (Mills, Pitt, and Ferguson 2019).

For podcasting, the introduction of programmatic advertising has meant that creators and publishers can provide their content or RSS feed to an SSP and make that content available to any DSP that would like to run an audio advertisement within their podcast. The key element to the success of this "just in time" advertising strategy is the deployment of dynamic advertising insertion (DAI). A dynamically inserted ad is "piece of audio (referred to as the 'creative' from here) that is recorded and produced separately from a podcast episode. The creative is 'stitched' into the podcast episode file at the time of download when the ad targeting conditions are met" (Resler 2020). This snippet of audio—the advertisement—is separately created and then dropped into the podcast at specific time codes within the podcast audio file that are tagged by the creator. For podcasts that are downloaded via an RSS feed to a podcast app, the DAI process occurs at the point of download, thereby locking in a particular set of advertisements into the resulting podcast audio file until it is played by the listener. For streaming podcast audio via platforms such as Spotify, for example, the DAI process occurs on the fly as the audio file is being streamed to the client app. DAI enables a whole new range of capabilities for podcast advertising, such as the ability to place advertisements instantly across hundreds or thousands of podcasts episodes, to place limits or caps on either the time range for a particular campaign (thirty days long, for example) or the number of times the ad is played (to reduce advertising load on listeners), or even to offer slightly different versions of the same campaign to the same listener across multiple podcasts (Barletta 2022). Dynamically inserted advertising also means that even older podcast inventory with "evergreen" content that continues to be downloaded and consumed by listeners can continue to be monetized with current advertising clients and campaigns. Another major consequence of the shift toward programmatic advertising in podcasting is that digital advertisers can now simply add their content to podcasts with the click of a button, expanding their reach across multiple audio-visual media. There are several large DSPs catering to digital advertising such as The Trade Desk and Basis that allow advertisers to reach consumer via webpages, search queries, YouTube videos, and podcasting. Within the podcast ecosystem, DSP companies have emerged that specialize in audio-first sales such as Adswizz, AudioHook, Acast, and Triton Digital. Spotify also acts as an SSP and DSP together, offering its vast repository of user-generated podcast content via its Anchor service as well as more professionalized content via its exclusive carriage arrangements with popular podcasts like the *Joe Rogan Experience* and *Call Her Daddy*. Spotify's purchase of Megaphone for $235 million in 2020 enabled the company to expand its SSP for advertisers to include the professionalized content of over 5,500 podcast shots from publishers such as Slate, Disney, and Vox Media (Carman 2020c). Of course, there are more potential uses of DAI that go beyond the delivery of advertising, such as syndicated content to podcasts, but the predominant use of DAI has been to deliver advertising content to podcasting.

Programmatic advertising and DAI are placing the larger publishers and podcast platforms at the strategic center of the industry because these players have made all their podcast inventory available to SSPs for the purpose of selling advertising. After its acquisition of the How Stuff Works podcast network in 2018, for example, iHeartMedia adopted a fully dynamic-insertion model for monetizing its over 700 shows, though it recorded dynamically inserted ads with its hosts own voices to avoid the jarring nature of a dropped in advertisement into its podcasts (Guaglione 2022). Despite the convenience and the scalability of programmatic advertising, some in the industry are actively worried that the desire to relentlessly monetize podcasts will lead to an ever-expanding number of ads cluttering the content (leading to higher ad loads), and that those ads will be of lower quality, essentially turning podcasting into the online equivalent of commercial broadcast radio (Guaglione 2022). Along with the industry concerns, there are consumer concerns as well, especially since the dynamic ad insertion process requires extensive amount of surveillance of listener behavior, such as tracking IP addresses, app usage, and listening of specific podcasts and moments within those podcasts, as noted in the previous chapter. These all hold the potential to disrupt the experience of intimacy and trust between the podcaster and the audience.

Programmatic approaches to podcast advertising have the potential to indirectly alter or censor forms of creative production as well. Since programmatic approaches automate the buying and selling of ad content within podcasting, advertisers no longer have a personal connection with the individual podcaster and indeed may be wholly unfamiliar with the content of their show. Buying ad impressions in bulk via a DSP may also mean that an advertiser may find their advertisement on a podcast with controversial content, creating a concern for what advertisers call *brand safety*. As Bishop explores in her analysis of social media influencer tools on sites like Facebook and Instagram, brand safety refers to "a positive reproduction of a brand's ideals, an avoidance of controversy, and a circumvention of sex, violence, and profanity" (Bishop 2021, 4).

Bishop catalogs how brands manage the risk of purchasing space on blogs and social media accounts of popular influencers by relying upon extensive and constant AI-driven surveillance tools. These tools make "value-laden algorithmic judgments [that] map onto well-worn hierarchies of desirability and employability, originating from systemic bias along the lines of race, sexuality, and gender" (Bishop 2021, 2).

Much like the social media influencers discussed by Bishop, podcast advertisers have also recently expressed concern about their ability to avoid controversial content as an environment for their programmatic ad buys. Spotify has been a lightning rod for controversy about its most prominent podcaster, Joe Rogan, who attracted major negative attention in early 2022 when recording artists Neil Young, Joni Mitchell, India Arie, and others demanded that their music be removed from Spotify's service in protest over Rogan's false information about COVID-19 vaccines (Jurgensen 2022). They drew international attention to Spotify's marquee podcaster and to the company's rather opaque content moderation policies. Advertisers pointed to the Rogan controversy as evidence that more robust brand safety techniques were needed to ensure the continued viability of programmatic advertising. In summer 2021, for example, Acast partnered with Comscore (2021) to use "natural language processing, machine learning, an AI" to filter and evaluate all podcast episode transcripts in its inventory to ensure brand safety requirements, with AdsWizz following suit in 2022 (Dua 2022). Acast relied upon controversial content categories developed by the Global Alliance for Responsible Media (GARM), an industry trade group created in 2019 to monitor and rationalize social media content to assuage fears of advertisers about damaging or controversial content.[6] GARM identifies twelve separate categories of harmful or controversial content such as "terrorism," "debated sensitive social issues," "misinformation," and "arms and ammunition" (Meyers 2022). Similarly, in early 2022, iHeartMedia (2022) announced its own partnership with Sounder, "an audio intelligence platform that builds foundational podcasting technology" to evaluate all podcast episode transcripts in its inventory in order to "perform brand suitability analysis, topic analysis, content summarization, and dynamic segmentation."

---

[6]https://wfanet.org/leadership/garm/about-garm

Spotify's acquisition of Kinzen, a startup company that develops machine learning to identify harmful content within audio files, is another indication that platforms are seeking to reassure advertisers about avoiding controversial content (Clark 2022). Podcast media-planning platform Magellan AI has gone further, developing an online tool to allow advertising agencies to use their own keywords and criteria to evaluate podcast content rather than relying upon GARM content categories. Thus, the emergence of platforms, advertising supply side platforms, and DAI has not only rationalized the buying and selling of advertising across the industry, but it has opened new vistas of podcast content surveillance as well.

Branded Content

Finally, a comparatively small (roughly 4 percent of all advertising revenue, according to the IAB) but growing form of third-party podcast monetization is *branded content*. Branded content refers to a whole constellation of media either sponsored by or directly produced by interested parties. In his book *Branded Content*, Jonathan Hardy (2021, 4) describes one type of branded content as "entertaining or informational media content controlled by brand owners ('owned media')," while another refers to "brand communications that appear within independently owned, 'third-party' media publications, channels, platforms, and social media spaces that are subject to control by parties other than brands." This type of content can take many forms, including advertorials in news media and magazines, wholly sponsored television programs, and sponsored posts on social media like Facebook and Instagram. Branded content within the podcasting arena consists of advertising messages that take the form of audio files that are downloaded and consumed as podcasts, with a traditional "show" and "episode" format. As such, these forms of brand awareness outreach are mostly indistinguishable from other podcasts to the untrained eye. Indeed, one of the hallmarks of success within the field of branded content is to conceal the core advertising purpose of the podcast from listeners. As one podcasting consultant I interviewed explained, branded podcasts are "typically good content that really tells the brand's story in a unique and interesting way. And there's a huge interest in those shows. They're also terribly expensive, and really, really hard to make."

Branded content has been a part of podcasting from its early years. *The Bungie Podcast* (2006–17), produced by the studio that developed the popular video game Halo, was perhaps the first podcast produced by a company that focused listener attention on the company and extended its outreach to fans of the game who desired an inside look at the creative decision-making surrounding its development. Perhaps the most consequential branded podcast, however, was *The Message*, which was an eight-episode sci-fi podcast series produced by Panoply, though entirely sponsored by General Electric (GE) (Quirk 2015). The series attracted a large audience and briefly hit #1 on the iTunes (now Apple Podcasts) podcast charts in 2015 (Owen 2015). While Panoply was transparent in noting that this fictional podcast was sponsored by GE, there are potential ethical challenges for nonfictional podcasts in featuring content that has been designed solely to extend positive brand awareness for a particular company or product. Alex Blumberg, co-founder of Gimlet Media and host of the *Start Up* podcast about the founding of his podcast production company, considered the potential ethical dilemmas of sponsored, branded content in episode 17 of his podcast when his company launched its own division dedicated to such content. Blumberg was in talks with real estate platform Zillow to develop a number of branded podcast episodes, but balked at the idea of incorporating that content into a Gimlet podcast. Blumberg commented, "[If Zillow executives] are involved in the editorial process, like if you guys have an editing say in the content, then that is branded content for us. It's not editorial content for us. You know what I mean? That's kind of a red line for us." Gimlet ultimately abandoned the project with Zillow because it blurred the line between promotional and editorial content.

In the past several years, the production of branded podcast content has grown considerably. Chartable, a podcast advertising metrics company purchased by Spotify in 2022, has tracked the number of branded podcasts available in the Apple Podcasts directory, and discovered over 8,000 such podcasts in 2021, up from less than 500 in 2015 (Zohrob 2021). Some popular branded podcasts bear the name of the companies that produce them, such as *Trader Joe's Inside* (with stories about the company and those who work there) and Duolingo's *Spanish* podcast, while other branded podcasts feature content that is related to the core business of the sponsor, such as computer antivirus company McAfee Security's *Hackable?*, the *Work in Progress* podcast by online productivity platform Slack, and *C Suite*, a podcast produced by TD Bank and hosted by Claudette McGowan, TD Bank's Global Executive Officer for Cyber Security.

One of the catalysts of such a dramatic expansion in branded podcasting is the emergence of divisions within podcast publishers and networks dedicated to producing such content. Independent podcast consultants and experts have also built their own businesses largely to support corporate clients wishing to launch their own podcast, either to raise brand awareness, to generate leads for new business opportunities, or to strengthen existing client or customer relationships. As one podcast consultant noted, "my clients are getting into [branded podcasting] because they feel compelled … They know that it's a vehicle to give to prospects to give to existing customers to strengthen the relationship." Recently, however, less transparent forms of branded content have surfaced that stretch both the definition and ethical boundaries of branded content. In late 2022, for example, journalist Ashley Carman (2022b) uncovered a "pay-to-play" scheme whereby some individuals were paying popular podcasters anywhere from $3,500 to $50,000 to be a guest on their popular podcasts in order to reach their audience and advertise their services. Dubbed "podcast payola," this practice amounts to a form of branded content, though in this case the audience is not aware that they are listening to sponsored podcast content.

Conclusion

One of the key drivers of the formalization in the podcasting industry has been the expansion of options for monetization of the content. As this chapter has outlined, early independent podcasters relied largely on first-party monetization to underwrite the costs associated with production, if they monetized at all. Cunningham and Craig's analysis of creators in the SME field is a helpful guide for contextualizing the informal economies that surround forms of online media creation such as podcasting. Unlike the social media influencers and YouTube vidders that Cunningham and Craig explore, however, podcasters are not necessarily bound to platform-based infrastructures to distribute and monetize their creativity. Due to the open nature of RSS and the subsequent freedom from the strictures of a centralized platform for distributing and monetizing content, podcasters have developed several strategies for transforming their listeners into financial supporters. Selling T-shirts and other merchandise, leveraging crowdfunding sites like Patreon, along with micropayments and even the "value for value" model pioneered by the Podcasting 2.0 project are all methods for podcasters to derive direct financial support from their fans and listeners. Paywalls, bonus content, and subscription-based podcasting are newer options for podcasters to monetize. These revenue models are focused on the content market by essentially charging listeners money to access podcast content.

In the past several years, however, the advertising industry has demonstrated a much greater interest in podcasting, bringing with it an influx of billions of dollars and catalyzing a cascade of acquisitions within the industry. This has resulted in an important shift within the industry away from the content market and toward the *audience market*. Advertisers are not as interested in buying or supporting specific types of podcast content as much as they are keen to buy access to specific audiences. The key attraction for advertisers lies in podcasting's sense of authenticity and strong psychic connection between listener and podcaster, since it not only enhances audience engagement with their brand, but listeners may be less inclined to tune out promotional messages if they are delivered by a podcaster they know and trust. Direct response advertising, whereby podcast listeners are encouraged to purchase a product or service with a coupon or discount code, has been a mainstay of podcasting, but increasingly, brand advertisers with sizeable budgets are moving into the ecosystem and purchasing either host-read spots or are producing their own audio campaigns.

The waves of mergers and acquisitions outlined in Chapter 2 have now made it possible for supply side platforms to bundle audiences across hundreds of different podcasts, allowing advertisers to pursue *scale* in their podcast buys. The introduction of programmatic advertising has similarly transformed the landscape by allowing vast inventories of audio content to be paired with advertisers' demographic targets. The emergence of key players in the podcast advertising scene such as podcast-specific ad agencies has largely institutionalized the process of buying and selling advertising for the medium. Major platforms like Anchor, Google, and Spotify are beginning to shift the terms of the market by pursuing "dynamic ad insertion," whereby advertising is digitally inserted into podcasts (post-production), much as it is done in commercial broadcast radio. Through this pursuit of programmatic advertising, advertisers can spread their ad messages over a wide range of podcasts in an efficient manner, much as they do on other forms of media.

While some of the rush of companies to acquire and merge within podcasting is certainly to achieve economies of scale in production and reach of audience, another clear goal of much of this activity is to eliminate the organizational boundaries separating different proprietary databases of podcast listener data. The sharing of information allows for podcast hosts, platform services, creators, and advertisers to obtain a more complete view of the podcast audience with the twin goals of greater *efficiency* for ad buys (not wasting money advertising to listeners you don't care to reach), as well as greater *accountability* for advertising buys (to ensure that a specific number and type of listeners attended to an advertisement). The end goal of this, as Zuboff (2019, 399) writes, is "a utopia of certainty" in which all barriers to information have been wiped clear by the "application of instrumentarian power" in the service of optimization for more efficient capitalist exchange. According to Zuboff's analysis, the concentration of information in the hands of centralized services—such as those operated by platforms such as Spotify, Facebook, and Amazon—allows for sophisticated machine learning to eliminate "chaotic elements" of any information system and ensure "guaranteed outcomes" (2019, 413). While Zuboff is arguing here that individual freedoms—both political and expressive—have been drastically curtailed by the deployment of AI knowledge generation via that parsing of data about online human actions, it is not a great stretch to see similar forces at work within podcasting. In essence, by making podcasting a "safe" medium for programmatic, brand advertising, platforms are creating centralized repositories of both listener data and podcaster content, raising important questions about privacy and censorship. Ironically, the influx of pervasive advertising into podcasting, particularly via stealth through branded content, threatens to erode the podcaster-listener relationship by slowly transforming the medium into one that looks increasingly like other legacy mass media. In other words, the influx of traditional, pre-produced advertising "spots" into podcast content may eventually make podcasting sound more like traditional commercial radio.

Conclusion: Platformization and Podcasting's Third Decade

Spotify CEO Daniel Ek took to the stage at its co-called Investor Day on June 8, 2022, which was broadcast online as a live webcast (Spotify 2022b). The event was billed as a chance for the senior management team at Spotify to explain "how you should be thinking out our business as investors." He explained that Spotify had "morphed pretty dramatically as a business" since its initial public stock offering in 2018. Spotify, he said, had successfully leveraged its "ubiquity" on multiple mobile devices and operating systems to become the largest audio streaming platform in the world. He also emphasized that Spotify users overwhelmingly cited the service's algorithmically driven personalization functions as a key driver of their use, particularly when these algorithms assisted them in discovering new content.

Aside from their focus on audio streaming and investments in data extraction and personalization, Spotify's investor-oriented presentation also laid out some of their expectations for the future of podcasting as well. As noted throughout the book, Spotify has almost single-handedly transformed podcasting through its aggressive strategy of acquisitions of podcasting production companies, metrics and advertising firms specializing in podcasting, and exclusive carriage agreements with popular podcasts such as

The Joe Rogan Experience, *Armchair Expert with Dax Sheppard*, and *Call Her Daddy*, among many others.[1] What's perhaps most notable about Spotify's moves into podcasting has been the sheer scope of its investment: over $1 billion since 2018 with few assurances that these bets would pay off in the near future, or ever. Even in his remarks to investors during this event, Ek acknowledged that Spotify's podcasting ventures were "still largely in investment mode, and not yet profitable," but with the potential for a "40 to 50 percent" profit margin in the future (Spotify 2022b).

The most controversial and revealing moment during Spotify's Investor Day presentation, however, came when Spotify's Head of Talk Verticals, Maya Prohovnik, publicly addressed Spotify's approach to podcasting. In her remarks, she took direct aim at RSS, podcasting's open distribution mechanism and arguably one of the most central features of its identity. In touting Spotify's innovations in podcasting, she noted that "We've been able to replace RSS for our platform distribution, which means that podcasts created on our platform are no longer held back by this outdated technology" (Spotify 2022c). Prohovnik noted a series of supposed limitations of RSS that were now easily overcome by Spotify's unified platform such as: the inability to easily license recorded music rights for podcasts; the difficulty of interactivity between fans and creators (solved because Spotify also acts as a social medium via its Spotify Live feature—a copycat of social audio platform Clubhouse); and inability to access key consumption data due to RSS's "anonymized, aggregated analytics."

The phrase "outdated technology" was a provocative shot across the bow for traditional podcasters. In essence, Spotify's management argued that RSS was a major limiting factor for the medium and that the centralized architecture of content platforms like Spotify represented the future of podcasting. Spotify's disparagement of RSS was met with pushback from around the podcasting space. Podcasting 2.0 lead developer Dave Jones (2022) observed, for example, "if RSS is 'outdated technology' then so is HTML," yet both have been integral to creative innovation online. iHeartMedia CEO Conal Byrne also came to RSS's defense, pointing out that "RSS

---

[1] See https://ads.spotify.com/en-US/news-and-insights/spotify-podcast-library-ad-space/ for a full list.

feeds gives creators or publishers all the control ... That's unique to this medium" (Byrne 2022). Spotify's public broadside against RSS laid bare a tension at the heart of podcasting's expansion and commercialization: the struggle over distribution. The emerging centrality of digital content platforms like Spotify, Amazon Music, and now YouTube (Google) to podcast listening has for the first time offered audiences an alternative future for the medium, one that revolves around a closed "walled garden" of content services in contrast to the open ecosystem of RSS.

The continued survival of RSS as the distribution mechanism of podcasting content is one of several issues that will occupy central importance in the medium's third decade. In this concluding chapter, I draw together the threads of the book and raise questions that I believe should occupy political economic and media industry scholars regarding the continued development of podcasting. The study of podcasting itself is inherently fraught, chiefly because it is not a stable object, but is instead subject to continual churn. As I have developed this book over the years, I have witnessed a radical transformation of the podcasting industry from an amateur-driven cultural form to a rapidly expanding industry searching for new audiences and business models. Industry insiders are convinced that the future of podcasting is bright, especially since there is still major room for audience growth to bring it up to par with other forms of online media consumption. Despite these rosy projections about continued growth, the platformization of podcasting raises major questions about *what podcasting will look like* in the next five to ten years. The questions are central not just for podcast creators and practitioners, but for scholars alike as we come to terms with a medium that is in a constant state of flux. Indeed, *how* podcasting—perhaps one of the few lingering technical relics of the early web still in use today—adapts to an online world dominated by platforms will reveal some important truths about the future of the digital economy.

Distribution Battles and the Future of Podcasting: Is Podcasting a Social Medium?

As I've explored in the book, platform services have flocked to podcasting as its popularity has skyrocketed. On the surface, the ostensible goal of players like Spotify, Google, and Amazon is to secure their own "piece of the pie" and to fashion new means for expanding their own user bases by making it that much easier to consume many different types of content within a single platform. But Spotify VP Maya Prohovnik's remarks in June of 2022 revealed a much longer-term project at work: to decouple podcasting from the open architecture of RSS and to refashion it as a platform-centric medium. Spotify and other platform providers envision a future in which listeners will stream podcast content either directly from their servers or via "pass through" of the content from the podcast host, via the platform app, to audiences. Much like audio streaming, platform listeners will receive AI-generated recommendations about new podcasts, and users will be empowered to share their favorite episodes to friends and followers via platform-specific apps. All the while, platform services will be able to track listening behaviors more carefully and more efficiently deliver targeted advertising to those listeners through sophisticated algorithms and digital advertising insertion (DAI). There are, of course, numerous conveniences associated with platform-centric listening, such as ease of podcast discoverability, the ability to provide feedback and reviews to podcasts, and, in the case of Spotify, the opportunity for creators to include copyrighted music in their podcasts for the very first time, provided that those shows remain exclusive to the platform itself. Finally, platform services such as Spotify and Apple Podcasts have offered themselves up as convenient intermediaries for the monetization of content by introducing paid subscriptions, with the platform taking a portion of the subscription revenue. As I outlined in the previous chapter, Spotify has also leveraged its purchase of Megaphone to create the "Spotify Audience Network" which will create a vast podcast content inventory to sell targeted advertising (Carman 2021a; Spotify 2021). While these industry moves have been billed as efforts to help indie podcasters support their own creative labor, they are also geared toward increasing the financial bottom line for platform providers by increasing the metric that matters most: monthly active users (MAUs). In this sense, platforms are creating their own centrifugal forces to bring users to the platform for podcasts and keep them there for other types of content consumption.

A key allure of platforms is their ability to facilitate social interactions among their users. These recent moves in the industry have also endeavored to more closely align podcast listening with the social features that make their services so attractive: to essentially transform podcasting into a *social medium*. Podcasting has always been associated with a strong sense of community and intimacy between creators and listeners. It encourages practitioners and audiences alike to engage more deeply with audio content and with each other, something that Bonini et al. (2020, 6) describe as "conviviality," "or being vigorously engaged in relationships, conscious of values and meanings." This sense of community surrounding podcasting has to some extent been co-opted by platform services, which have sought to re-cast podcasting in the mold of other social media such as YouTube, Twitter, and Instagram. For example, the past several years have seen the rise of so-called social audio services such as Clubhouse, Twitter Spaces, and Spotify's Greenroom (renamed "Spotify Live" in April 2022). These services have leveraged podcasting communities by enabling live, real-time broadcasts with audiences that are essentially co-present, commenting via the text functions of the social medium and even via audio when invited by the host. Additionally, Spotify has begun rolling out added features in its app that enables users to easily record and upload audio directly from their mobile device (Mehta 2022a), much as it has already done in its Anchor app. In another new in-app trial in August 2022, Spotify users in New Zealand and Vietnam were even prompted to record voice reactions to music playlists that would be posted as a podcast episode to that user's profile, where their followers would be able to listen (Mehta 2022b). Apple Podcasts and Spotify even adopted the social media term "followers" within their apps in 2022, re-purposing the previous "subscribers" moniker to refer to those who paid a monthly in-app fee to access a specific podcast that was behind a paywall (Silberling 2022).

The efforts of platforms to transform podcasting into the next big social media service have not necessarily been all that successful, however, at least in the short term. For example, the podcasting world was stunned in May of 2022 when Facebook's parent corporation Meta announced that it was abruptly closing down its podcast integration, barely a year after it had been launched (Carman 2022a). Even Spotify's own expensive gamble on podcast integration within its music streaming service hasn't resulted in the surge of new listeners that it had hoped (Salzman 2022). And what about the pivot of podcasting toward social audio platforms like Clubhouse? Well, after its meteoric rise in 2021 during the height of the global pandemic, Clubhouse has seen major declines in app installs (Fatemi 2022), in part due to the rise in competing services like Twitter Spaces and Spotify Live (Conger 2021). In this sense, the anticipated "pivot" of podcasting toward social audio is likely not a foregone conclusion. This does not necessarily mean that social media are not influencing the formalization of podcasting, however. In fact, the logics of social media labor, whereby content creators are encouraged to work long hours to facilitate ongoing social relationships with their audiences, are becoming increasingly important within the podcasting industry. The rhetoric of podcast production as discussed in the "how to" podcasts of Daniel J. Lewis and Dave Jackson, along with the entrepreneurism of annual conventions like Podcast Movement and International PodFest, captures the ethos of this embrace of the gig labor ethos. Podcast hosts have even been re-imagined by advertisers as "influencers" who can leverage their visceral connections with listeners to seamlessly interweave native advertising into those interactions. Perhaps the most direct indication that social media will play an important role in the future of podcasting was YouTube's August 2022 announcement that it would launch its own podcast service[2] which would link viewers to videos of podcast recordings (Shapiro 2022). Indeed, according to an industry report released by Cumulus Media, six out of ten weekly podcast listeners report that they preferred podcasts with video, and that YouTube was their most preferred platform for viewing them (Sharma 2022). The emergence of video podcasts looks to be much more disruptive than social audio, and this in turn will further push audiences toward platform services to consume their favorite podcasts.

There is one more potential challenge to podcast distribution that may have an outsized impact on its development in the next several years: the atomization of the medium itself. First, platforms such as Spotify along with new independent podcasting apps begin to offer new types of listening affordances to audiences, some of which have the potential to disrupt the traditional flow of

---

[2] https://www.youtube.com/podcasts

"shows" and "episodes" (which are themselves holdover concepts from broadcast media like radio and television). By leveraging the concept of "playlists" from its music streaming service, users can now share create and share lists of individual podcast episodes. Much like their streaming audio counterparts, Spotify's podcast playlists can be centered around a theme or topic, or may just comprise a list of one user's favorite podcast episodes of all time (Misener 2019b). Spotify's integration of podcast playlists in 2019 wasn't necessarily new. In fact, other podcast discovery services such as Podchaser, which was acquired by Acast in July 2022 (Inside Radio 2022b), and Listennotes have provided this functionality for some time. Podcast app Hark also curates lists of podcast episodes and selections based on a particular theme or idea (Banton 2021). Instead, what is noteworthy about Spotify's integration of playlists is the fact that Spotify is the single largest platform for audio consumption,[3] ensuring that those playlists enjoy perhaps the largest audience reach. Additionally, as it does with its audio streaming service, Spotify has also created podcast playlists of its own, offering its own staff as potential editorial and creative gatekeepers who are capable of steering listeners toward a small group of selected podcasts.

The second front in the atomization of podcasting is the development of new mobile apps that allow for tagging, clipping, and sharing podcast content; essentially chopping up specific episodes into smaller, easily digestible information nuggets. The increasing popularity of podcasting has incentivized app developers to launch scores of new mobile apps, some of them going beyond the traditional functions of searching, subscribing, and playing podcasts to include notetaking, audio annotations, and the clipping and sharing of small bits of audio to other app users. Apps such as Podverse, Momento, Snipd, Airr, and IQ-Notecast/Inflo, for example, enable users to tag snippets of audio, which are then transcribed via AI and saved as individual notes, which can be shared with other users. Users can then create their own playlists of these audio snippets or even listen to the "top" most popular shared podcast audio selections through the app itself. Mobile podcatching apps such as these have vastly

---

[3]According to Edison Research, Spotify became the top podcast platform in the United States in 2022, surpassing SiriusXM, iHeartRadio, NPR, and *The New York Times* (Edison Research 2022b).

expanded the range of access that listeners can have with podcasts, but it also threatens the *seriality* of podcasting—a core aspect of its identity (Sterne et al. 2008a)—by altering the nature of the listening experience from a long form medium into a series of brief audio encounters. Google has also begun contributing to this potential fracturing of the medium by transcribing all podcast content in the background and then leveraging its formidable search algorithms to surface specific podcast episodes, and even *specific moments within those episodes*, for users search on a particular keyword or topic (Carman 2019c). All of these developments point to a central problematic for podcasting as it enters its third decade: What happens when podcasting is effectively decoupled from RSS, the open distribution mechanism that has been so integral to its identity and central to its popularization? While the Podcasting 2.0 effort pioneered by Adam Curry and David Jones has aimed to revitalize the open ecosystem of RSS by developing new namespaces, they have thus far encouraged only a few app developers to implement these new additions to RSS, and their efforts have been largely ignored by larger platform services like Apple Podcasts, Spotify, Amazon Music, and Google Podcasts. The result is that listeners who access podcast content via these platforms will not be able to take advantage of these new features of RSS, and with little to no user adoption of these new features, the future utility of RSS as a dynamic distribution mechanism for podcasting will be greatly diminished.

Content Exclusivity and the Perils of Platform Governance

Another industry trend in podcasting is also challenging the primacy of open distribution via RSS: content exclusivity. As I have explored in previous chapters, large platforms and podcast publishers such as Spotify, Amazon, and Apple have integrated digital paywalls into their services, while also signing high-profile podcast talent with huge audiences to exclusive carriage deals on their services. Luminary, the $100 million venture capital funded podcast subscription service, launched to much fanfare and controversy (Carman 2019a), only to struggle to find enough listeners willing to purchase a monthly subscription (Shaw and Anand 2020). Despite the public backlash from podcasters surrounding Luminary's pay-to-play structure, three years on, exclusive content has become a standard feature of the medium. Most notably, in May 2020 Spotify signed an exclusive deal with Joe Rogan (Steele 2020), the most popular podcaster, one that was reportedly valued $200 million (Rosman et al. 2022). Other major exclusivity deals have included Spotify's $60 million for *Call Her Daddy* in 2021 (Blasi 2021). Even podcast pioneer Roman Mars sold the exclusive rights to produce and distribute *99 percent Invisible* to radio giant SiriusXM, though the podcast will remain freely available on all platforms for the time being (Ugwu 2021a).

By signing high-profile podcast talent to exclusive carriage deals, platform services are catering to their own bottom line by not only bringing attention and new users to their platforms, but by encouraging those users to spend more time and money on these platforms. In stark contrast to the open-ness of RSS distribution, platforms are purposely designed as closed systems—elaborate technical "walled gardens." But podcasts with dedicated followings are also emerging as coveted forms of intellectual property in a media environment hungry for new content. Podcast production studio Wondery, for example, aggressively pursued cross-licensing deals for its original audio dramas, including *Dr. Death*, *Dirty John*, and *Gladiator* which have all appeared as television series (Locker 2019). Indeed, the collective value of these creative properties no doubt made it an attractive acquisition target for Amazon, which paid $300 million for it in late 2020 (L. Hirsch 2020). A good deal of industry formalization has emerged around professionalized podcast content, particularly among the larger podcast networks such a Wondery, Gimlet Media, The Ringer, and Earwolf, especially since these networks have largely been acquired by the giant tech platforms in the past several years. Additionally, the content pipeline from podcasting to television and feature films is also now well-established, thanks in large part to the emerging centrality of traditional entertainment talent agencies into podcasting as well (Chan 2022). New podcasts with bankable Hollywood talent often now launch as part of multi-media deals that include books, made-for-TV dramas, or documentaries. Original podcast programming will continue to become more and more valuable to television and film production as they search for new forms of intellectual property for their own production apparatus.

There is another important consequence of the shift of platforms into podcast production. These purportedly "neutral" platforms that had previously positioned themselves as directories and distribution hubs for podcast content that was created and stored elsewhere have now essentially become *publishers themselves*. For example, thanks to its acquisition of podcast production companies such as Gimlet Media and The Ringer, Spotify is now firmly in the business of producing original podcast content, as is Amazon through its acquisition of Wondery. An emerging question for podcasting has become: How will these new publishers accept the new responsibilities accorded with publishing podcasts by establishing some kind of editorial standards or codes of ethics? Unlike some of their platform counterparts with established histories in broadcast radio (and regulatory standards) such as NPR, the BBC, and even iHeartRadio and SiriusXM, technology companies like Spotify and Amazon are struggling with issues of *platform governance* much as Google has done with YouTube. This struggle was brought into sharp relief, for instance, in early 2022, when popular music recording artists Neil Young and Joni Mitchell removed their albums from Spotify in protest over the anti-vaccine rhetoric regularly found on the Spotify-exclusive *Joe Rogan Experience* (Tsioulcas 2022). Spotify CEO Daniel Ek was slow to respond to the public criticism of Rogan, arguing that Spotify was simply a distributor of content and not a publisher, and that he respected the free speech rights of the content carried on the platform. Spotify eventually responded with a set of "Platform Rules" and agreed to place a "controversial" label on specific episodes of Rogan's podcast (Spotify 2022a). Rogan himself posted a 10 minute video to his Instagram account pledging to do better to strike a balance of content on his show. Much like the Alex Jones *Infowars* debacle explored earlier in the book, platforms will increasingly take on the role of podcast publishers, though with only fledgling editorial infrastructures to ensure the accuracy of information contained in those podcasts. The entire podcasting industry has only just begun to grapple with the rising tide of public misinformation and its potential role in preventing its spread.

Platform Optimization and the Economy of Attention

As noted earlier in the book, podcasting is a classic "Long Tail" media format. This means that there are a small handful of large, big budget podcasts that garner most of the available revenue, and an increasingly large number of very small, niche podcasts that make up the long tail of the industry. As podcasting moves into its third decade, several important trends are emerging here. First, the number of podcasts continues to mushroom, with now well over 4 million available, according to the Podcast Index.[4] This represents a staggering amount of growth in creative output, particularly since the early days of the pandemic in 2020. Essentially, the Long Tail of podcasting is becoming ever longer, with more hyperniche content launches expanding the offerings for listeners. This trend has been accelerated by Spotify's acquisition and promotion of Anchor, the podcast hosting service that offers free podcast uploads for users in exchange for its ability to monetize that user-generated content via advertising, similar to YouTube. Second, podcasting continues to draw in new listeners to the medium, thereby expanding the size of the global podcast audience. According to Statista, for example, the size of the global podcast audience in 2022 is 383.7 million, and projected to cross a half billion listeners by 2024 (Statista Research Department 2022). Similarly, Edison Research reported that an estimated 177 million people in the United States had "ever" listened to a podcast in 2022, and that an estimated 109 million people had listened to a podcast in the past month (T. Webster 2022). These growth trend lines are all signs of a vibrant and expanding medium.

Despite all this growth, industry consolidation and platformization have had significant impacts. While the tail of the industry has been expanding, the head of that graph has also seen major changes. Revenues in the head have been increasing, expanding the profit ceiling in podcasting. However, these new revenues have been unevenly distributed, going mainly to the largest networks and platform services like Amazon, Spotify, and SiriusXM, all of which have made substantial investments in the industry

---

[4] www.podcastindex.org

by purchasing podcasting production companies or by securing exclusive distribution agreements with popular podcasters. Along with the industry consolidation among major platform players, there has been a consolidation of audience as well. A recent analysis (Soto 2022) discovered that advertisers can reach 59 percent of all US podcast audiences just by distributing their ads in the top 100 most popular podcasts. Extending out further, the report noted that expanding to the top 500 podcasts only accounted for another 16 percent of the total US audience (at 75 percent), and extending that advertising buy out to the top 1,000 podcasts achieved an 82 percent reach, only a paltry 7 percent more audience share over the top 500. This makes plain that the podcast attention economy is concentrated among the most popular podcasts. These podcasts have the highest production budgets, often feature celebrity hosts, and are created by the networks and platform producers that have emerged as industry leaders within podcasting. Looking for more efficient buys, advertisers will go where the audiences are, and pursue deals with these top podcasts, making for a synergy between the attention economy and the advertising economy. To be clear, there will continue to be opportunities for small-scale monetization for niche and independent podcasts, but the bulk of the advertising revenues will be concentrated within an ever-shrinking collection of hit podcasts. These podcasts also have extensive promotion budgets supporting them, and platform providers will increasingly direct their users' attention toward these podcasts via their platform algorithms in a kind of promotional cycle. Within this context, smaller independents and new podcasters may find it increasingly challenging to build an audience for their creative content.

In some ways, podcasting may become something of a victim of its own runaway success. As a hyper niche cultural form, successfully connecting listeners to content that sparks their interests and passions is key to the continued expansion of the medium. As more and more podcasts are launched, many of them likely via the Spotify-owned Anchor platform, it will become increasingly challenging for listeners to locate content that may resonate with them simply due to the clutter in the marketplace. Listeners will have to wade through a dizzying variety of podcast choices, with many of these shows no longer being updated (they will have "podfaded"), adding to the chaos. In other words, *discoverability* will become central to the medium in an increasingly crowded content landscape. As the above data suggests, professional podcasts will inevitably have a leg up in the attention economy due to their marketing budgets, and because some of them are in fact exclusive to a single platform (like Spotify's exclusive podcasts), which will place these shows in front of their users at every opportunity. For independent podcasters, then, the most efficient strategy for reaching new listeners will inevitably run through the platforms due to their large user base. Like other cultural creators that rely on platforms as key intermediaries, podcasters are developing *platform optimization* strategies in order to ensure that their content becomes algorithmically visible to listeners. As I discussed in Chapter 3, some of these optimization strategies involve "gaming" the algorithm to appear in Apple's "Top Podcasts," while others involve a careful analysis of the most popular genres and podcasts on the "Top 10" lists of platform distributors and reverse engineering similar types of content for a new podcast.[5] Examining the impacts of platform optimization on the creative process is therefore an important goal of scholarly research, and work by Bishop (2020), Morris (2020), and Prey (2020) have pointed the way.

Professionalism, Creative Labor, and the Emergence of Workers' Rights

As I have outlined in the book, podcasting is a cultural form that has become increasingly professionalized, particularly following the runaway success of *Serial* in 2014. The dramatic increase in the size of the listening audience as well as the cultural awareness and relevance of the medium has created viable avenues for independents to pursue podcasting as a career path. Like moths to a flame, the low barriers to entry and camaraderie among independent podcasters

---

[5]This is not to mention the optimization strategy of copying a podcast's title, audio files, and cover art and re-distributing it under a different RSS feed to sell advertising against someone else's content. Podcast industry journalist James Cridland (2020b) demonstrated how easy it was to pirate someone's podcast by creating a duplicate RSS feed with the same content on the Anchor (Spotify for Podcasters) hosting service. Despite the illegal and unsavory nature of the practice, it is nevertheless a form of platform optimization.

operate as the lure to bring hundreds of thousands of new entrants into a medium that may offer limited avenues to economic viability. New podcast creators are encountering a much more diversified and complex industry than they would have found a decade ago, with major platform services like Spotify, Apple, and Amazon offering streamlined and often low-cost (or free) entry points into podcast production. The simplified mobile-centered recording, editing, and publishing features of Anchor, for example, have enticed millions of new audio creators to venture into podcasting to tell their own unique stories to the world. These new podcasters may be less aware, however, that they may not enjoy full rights of ownership of content that they create and distribute via platform services, nor can they claim the full benefits of monetization.

Public service broadcasters, commercial radio companies, and tech companies have all made significant investments in the industry, perhaps sensing that broadcast radio's future destiny is intertwined with podcasting. This major cash influx into podcasting has also created many new jobs and career opportunities and has accelerated the professionalization of the medium. The significant consolidation of ownership within the past several years, as well as the resulting major injection of capital into the industry by large platform providers, has placed companies like Spotify at the center of the podcast universe. Podcast platforms like Spotify have created numerous new jobs, but labor conditions among those who work exclusively for platform-owned services have not necessarily proven to be a panacea for creators. In fact, there have been more than a handful of cases wherein podcast creators with large followings have been enticed by exclusive deals with large platforms like Spotify, only to later leave and return to the open ecosystem of RSS due to creative disagreements or other restrictions on the production process. Comedy-horror podcast *Last Podcast On the Left*, for example, decided not to renew its exclusive deal with Spotify in 2021, opting instead to sign a deal with SiriusXM that allowed them to distribute its content once again for free via RSS in order to more efficiently monetize via advertising (Lee 2021). Hip-hop musician and Spotify-exclusive podcaster Joe Budden had an even more rancorous exit from Spotify in 2020, which he accused of "pillaging" his audience in order to maximize the revenue for the platform. Budden also described some rather regressive labor practices imposed upon his production company by Spotify, such as preventing him and his team from taking time off for Christmas and New Year's Eve because it would have required them to miss the recording of episodes (Carman 2020a).

Despite some of these negative experiences of high-profile podcasters working under contract with platform providers, independent creators with whom I spoke for this project expressed a sense of possibility and optimism about podcasting, due largely to the creative freedom it provides thanks to the lack of institutional gatekeepers. The sense of community among creators and the ability to connect directly to listeners were also strong attractors for independent podcasters. As I have outlined in previous chapters, podcast creators play an important role in the professionalization of the medium by dispensing advice and mentorship to new market entrants. Indeed, some of these creators have developed their own business niches as industry insiders or cultural intermediaries by offering their mentorship to other podcasters for a fee. This entrepreneurial fervor is also readily apparent at industry conventions and meetups, where podcasters swap stories and strategies about production practices, marketing, and listener community management.

There is also a genuine sense of camaraderie among independent podcasters, and this has created some ideal conditions for the emergence of labor collectives and other types of communities of practice. Some, like Multitude Productions,[6] aim to both educate and socialize new podcasters by demonstrating the economic viability of the medium for creators with small, hyperniche, but enthusiastic audiences. Other labor collectives focus on one specific aspect of the industry such as podcasting editing, as seen with groups such as the Global Podcast Editors[7] or the Podcast Editors Academy.[8] These organizations not only educate members about the skills required to edit podcast audio, but they also act as sites of informal mentorship and job clearinghouses. Other informal groups like Podcasts in Color[9] have helped diversify the medium by creating a searchable database of BIPOC podcasts and by drawing listener

---

[6] https://multitude.productions/about
[7] https://www.stephfuccio.com/globalpodcasteditors
[8] https://www.podcasteditoracademy.com/
[9] https://www.podcastsincolor.com/

attention to independent podcasts that feature underrepresented voices. These informal labor collectives can serve as bulwarks against the excesses of platforms, though their ability to shift the terms of their labor relationship with larger platforms are limited.

The prospects for greater labor autonomy are slightly more positive for salaried employees of companies owned by larger podcast platforms, where more formal podcast unionization has begun to take hold. For example, the salaried staff of Gimlet Media and The Ringer joined the Writers Guild of American East (WGAE) Union in 2020 and successfully negotiated a three-year contract with Spotify in 2021 that covered salaries, annual increases, benefits, and assurances for hiring of employees from diverse backgrounds (Carman 2021b). Inspired by the Gimlet and Ringer Union contracts, Spotify-owned podcast production company Parcast also joined the WGA and threatened to strike before it too reached a multi-year contract agreement with Spotify in 2022 (Kilkenny 2022). An important emerging research area within podcast studies focuses on the labor practices of podcast creators in a platform-driven environment. More specifically, scholars should interrogate how creators navigate the crosscurrents of podcast platformization in their search for more listeners. One recent study by Freja Adler Berg (2021), for example, considers the calculations made by independent Danish podcasters in switching to paid podcasting platform Podimo as a means to pursue financial independence for their productions. Much more research is needed here on the lived experiences of creators as they adjust to the increasing centrality of platforms in their production processes.

The Emerging Duality of Podcasting

To listeners, the podcasting landscape looks much the same as it did a decade ago, though the process of discovering new shows, subscribing to them, and downloading or streaming content has been greatly simplified. Behind the scenes, however, in terms of the technical and institutional structures that create and distribute that content to audiences, major changes are reshaping the medium in ways that are not immediately transparent for listeners. Platformization aims to consolidate the listening experience into one unified interface, to essentially domesticate the fragmented and somewhat chaotic landscape of podcasting. In their moves to transform podcast listening into a platform-centric experience, however, companies like Spotify, Google, and Amazon are working to shift the very definition of the medium itself. Podcasting is slowly moving away from the long-form, serialized experience and into a mode that looks more like social media and, of course, YouTube: shared clips, intense social engagement online around podcast content, and fragmented, bite-sized consumption fueled by ever more sophisticated AI-driven discovery tools. Peer recommendations and word of mouth will no doubt continue to be important as a means for podcasters to expand their audience base, but AI-driven discovery tools are gradually becoming the norm in the industry, which will drive independent podcasters to more carefully optimize their production and distribution strategies to match the requirements of platforms.

In short, the story of podcasting's third decade will center on the development of two divergent versions of podcasting existing side by side. On the one hand, the scrappy, upstart version of podcasting that features largely amateur content—the cornerstone of the medium from its early years—will survive thanks to the open architecture of RSS. But the explosion of independent, amateur-driven content is not necessarily incontrovertible evidence of a thriving podcast ecosystem. In fact, one analysis conducted in April 2021 by James Cridland of Podnews and Steven Goldstein of Amplifi Media found that only 8 percent (or roughly 156,000) of over 2 million podcasts available on Apple Podcasts had both ten or more episodes and a fresh episode produced in the past week (Goldstein 2021). A follow up in 2022 of the same metric of over 4 million podcasts available on the Podcast Index discovered that, despite the explosion in the number of new podcasts in the ecosystem, about the same number of total podcasts were being regularly updated, now only 4 percent of the total (Goldstein 2022). On the one hand, this analysis reveals that amateur content is alive and well, as new entrants have flooded the ecosystem with new content. On the other hand, this also suggests that "podfading" is becoming more common, perhaps as yeoman podcast creators discover both the demands of producing a regular show as well as the increased competition for listeners with larger, more established podcasts. Thanks to the open architecture of RSS and its continued viability as an easy "on ramp" for amateur podcasters, it is likely that the scrappy, upstart aura of podcasting will continue to survive.

This version of podcasting will co-exist with the professionalized, platform-dominated medium. As companies like Spotify, Amazon, NPR, SiriusXM, and iHeartMedia aggressively monetize and market exclusive podcast content on their platforms, they have positioned themselves as the new gatekeepers with the keys to an ever-expanding global podcast audience. These platform-driven podcasts—already with substantial audience share of the podcast listening universe—are likely to grow their listenership at a much faster rate than smaller, independent podcasts, thanks in part to the built-in advantages they may enjoy by being featured on major platform services like Apple Podcasts or Spotify, particularly if those podcasts are continually surfaced for listeners in the form of AI-driven recommendations. In other words, the differences between the "head" and "tail" of the podcast industry will likely become more pronounced. Professional indie podcasters with large followings (especially celebrities) or those working for major networks or production companies will continue to produce shows that will be highly visible to listeners and will also command the bulk of the industry's advertising revenue. "Big" podcasting will begin to look quite different from amateur, independent podcasts, and will become more integrated into the commercial apparatus thanks to cross-promotions and the translation of podcast IP into other media such as television.

Thus, podcasting's role as a forum for independent, amateur, and "authentic" cultural expression is being challenged by distinct formalization processes: the increased focus on effective methods of audience monitoring, monetization via advertising, standardization of production techniques, and aggressive forms of self-branding found in other forms of online cultural production. The processes of formalization are not totalizing and irreversible, however, but are instead often contradictory and chaotic. Amid the increasing commercialization of podcasting, for example, amateur podcasters have banded together to form networks, collectives, and informal communities of practice that has established a powerful communitarian ethos at the heart of the medium. Podcasting is at a historic crossroads: formalization, specialization, and monetization may fundamentally challenge the democratic ethos of the medium, and it is imperative that we consider what might be lost in a future that may be dominated by major online platforms.

REFERENCES

Abbruzzese, Jason. 2017. "The Latest Trend in Podcasts? Making Them into Movies." *Mashable* (blog). August 2, 2017. http://mashable.com/2017/08/02/gimlet-media-fundraising-podcast-movies/#rcqvzyFiaiqR/.

Abidin, Crystal. 2016. "Visibility Labour: Engaging with Influencers' Fashion Brands and #OOTD Advertorial Campaigns on Instagram." *Media International Australia* 161 (1): 86–100. https://doi.org/10.1177/1329878X16665177.

"About Hot Pod." 2022. *Hot Pod News*. January 1, 2022. https://hotpodnews.com/about/.

Adgate, Brad. 2021. "As Podcasts Continue to Grow in Popularity, Ad Dollars Follow." *Forbes* (blog). February 11, 2021. https://www.forbes.com/sites/bradadgate/2021/02/11/podcasting-has-become-a-big-business/.

Adler Berg, Freja Sørine. 2021. "The Tension between Podcasters and Platforms: Independent Podcasters' Experiences of the Paid Subscription Model." *Creative Industries Journal* 15 (1): 58–78. https://doi.org/10.1080/17510694.2021.1890417.

AdvertiseCast. 2022. "Podcast Advertising Rates 2022." October 1, 2022. https://www.advertisecast.com/podcast-advertising-rates.

Alexander, Neta. 2016. "Catered to Your Future Self: Netflix's 'Predictive Personalization' and the Mathematization of Taste." In *The Netflix Effect: Technology and Entertainment in the 21st Century*, edited by K. McDonald and D. Smith-Rowsey, 81–100. New York: Bloomsbury Academic.

Ali, Rafat. 2009. "Leo Laporte on Media, Tech and Journalism." PaidContent. October 3, 2009. http://paidcontent.org/2009/10/03/419-weekend-viewing-ona09-leo-laporte-on/.

Almo, Laura. 2016. "Listen Up! Dispatches from Podcast Movement 2016." *Documentary* (blog). September 23, 2016. https://www.documentary.org/online-feature/listen-dispatches-podcast-movement-2016/.

Amadeo, Ron. 2023. "YouTube Podcasts Go Live in the US with Inclusion in YouTube Music." *Ars Technica* (blog). April 28, 2023. https://arstechnica.com/gadgets/2023/04/youtube-podcasts-go-live-in-the-us-with-inclusion-in-youtube-music/.

Anand, N., and Richard A. Peterson. 2000. "When Market Information Constitutes Fields: Sensemaking of Markets in the Commercial Music Industry." *Organization Science* 11 (3): 270–84.

Anderson, Chris. 2006. *The Long Tail: Why the Future of Business Is Selling Less of More*. New York: Hyperion Books.

Andrejevic, Mark. 2009. "Exploiting YouTube: Contradictions of User-Generated Labor." In *The YouTube Reader*, edited by Patrick Vonderau, Pelle Snickars and Jean Burgess, 406–23. Stockholm: National Library of Sweden.

Andrejevic, Mark. 2011. "The Work That Affective Economics Does." *Cultural Studies* 25 (4–5): 604–20. https://doi.org/10.1080/09502386.2011.600551.

Andrejevic, Mark. 2013. "Estranged Free Labor." In *Digital Labor: The Internet as Playground and Factory*, edited by Trebor Scholz, 149–64. New York: Routledge.

Apple. 2005. "Apple Takes Podcasting Mainstream." Apple Newsroom. June 28, 2005. https://www.apple.com/newsroom/2005/06/28Apple-Takes-Podcasting-Mainstream/.

Apple. 2011. "Apple Introduces ICloud." Apple Newsroom. June 6, 2011. https://www.apple.com/newsroom/2011/06/06Apple-Introduces-iCloud/.

Apple. n.d. "Apple Podcasts Categories." A Podcaster's Guide to RSS. Accessed July 31, 2021. https://help.apple.com/itc/podcasts_connect/#/itc9267a2f12.

Arditi, David. 2021. *Streaming Culture: Subscription Platforms and the Unending Consumption of Culture*. Bingley: Emerald Publishing.

Arriagada, Arturo, and Sophie Bishop. 2021. "Between Commerciality and Authenticity: The Imaginary of Social Media Influencers in the Platform Economy." *Communication, Culture and Critique* 14 (4): 568–86. https://doi.org/10.1093/ccc/tcab050.

Arriagada, Arturo, and Francisco Ibáñez. 2020. "'You Need at Least One Picture Daily, If Not, You're Dead': Content Creators and Platform Evolution in the Social Media Ecology." *Social Media + Society* 6 (3): 2056305120944624. https://doi.org/10.1177/2056305120944624.

Arvidsson, Adam. 2019. *Changemakers: The Industrious Future of the Digital Economy*. Cambridge, UK: John Wiley & Sons.

Attig, Christiane. 2020. "Männlich, Mittelalt, Gebildet – Oder? Eine Charakterisierung Deutschsprachiger Podcaster:Innen [Male, Middle-Aged, Educated – Right? A Characterization of German-Speaking

Podcasters]." *Kommunikation@gesellschaft* 21 (2): 1–13. https://doi.org/10.15460/kommges.2020.21.2.626.

Axon, Samuel. 2021. "Apple's Podcast Subscriptions Went Live Today—with a 30 Percent Cut." *Ars Technica*. June 15, 2021. https://arstechnica.com/gadgets/2021/06/apples-podcast-subscriptions-went-live-today-with-a-30-percent-cut/.

Banton, Lawrence. 2021. "Hark Audio Turns Hours-Long Podcasts Into Big Moment Playlists." *Cheddar News* (blog). April 30, 2021. https://cheddar.com/media/hark-audio-turns-hours-long-podcasts-into-big-moment-playlists/.

Barletta, Bryan. 2021. "Podcast Prefix Analytics Explained." *Sounds Profitable* (blog). March 24, 2021. https://soundsprofitable.com/update/prefix-analytics.

Barletta, Bryan. 2022. "Programmatic Advertising for Buyers." *Sounds Profitable* (blog). September 13, 2022. https://soundsprofitable.com/update/programmatic-ads-for-buyers.

Barlow, John Perry. 2019. "A Declaration of the Independence of Cyberspace." *Duke Law & Technology Review* 18 (1): 5–7.

Barrett, Jason. 2016. "Takeaways from the Podcast Movement Conference." *Barrett Sports Media* (blog). July 12, 2016. http://sportsradiopd.com/2016/07/takeaways-from-the-podcast-movement-conference/.

Basu, Shumita. 2017. "The Delightful World of Super-Niche Podcasts." *WNYC News* (blog). April 12, 2017. http://www.wnyc.org/story/super-niche-podcasts/?utm_source=sharedUrl&utm_medium=metatag&utm_campaign=sharedUrl.

Baym, Nancy K. 2015. "Connect with Your Audience! The Relational Labor of Connection." *The Communication Review* 18 (1): 14–22.

Baym, Nancy K. 2018. *Playing to the Crowd: Musicians, Audiences, and the Intimate Work of Connection*. 1st edn. New York: NYU Press.

BBC News. 2014. "BBC Marks 10 Years of Podcasting with Record Figures." October 15, 2014. bbc.com/mediacentre//latestnews/2014/10years–podcasting/.

BBC News. 2018. "New BBC Sounds App Aims to Woo Younger Listeners." *BBC News*. October 29, 2018. sec. Entertainment & Arts. https://www.bbc.com/news/46017079/.

BBC News. 2020. "BBC Launches New Creative Development Unit in Bristol Focused on Podcasts." June 26, 2020. bbc.com/mediacentre//latestnews/2020/creative-development-unit/.

Benkler, Yochai. 2006. *The Wealth of Networks: How Social Production Transforms Markets and Freedom*. New Haven [Conn.]: Yale University Press.

Bermejo, Fernando. 2009. "Audience Manufacture in Historical Perspective: From Broadcasting to Google." *New Media & Society* 11 (1–2): 133–54.

Berry, Richard. 2006. "Will the IPod Kill the Radio Star? Profiling Podcasting as Radio." *Convergence: The International Journal of Research into New Media Technologies* 12 (2): 143–62. https://doi.org/10.1177/1354856506066522.

Berry, Richard. 2015. "A Golden Age of Podcasting? Evaluating Serial in the Context of Podcast Histories." *Journal of Radio & Audio Media* 22 (2): 170–8.

Berry, Richard. 2016. "Podcasting: Considering the Evolution of the Medium and Its Association with the Word 'Radio.'" *Radio Journal: International Studies in Broadcast & Audio Media* 14 (1): 7–22. https://doi.org/10.1386/rjao.14.1.7_1.

Berry, Richard. 2020. "Radio, Music, Podcasts – BBC Sounds: Public Service Radio and Podcasts in a Platform World." *Radio Journal: International Studies in Broadcast & Audio Media* 18 (1): 63–78. https://doi.org/10.1386/rjao_00016_1.

Berry, Richard. 2021. "What Is a Podcast? Mapping the Technical, Cultural, and Sonic Boundaries between Radio and Podcasting." In *Routledge Companion to Radio Studies*, edited by Jason Loviglio and Mia Lindgren. Abingdon, Oxon, UK: Routledge.

Bierma, Nathan. 2005. "'Podcast' Is Lexicon's Word of the Year." *Chicago Tribune*. December 28, 2005. https://www.chicagotribune.com/news/ct-xpm-2005-12-28-0512270256-story.html.

Bijker, W. E. 1997. *Of Bicycles, Bakelites, and Bulbs: Toward a Theory of Sociotechnical Change*. Cambridge, MA: The MIT Press.

Bilton, Ricardo. 2014. "Public Radio's Complicated Digital Journey." *Digiday* (blog). December 19, 2014. https://digiday.com/media/public-radios-complicated-digital-journey/.

Bishop, Sophie. 2018a. "Vlogging Parlance." In *Microcelebrity around the Globe*, edited by Crystal Abidin and Megan Lindsay Brown, 21–32. Bingley, UK: Emerald Publishing Limited. https://doi.org/10.1108/978-1-78756-749-820181002.

Bishop, Sophie. 2018b. "Anxiety, Panic and Self-Optimization: Inequalities and the YouTube Algorithm." *Convergence* 24 (1): 69–84. https://doi.org/10.1177/1354856517736978.

Bishop, Sophie. 2020. "Algorithmic Experts: Selling Algorithmic Lore on YouTube." *Social Media + Society* 6 (1): 2056305119897323. https://doi.org/10.1177/2056305119897323.

Bishop, Sophie. 2021. "Influencer Management Tools: Algorithmic Cultures, Brand Safety, and Bias." *Social Media + Society* 7 (1): 205630512110030. https://doi.org/10.1177/20563051211003066.

Blasi, Weston. 2021. "Spotify Strikes $60 Million Podcast Deal with Barstool's 'Call Her Daddy.'" *MarketWatch* (blog). June 17, 2021. https://www.marketwatch.com/story/spotify-strikes-60-million-podcast-deal-with-barstools-call-her-daddy-11623875822.

Blattberg, Eric. 2015. "The Measurement Challenge Facing Podcast Advertising." *Digiday* (blog). February 5, 2015. https://digiday.com/media/measurement-challenge-podcast-advertising.

Bodle, Robert. 2011. "Regimes of Sharing." *Information, Communication & Society* 14 (3): 320–37. https://doi.org/10.1080/1369118X.2010.542825.

Bollier, David. 2008. *Viral Spiral: How the Commoners Built a Digital Republic of Their Own*. New York, NY: New Press.

Bolter, Jay David, and Richard Grusin. 2000. *Remediation: Understanding New Media*, Revised edn. Cambridge, MA: The MIT Press.

Bonifacio, Ross, and Donghee Yvette Wohn. 2020. "Digital Patronage Platforms." In *Conference Companion Publication of the 2020 on Computer Supported Cooperative Work and Social Computing*, 221–6.

Bonifacio, Ross, Lee Hair, and Donghee Yvette Wohn. 2021. "Beyond Fans: The Relational Labor and Communication Practices of Creators on Patreon." *New Media & Society*. 25(10), 2684–2703. https://doi.org/10.1177/14614448211027961.

Bonini, Tiziano. 2015. "The 'Second Age' of Podcasting: Reframing Podcasting as a New Digital Mass Medium." *Quaderns Del CAC* 41 (18): 21–30.

Bonini, Tiziano, Belén Monclús, and Salvatore Scifo. 2020. "Radio as a Social Media." *Radio Journal: International Studies in Broadcast & Audio Media* 18 (1): 5–12. https://doi.org/10.1386/rjao_00012_2.

Bottomley, Andrew J. 2015a. "Podcasting: A Decade in the Life of a 'New' Audio Medium: Introduction." *Journal of Radio & Audio Media* 22 (2): 164–9. https://doi.org/10.1080/19376529.2015.1082880.

Bottomley, Andrew J. 2015b. "Podcasting, Welcome to Night Vale, and the Revival of Radio Drama." *Journal of Radio & Audio Media* 22 (2): 179–89. https://doi.org/10.1080/19376529.2015.1083370.

Bottomley, Andrew J. 2020. *Sound Streams: A Cultural History of Radio-Internet Convergence*. Ann Arbor, Michigan: University of Michigan Press. https://www.press.umich.edu/9978838/sound_streams.

Bottomley, Andrew J. 2021. "Podcast Archaeology: Researching Proto-Podcasts and Early Born-Digital Audio Formats." In *Saving New Sounds*, edited by Jeremy Wade Morris and Eric Hoyt, 29–50. Ann Arbor, MI: University of Michigan Press. https://www.press.umich.edu/11435021/saving_new_sounds.

Braun, Joshua. 2014. "Transparent Intermediaries: Building the Infrastructures of Connected Viewing." In *Connected Viewing: Selling, Streaming, & Sharing Media in the Digital Age*, edited by Jennifer Holt and Kevin Sanson, 134–53. London: Routledge.

Braun, Joshua A. 2021. "Points of Origin: Asking Questions in Distribution Research." In *Digital Media Distribution*, edited by Paul McDonald, Courtney Brannon Donoghue and Timothy Havens, 27–46. New York: NYU Press. https://nyupress.org/9781479806782/digital-media-distribution.

Bruns, Axel. 2006. "Towards Produsage: Futures for User-Led Content Production." In *Creative Industries Faculty*, edited by Fay Sudweeks, Herbert Hrachovec and Charles Ess, 275–84. Tartu, Estonia: Murdoch University. http://eprints.qut.edu.au/4863.

Bruns, Axel. 2008. *Blogs, Wikipedia, Second Life, and Beyond*. New York, NY: Peter Lang.

Bruns, Axel, and Joanne Jacobs, eds. 2006. *Uses of Blogs*. Digital Formations, v. 38. New York: Peter Lang.

Bucher, Taina. 2012. "Want to Be on the Top? Algorithmic Power and the Threat of Invisibility on Facebook." *New Media & Society* 14 (7): 1164–80.

Burgess, Jean. 2012. "YouTube and the Formalisation of Amateur Media." In *Amateur Media: Social, Culturual and Legal Perspectives*, edited by Dan Hunter, Ramon Lobato, Megan Richardson and Julian Thomas, 53–8. New York: Routledge.

Burgess, Jean, and Axel Bruns. 2012. "Twitter Archives and the Challenges of 'Big Social Data' for Media and Communication Research." *M/C Journal* 15 (5). http://journal.media-culture.org.au/index.php/mcjournal/article/view/561.

Burgess, Jean, and Joshua Green. 2009. *YouTube: Online Video and Participatory Culture*. Cambridge, MA: Polity.

Burgess, Jean, and Joshua Green. 2018. *YouTube: Online Video and Participatory Culture*, 2nd edn. Cambridge, UK: Polity.

Busch, Oliver. 2016. "The Programmatic Advertising Principle." In *Programmatic Advertising: The Successful Transformation to Automated, Data-Driven Marketing in Real-Time*, edited by Oliver Busch, 1st edn., 3–16. New York, NY: Springer.

Buzzard, Karen S.F. 2015. "The Rise of Market Information Regimes and the Historical Development of Audience Ratings." *Historical Journal of Film, Radio & Television* 35 (3): 511–17. https://doi.org/10.1080/01439685.2015.1052219.

Buzzsprout. 2018. "Apple Podcasts Analytics: How to Find & Use These Podcast Statistics." *Buzzsprout Blog* (blog). November 20, 2018. https://www.buzzsprout.com/blog/apple-podcasts-analytics.

Buzzsprout. 2021. "Podcasting Industry Stats." December 31, 2021. https://www.buzzsprout.com/global_stats.

Byrne, Conal. 2022. "Get Primed for a Level Set: Three Lessons on Audio Marketing." *Forbes*. June 8, 2022. https://www.forbes.com/sites/forbestechcouncil/2022/06/08/get-primed-for-a-level-set-three-lessons-on-audio-marketing.

Caldwell, John Thornton. 2008. *Production Culture: Industrial Reflexivity and Critical Practice in Film and Television*. Durham, NC: Duke University Press.

Caldwell, John Thornton. 2011. "Cultures of Production: Studying Industry's Deep Texts, Reflexive Rituals, and Managed Self-Disclosures." In *Media Industries: History, Theory, and Method*, edited by Jennifer Holt and Alisa Perren, 199–212. West Sussex, UK: John Wiley & Sons.

Caraway, Brett. 2011. "Audience Labor in the New Media Environment: A Marxian Revisiting of the Audience Commodity." *Media, Culture & Society* 33 (5): 693–708. https://doi.org/10.1177/0163443711404463.

Carman, Ashley. 2018. "NPR Wants to Know What Podcast Ads You Skip." *The Verge* (blog). December 27, 2018. https://www.theverge.com/2018/12/27/18156895/npr-remote-audio-data-rad-analytics-podcast-tracking-apple-spotify.

Carman, Ashley. 2019a. "Podcast Wars: $100 Million Startup Luminary Launches Tuesday without Reply All or The Daily." *The Verge* (blog). April 22, 2019. https://www.theverge.com/2019/4/22/18510897/luminary-podcast-app-launch-the-daily-gimlet-media-spotify.

Carman, Ashley. 2019b. "Chartable Will Help Podcasters Track How Listeners Find Their Show." *The Verge* (blog). May 13, 2019. https://www.theverge.com/2019/5/13/18617188/chartable-smartlinks-url-podcast-marketing-tracking.

Carman, Ashley. 2019c. "Google Will Start Surfacing Individual Podcast Episodes in Search Results." *The Verge* (blog). August 8, 2019. https://www.theverge.com/2019/8/8/20759394/google-podcast-episodes-search-results-transcriber.

Carman, Ashley. 2020a. "Joe Budden Is Taking His Podcast off Spotify Because the Company 'Is Pillaging' His Audience." *The Verge* (blog). August 26, 2020. https://www.theverge.com/2020/8/26/21403282/joe-budden-spotify-exclusive-leaving-host-podcast.

Carman, Ashley. 2020b. "Amazon Music Now Has Podcasts." *The Verge* (blog). September 16, 2020. https://www.theverge.com/2020/9/16/21439531/amazon-music-podcasts-prime-titles.

Carman, Ashley. 2020c. "Spotify Is Acquiring Podcast Hosting Company Megaphone for $235 Million." *The Verge* (blog). November 10, 2020.

https://www.theverge.com/2020/11/10/21557458/spotify-megaphone-podcast-streaming-ad-insertion.

Carman, Ashley. 2021a. "Spotify CEO Daniel Ek Explains How the Company Plans to Help Artists (and Itself) Make Money." *The Verge* (blog). February 23, 2021. https://www.theverge.com/2021/2/23/22295315/spotify-ceo-interview-podcast-daniel-ek-music-stream-on.

Carman, Ashley. 2021b. "Gimlet and Ringer Unions Detail Their First Historic Contracts with Spotify." *The Verge* (blog). April 7, 2021. https://www.theverge.com/2021/4/7/22327090/gimlet-media-union-spotify-contract-agreement.

Carman, Ashley. 2021c. "Spotify Launches Podcast Subscriptions, but You Can't Subscribe in-App." *The Verge* (blog). April 27, 2021. https://www.theverge.com/2021/4/27/22404273/spotify-podcast-subscriptions-monetize-subscriber-shows.

Carman, Ashley. 2021d. "Dax Shepard's Armchair Expert Podcast Is Going Exclusive to Spotify." *The Verge* (blog). May 12, 2021. https://www.theverge.com/2021/5/12/22432286/dax-shepard-armchair-expert-spotify-exclusive.

Carman, Ashley. 2021e. "Automattic, Owner of Tumblr and WordPress.Com, Buys Podcast App Pocket Casts." *The Verge* (blog). July 16, 2021. https://www.theverge.com/2021/7/16/22580023/automattic-pocket-casts-podcast-app-tumble-wordpress.

Carman, Ashley. 2021f. "Say Goodbye to Your Favorite Podcast Promo Codes." *The Verge* (blog). December 14, 2021. https://www.theverge.com/2021/12/14/22832670/podcast-ads-direct-response-brands-industry-hot-pod.

Carman, Ashley. 2022a. "Facebook Pulls the Plug on Podcast Business after a Year." *Bloomberg.Com*. May 2, 2022. https://www.bloomberg.com/news/articles/2022-05-02/facebook-is-planning-to-leave-the-podcast-business-after-a-year.

Carman, Ashley. 2022b. "Podcast Guests Are Paying Up to $50,000 to Appear on Popular Shows." *Bloomberg.Com*. August 3, 2022. https://www.bloomberg.com/news/articles/2022-08-03/podcast-guests-can-pay-big-money-to-be-on-top-shows.

Casilli, Antonio. 2017. "How Venture Labor Sheds Light on the Digital Platform Economy." *International Journal of Communication* 11 (January): 2067–70.

Chambers, Bradley. 2022. "Podcasting 2.0, The Lightning Network, and Value4Value Usher in a New Era of Podcasting That's Free of Big Tech Control." *9to5Mac* (blog). June 26, 2022. https://9to5mac.com/2022/06/26/podcasting-2-0/.

Chan, J. Clara. 2021. "IHeartMedia Podcasters to Unionize with Writers Guild East." *The Hollywood Reporter* (blog). December 9, 2021.

https://www.hollywoodreporter.com/business/digital/iheartmedia-podcasts-union-wgae-1235060050.

Chan, J. Clara. 2022. "Agencies Look to Cash in on Podcasts' IP Gold Rush." *The Hollywood Reporter* (blog). February 14, 2022. https://www.hollywoodreporter.com/business/business-news/caa-wme-icm-uta-verve-podcasts-1235092122.

Cheatwood, Derral. 2010. "Images of Crime and Justice in Early Commercial Radio—1932 to 1958." *Criminal Justice Review* 35 (1): 32–51. https://doi.org/10.1177/0734016809348358.

Chia, Aleena. 2012. "Welcome to Me-Mart: The Politics of User-Generated Content in Personal Blogs." *American Behavioral Scientist* 56 (4): 421–38. https://doi.org/10.1177/0002764211429359.

Ciancutti, John. 2020. "A New Way for Podcasters to Understand and Grow Their Audiences." *Google* (blog). May 5, 2020. https://blog.google/products/search/new-way-podcasters-understand-and-grow-their-audiences/.

Clark, Mitchell. 2022. "Spotify Is Ramping up Its Efforts to Find Misinformation in Podcasts." *The Verge* (blog). October 5, 2022. https://www.theverge.com/2022/10/5/23389301/spotify-kinzen-audio-analysis-content-moderation-acquisition.

Clifton, Kieran. 2019. "BBC Podcasts on Third-Party Apps." *BBC Blog* (blog). March 26, 2019. https://www.bbc.co.uk/blogs/aboutthebbc/entries/d68712d7-bd24-440f-94a0-1c6a4cdee71a.

Cochrane, Todd. 2005. "History of Podcasting." *Blubrry Podcasting - Podcast Hosting, Statistics, WordPress Hosting, Syndication Tools and Directory* (blog). 2005. https://create.blubrry.com/manual/about-podcasting/history-of-podcasting-new/.

Cochrane, Todd. 2016. "RawVoice / Blubrry Responds to the Public Radio Podcast Measurement Guidelines." *PowerPress Podcast* (blog). February 8, 2016. https://powerpresspodcast.com/2016/02/08/blubrry-responds-to-public-radio-podcast-measurement-guidelines.

Cochrane, Todd, and Rob Greenlee, dirs. 2018. "Apple Editorial Control #218." *New Media Show*. https://newmediashow.com.

Comscore. 2021. "Comscore Brings Innovation to Podcast Advertising, Enabling Brand Safety Protections for Acast Podcast Inventory." Comscore, Inc. July 26, 2021. https://www.comscore.com/Insights/Press-Releases/2021/7/Comscore-Brings-Innovation-to-Podcast-Advertising-Enabling-Brand-Safety-Protections-for-Acast-Podcast-Inventory.

Confessore, Nicholas. 2018. "The Follower Factory." *The New York Times*. January 27, 2018. sec. Technology. https://www.nytimes.com/interactive/2018/01/27/technology/social-media-bots.html, https://www.nytimes.com/interactive/2018/01/27/technology/social-media-bots.html.

Conger, Kate. 2021. "How the Copycats Came for Clubhouse." *The New York Times*. December 21, 2021. sec. Technology. https://www.nytimes.com/2021/12/21/technology/clubhouse-twitter-spaces.html.

Corcoran, John. 2014. "How the First National Podcasting Conference Launched with a $30,000 Kickstarter Campaign." *Huffington Post* (blog). October 21, 2014. http://www.huffingtonpost.com/john-corcoran/how-dan-franks-helped-lau_b_6014558.html.

Corrigan, Thomas F. 2018. "Making Implicit Methods Explicit: Trade Press Analysis in the Political Economy of Communication." *International Journal of Communication* 12 (0): 22.

Craig, David. 2022. "A Pedagogue's Progress, the Cunningham Turn, and the Birth of Creator Studies." *Media International Australia* 182 (1): 59–66. https://doi.org/10.1177/1329878X211043898.

Cramer, Maria. 2020. "Joe Rogan Strikes an Exclusive, Multiyear Deal with Spotify." *The New York Times*. May 20, 2020. sec. Business. https://www.nytimes.com/2020/05/20/business/media/joe-rogan-spotify-contract.html.

Cridland, James. 2018a. "Placings on Apple's Podcast Chart Can Be Bought." *Podnews.Net* (blog). May 13, 2018. https://podnews.net/article/rotten-apple-podcast-charts.

Cridland, James. 2018b. "Is This Proof That Apple's Podcast Charts Are Being Manipulated?" *Podnews.Net* (blog). May 16, 2018. https://podnews.net/article/apple-podcast-charts-manipulated-proof.

Cridland, James. 2018c. "About This Website." *Podnews.Net*. August 23, 2018. https://podnews.net/about.

Cridland, James. 2018d. "Blubrry and NPR Are First with IAB Certification." *Podnews.Net* (blog). December 19, 2018. https://podnews.net/update/blubrry-npr-iab-certification.

Cridland, James. 2019. "The End of Open: BBC Blocks Its Podcasts on Google [UPDATED]." *Podnews.Net* (blog). March 25, 2019. https://podnews.net/article/bbc-blocks-google.

Cridland, James. 2020a. "The Podfather Launches a New, Open Podcast Directory." *Podnews.Net* (blog). September 8, 2020. https://podnews.net/update/podcast-index-open-directory.

Cridland, James. 2020b. "How to Pirate Someone Else's Podcast onto Anchor." *Podnews* (blog). October 6, 2020. https://podnews.net/article/how-to-pirate-anchor.

Cridland, James. 2020c. "The Ambies Are Coming." *Podnews.Net* (blog). October 14, 2020. https://podnews.net/update/ambies-coming.

Cridland, James. 2021a. "There Are Now 2 Million Podcasts." *Podnews.Net* (blog). March 24, 2021. https://podnews.net/update/2-million-podcasts.

Cridland, James. 2021b. "Mythbusting: Is Anchor Full of Dead Shows, and Does It Matter?" *Podnews.Net* (blog). June 11, 2021. https://podnews.net/article/anchor-dead-shows-mythbusting.

Cridland, James. 2022. "New Podcast Apps." *Podnews.Net* August 8, 2022. https://podnews.net/article/podcast-apps.

Cridland, James. 2023. "Payne Lindsey's New Show." *Podnews.Net* (blog). January 16, 2023. https://podnews.net/update/payne-lindsey-ufo.

Crofts, Sheri, Jon Dilley, Mark Fox, Andrew Retsema, and Bob Williams. 2005. "Podcasting: A New Technology in Search of Viable Business Models." *First Monday* 10 (9). http://pear.accc.uic.edu/htbin/cgiwrap/bin/ojs/index.php/fm/article/viewArticle/1273/1193.

Cundill, Matt. 2016. "The Podcast Movement Is Indeed a Thing." *The Sound Off Podcast with Matt Cundill* (blog). July 12, 2016. http://www.mattcundill.com/single-post/2016/07/12/The-Podcast-Movement-is-Indeed-a-Thing.

Cunningham, Stuart. 2012. "Emergent Innovation through the Coevolution of Informal and Formal Media Economies." *Television & New Media* 13 (5): 415–30. https://doi.org/10.1177/1527476412443091.

Cunningham, Stuart, and David Craig. 2019. *Social Media Entertainment: The New Intersection of Hollywood and Silicon Valley*. New York: NYU Press.

Cunningham, Stuart, and David Craig, eds. 2021. *Creator Culture: An Introduction to Global Social Media Entertainment*. New York: NYU Press.

Cutting Edge Events. 2022. "Podfest Expo Returns May 26–29 at the Hilton Orlando after Setting Two World Records during Covid." *GlobeNewswire*. May 18, 2022. https://www.globenewswire.com/en/news-release/2022/05/18/2446173/0/en/Podfest-Expo-Returns-May-26-29-at-the-Hilton-Orlando-After-Setting-Two-World-Records-During-Covid.html.

Cwynar, Christopher. 2015. "More Than a 'VCR for Radio': The CBC, the Radio 3 Podcast, and the Uses of an Emerging Medium." *Journal of Radio & Audio Media* 22 (2): 190–9. https://doi.org/10.1080/19376529.2015.1083371.

Cwynar, Christopher. 2019. "Self-Service Media: Public Radio Personalities, Reality Podcasting, and Entrepreneurial Culture." *Popular Communication* 17 (4): 317–332. https://doi.org/10.1080/1540570 2.2019.1634811.

D'Alessandro, Anthony. 2018. "Apple Acquires Global Rights to Documentary 'The Elephant Queen.'" *Deadline*. September 9, 2018. https://deadline.com/2018/09/apple-acquires-global-rights-to-documentary-the-elephant-queen-toronto-international-film-festival-1202460419/.

Davies, Jessica. 2017. "The Global State of Digital Advertising in 5 Charts." *Digiday* (blog). May 3, 2017. http://digiday.com/uk/global-state-digital-advertising-5-charts/.

Dean, Brian. 2022. "Patreon: Subscriber and Creator Statistics for 2022." *Backlinko* (blog). January 6, 2022. https://backlinko.com/patreon-users.

Dennis. 2021. "Podcast Merchandise to Grow Your Show: Examples and Advice." *Castos*. May 27, 2021. https://castos.com/podcast-merchandise/.

D'heer, Evelien, and Pieter Verdegem. 2015. "What Social Media Data Mean for Audience Studies: A Multidimensional Investigation of Twitter Use during a Current Affairs TV Programme." *Information, Communication & Society* 18 (2): 221–34. https://doi.org/10.1080/1369118X.2014.952318.

Douglas, Susan J. 1999. *Listening in: Radio and the American Imagination, from Amos "n" Andy and Edward R. Murrow to Wolfman Jack and Howard Stern*, 1st edn. New York: Times Books.

Dowling, David O., and Kyle J. Miller. 2019. "Immersive Audio Storytelling: Podcasting and Serial Documentary in the Digital Publishing Industry." *Journal of Radio & Audio Media* 26 (1): 167–84. https://doi.org/10.1080/19376529.2018.1509218.

Dua, Garrison. 2022. "How We Can Achieve Brand Safety In Podcasting." *Advertising Week* (blog). August 25, 2022. https://advertisingweek.com/how-we-can-achieve-brand-safety-in-podcasting/.

Duffy, Brooke Erin. 2015. "Amateur, Autonomous, and Collaborative: Myths of Aspiring Female Cultural Producers in Web 2.0." *Critical Studies in Media Communication* 32 (1): 48–64. https://doi.org/10.1080/15295036.2014.997832.

Duffy, Brooke Erin. 2017. *(Not) Getting Paid to Do What You Love: Gender, Social Media, and Aspirational Work*. New Haven: Yale University Press.

Duffy, Brooke Erin, and Jefferson D. Pooley. 2017. "'Facebook for Academics': The Convergence of Self-Branding and Social Media Logic on Academia. Edu." *Social Media+ Society* 3 (1): 2056305117696523.

Duffy, Brooke Erin, and Urszula Pruchniewska. 2017a. "Gender and Self-Enterprise in the Social Media Age: A Digital Double Bind." *Information, Communication & Society* 20 (6): 843–59. https://doi.org/10.1080/1369118X.2017.1291703.

Edison Research. 2016. "The Infinite Dial 2016." *Edison Research* (blog). March 8, 2016. https://www.edisonresearch.com/online-radio-crosses-crucial-threshold-now-listened-to-by-half-of-americans-weekly/infinite-dial-2016-weekly-online-radio-listening.

Edison Research. 2021. "About Us." *Edison Research* (blog). January 25, 2021. https://www.edisonresearch.com/about-us/.

Edison Research. 2022a. "Super Listeners 2021 from Edison Research and Ad Results Media." *Edison Research* (blog). February 16, 2022. https://www.edisonresearch.com/super-listeners-2021-from-edison-research-and-ad-results-media.

Edison Research. 2022b. "U.S. Top Podcast Networks, By Reach Q2 2022." *Edison Research* (blog). September 13, 2022. https://www.edisonresearch.com/u-s-top-podcast-networks-by-reach-q2-2022.

Edison Research. 2023. "The Infinite Dial 2023." *Edison Research* (blog). March 2, 2023. https://www.edisonresearch.com/infinite-dial-2023-from-edison-research-with-amazon-music-wondery-and-art19/.

Edison Research, and Sounds Profitable. 2022. "The Creators, from Sounds Profitable." https://soundsprofitable.com/article/the-creators-us-2022.

Eskin, Blake. 2020. "Watch Video from the Podcast Privacy Symposium." *Medium* (blog). March 19, 2020. https://medium.com/prxofficial/watch-video-from-the-podcast-privacy-symposium-d30a1231e5f2.

Euritt, Alyn. 2022. *Podcasting as an Intimate Medium*, 1st edn. New York, NY: Routledge.

Evans, Suzy, and Kwasi Boadi. 2020. "Audible Looks to Cultivate Diverse Storytelling Talent with Podcast Development Program." *The Hollywood Reporter* (blog). December 7, 2020. https://www.hollywoodreporter.com/business/business-news/audible-looks-to-cultivate-diverse-storytelling-talent-with-podcast-development-program-4101109.

Evetts, Julia. 2003. "The Sociological Analysis of Professionalism: Occupational Change in the Modern World." *International Sociology* 18 (2): 395–415. https://doi.org/10.1177/0268580903018002005.

Fang, Wenbin. 2018. "The Freedom of Podcasting and Netflix for Podcasts Won't Work." *Broadcast—The Official Listen Notes Blog* (blog). June 4, 2018. https://broadcast.listennotes.com/the-freedom-of-podcasting-and-netflix-for-podcasts-wont-work-50fde042c915.

Fatemi, Falon. 2022. "The Rise and Fall of Social Audio Will Continue to Impact the Entertainment Industry for the Next Generation." *Forbes* (blog). February 10, 2022. https://www.forbes.com/sites/falonfatemi/2022/02/10/the-rise-and-fall-of-social-audio-will-continue-to-impact-the-entertainment-industry-for-the-next-generation/.

Fingas, Jon. 2019. "Amazon Cancels Podcast-Inspired 'Lore' after Two Seasons." *Engadget* (blog). July 28, 2019. https://www.engadget.com/2019-07-27-amazon-cancels-lore.html.

Fischer, Sara. 2019. "Podcast Event Sales Have Increased by over 2000% in the Last 6 Years." *Axios* (blog). July 9, 2019. https://www.axios.com/2019/07/09/podcast-events-monetization-ticket-sales.

Fischer, Sara. 2021. "From Apple to Spotify and NPR, the Podcast Paywall Wars Have Arrived." *Axios* (blog). April 27, 2021. https://

www.axios.com/podcast-subscriptions-apple-spotify-npr-nytimes-223e42b7-3866-41b3-9d63-387d2a594d34.html.

Fisher, Eran. 2015. "'You Media': Audiencing as Marketing in Social Media." *Media, Culture & Society* 37 (1): 50–67. https://doi.org/10.1177/0163443714549088.

Fleck, Alissa. 2018. "Podcast Metrics Are Still the Wild West: But Networks Are Moving to Change That." *Adweek*. June 21, 2018. https://www.adweek.com/digital/podcast-metrics-are-still-the-wild-west-but-networks-are-moving-to-change-that/.

Florini, Sarah. 2015. "The Podcast 'Chitlin' Circuit': Black Podcasters, Alternative Media, and Audio Enclaves." *Journal of Radio & Audio Media* 22 (2): 209–19. https://doi.org/10.1080/19376529.2015.1083373.

Forristal, Lauren. 2022. "US Podcast Ad Revenue to Reach $2 Billion in 2022 and Top $4 Billion by 2024, Study Says." *TechCrunch* (blog). May 9, 2022. https://social.techcrunch.com/2022/05/09/u-s-podcast-ad-revenue-to-reach-2-billion-in-2022-and-top-4-billion-by-2024-study-says/.

Fox, Kim, David O. Dowling, and Kyle Miller. 2020. "A Curriculum for Blackness: Podcasts as Discursive Cultural Guides, 2010–2020." *Journal of Radio & Audio Media* 27 (2): 298–318. https://doi.org/10.1080/19376529.2020.1801687.

Freedman, Des. 2012. "Web 2.0 and the Death of the Blockbuster Economy." In *Misunderstanding the Internet*, edited by James Curran, Natalie Fenton and Des Freedman, 74–94. Communication and Society. New York: Routledge.

Freidson, Eliot. 2001. *Professionalism, the Third Logic: On the Practice of Knowledge*. Chicago, IL: University of Chicago Press.

Friess, Steve. 2015. "The Media Milestone the Media (Fittingly?) Forgot." *Columbia Journalism Review* (blog). July 1, 2015. https://www.cjr.org/analysis/podcast_milestone.php.

Frommer, Dan. 2009. "ITunes Now 25% of All Music Sold in U.S." *Business Insider*. August 18, 2009. https://www.businessinsider.com/itunes-now-25-of-all-music-sold-2009-8.

Fuchs, Christian. 2012. "Dallas Smythe Today – The Audience Commodity, the Digital Labour Debate, Marxist Political Economy and Critical Theory. Prolegomena to a Digital Labour Theory of Value." *TripleC: Communication, Capitalism & Critique. Open Access Journal for a Global Sustainable Information Society* 10 (2): 692–740.

Ganguly, Payal. 2021. "Wipro Invests in Squadcast, Sells Stake in Denim Group and Partners with Finastra." *Techcircle*. June 3, 2021. https://www.techcircle.in/2021/06/03/wipro-invests-in-squadcast-sells-stake-in-denim-group-and-partners-with-finastra.

Gartenberg, Chaim. 2020. "Google Podcasts Rolls out New Design, Launches on IOS." *The Verge* (blog). March 25, 2020. https://www.theverge.com/2020/3/25/21192325/google-podcasts-update-design-android-ios-recommendations.

Gillespie, Tarleton. 2010. "The Politics of 'Platforms.'" *New Media & Society* 12 (3): 347–64. https://doi.org/10.1177/1461444809342738.

Gillespie, Tarleton. 2018. "Governance of and by Platforms." In *The SAGE Handbook of Social Media*, edited by Jean Burgess, Alice E. Marwick and Thomas Poell, 254–78. Thousand Oaks, CA: SAGE Publications.

Goldberg, Kevin. 2018. "Is It Possible to Game the Apple Podcast Charts?" *Discover Pods* (blog). February 15, 2018. https://discoverpods.com/game-hack-manipulate-apple-podcast-charts-itunes/.

Goldstein, Steven. 2018. "How Many of the 540,000 Podcasts Have 'Podfaded?'" *Amplifi Media* (blog). August 22, 2018. https://www.amplifimedia.com/blogstein/2018/8/22/how-many-of-the-550000-podcasts-are-actually-active.

Goldstein, Steven. 2021. "Why There Really Aren't 2 Million Podcasts." *Amplifi Media* (blog). April 5, 2021. https://www.amplifimedia.com/blogstein/why-there-really-arent-2-million-podcasts.

Goldstein, Steven. 2022. "A Surprisingly Small Number of Podcasts Are Still in Production." *Amplifi Media* (blog). August 21, 2022. https://www.amplifimedia.com/blogstein/lyspqop3ylro9a2t7y2de820uwkgwx.

Götting, Marie Charlotte. 2023. "Most Used Podcast Providers in the U.S. 2022." *Statista*. January 17, 2023. https://www.statista.com/statistics/712306/podcast-providers-in-the-us/.

Gourraud, Anthony. 2020. "A New Model to Detect the Thousands of Fake but 'IAB Certified' Podcast Downloads I Got." *Medium* (blog). September 30, 2020. https://anthony-gourraud.medium.com/a-new-model-to-detect-the-thousands-of-fake-but-iab-certified-podcast-downloads-i-got-20cee2e2eb39.

Graphtreon. 2023. "Patreon Podcasts Statistics: Graphs + Analysis." *Graphtreon*. June 3, 2023. https://graphtreon.com/patreon-stats/podcasts.

Gray, Jonathan. 2010. *Show Sold Separately: Promos, Spoilers, and Other Media Paratexts*. New York: NYU Press.

Green, Joshua, and Henry Jenkins. 2011. "Spreadable Media: How Audiences Create Value and Meaning in a Networked Economy." In *The Handbook of Media Audiences*, edited by Virginia Nightingale, 1st edn., 109–27. Malden, MA: Wiley-Blackwell.

Gregg, Melissa. 2009. "Learning to (Love) Labour: Production Cultures and the Affective Turn." *Communication and Critical/Cultural Studies* 6 (2): 209–14. https://doi.org/10.1080/14791420902868045.

Grimson, Jennifer. 2020. "Micro Empires: Monetize Your Podcast with Rob Walch." *MicroEmpires*. https://micro-empires.libsyn.com/monetize-your-podcast-with-rob-walch.

Guaglione, Sara. 2022. "Why Podcast Agencies Are Warning about the Move to Dynamically-Inserted Ads." *Digiday* (blog). March 4, 2022. https://digiday.com/media/why-podcast-agencies-are-warning-about-the-move-to-dynamically-inserted-ads/.

Guinness World Records. 2021. "Largest Attendance for a Virtual Podcasting Conference in One Week." *Guinness World Records*. March 5, 2021. https://www.guinnessworldrecords.com/world-records/619872-largest-attendance-for-a-virtual-podcasting-conference-in-one-week.

Guttman, A. 2022. "Radio Ad Revenue in the U.S. 2022." *Statista*. February 5, 2022. https://www.statista.com/statistics/272412/radio-advertising-expenditure-in-the-us/.

Ha, Louisa. 2018. "Is YouTube Red the Ultimate Viewing Experience and What Is the Future of Online Video Audience Research?" In *The Audience and Business of YouTube and Online Videos*, edited by Louisa Ha, 161–76. Lexington Studies in Communication and Storytelling. Lanham, MD: Lexington Books. https://nls.ldls.org.uk/welcome.html?ark:/81055/vdc_100058676306.0x000001.

Hammersley, Ben. 2003. *Content Syndication with RSS*, 1st edn. Beijing : Farnham: O'Reilly Media.

Hammersley, Ben. 2004. "Audible Revolution." *The Guardian*. February 11, 2004. sec. Media. https://www.theguardian.com/media/2004/feb/12/broadcasting.digitalmedia.

Hansen, Samuel. 2021. "The Feed Is the Thing: How RSS Defined PodcastRE and Why Podcasts May Need to Move On." In *Saving New Sounds*, edited by Jeremy Wade Morris and Eric Hoyt, 195–207. Ann Arbor, MI: University of Michigan Press. https://www.press.umich.edu/11435021/saving_new_sounds.

Hardy, Jonathan. 2021. *Branded Content: The Fateful Merging of Media and Marketing*. London: Routledge. https://doi.org/10.4324/9781315641065.

Havens, Timothy, and Amanda D. Lotz. 2011. *Understanding Media Industries*. New York: Oxford University Press.

Havens, Timothy, Amanda D. Lotz, and Serra Tinic. 2009. "Critical Media Industry Studies: A Research Approach." *Communication, Culture & Critique* 2 (2): 234–53. https://doi.org/10.1111/j.1753-9137.2009.01037.x.

Haygood, Daniel M. 2007. "A Status Report on Podcast Advertising." *Journal of Advertising Research* 47 (4): 518–23. https://doi.org/10.2501/S0021849907070535.

Heater, Brian. 2019. "Spotify's Podcast Dashboard Comes out of Beta." *TechCrunch* (blog). August 13, 2019. https://social.techcrunch.com/2019/08/13/spotifys-podcast-dashboard-comes-out-of-beta/.

Heater, Brian. 2021. "Zencastr Raises $4.6M as Its Beta Video Offering Goes Live for All." *TechCrunch* (blog). February 16, 2021. https://social.techcrunch.com/2021/02/16/zencastr-raises-4-6m-as-its-video-offering-goes-live-for-all/.

Heeremans, Lieven. 2018. "Podcast Networks: Syndicating Production Culture." In *Podcasting: New Aural Cultures and Digital Media*, edited by Dario Llinares, Neil Fox and Richard Berry, 57–79. London: Palgrave Macmillan.

Heller, Nathan. 2013. "Bay Watched." *The New Yorker*. October 14, 2013. http://www.newyorker.com/magazine/2013/10/14/bay-watched.

Hemenway, Kevin. 2002. "Extending RSS 2.0 with Namespaces." September 1, 2002. https://www.disobey.com/detergent/2002/extendingrss2/.

Herbert, Daniel, Amanda D. Lotz, and Aswin Punathambekar. 2020. *Media Industry Studies*. Cambridge, UK ; Medford, MA: Polity.

Hesmondhalgh, David. 2007. *The Cultural Industries*, 2nd edn. Los Angeles, CA: Sage.

Hetcher, Steven. 2012. "Amateur Creative Digital Content and Proportional Commerce." In *Amateur Media: Social, Culturual and Legal Perspectives*, edited by Dan Hunter, Ramon Lobato, Megan Richardson and Julian Thomas, 35–52. New York: Routledge.

Hill, Brad. 2021. "A New Magazine (Yes, Print) for Podcast Transcripts." *RAIN News* (blog). August 24, 2021. https://rainnews.com/a-new-magazine-yes-print-for-podcast-transcripts/.

Hilmes, Michele. 1997. *Radio Voices: American Broadcasting, 1922-1952*. Minneapolis, MN: University of Minnesota Press.

Hirsch, Lauren. 2020. "Amazon Buys Wondery as Podcasting Race Continues." *The New York Times*. December 30, 2020. sec. Business. https://www.nytimes.com/2020/12/30/business/dealbook/wondery-amazon-podcasts.html.

Hirsch, Paul M., and Daniel A. Gruber. 2015. "Digitizing Fads and Fashions: Disintermediation and Glocalized Markets in Creative Industries." In *The Oxford Handbook of Creative Industries*, edited by Candace Jones, Mark Lorenzen and Jonathan Sapsed, 421–38. Oxford, UK: Oxford University Press. https://doi.org/10.1093/oxfordhb/9780199603510.013.013.

Hoover, Victoria. 2022. "The Missing Narrator: Fictional Podcasting and Kaleidosonic Remediation in Gimlet's Homecoming." *Journal of Radio & Audio Media* 29 (2): 256–273. https://doi.org/10.1080/19376529.2020. 1762195.

REFERENCES

HowStuffWorks. 2000. "About HowStuffWorks." *HowStuffWorks.* February 1, 2000. https://www.howstuffworks.com/about-hsw.htm.

Hunt, Forest. 2021. "The New Podcast Oligopoly." *FAIR* (blog). May 21, 2021. https://fair.org/home/the-new-podcast-oligopoly/.

iHeartMedia. 2022. "IHeartMedia Partners with Sounder to Launch Best-in-Class Brand Safety Tools across the Largest Global Podcast Network." February 2022. https://www.iheartmedia.com/press/iheartmedia-partners-sounder-launch-best-class-brand-safety-tools-across-largest-global.

Ingram, Mathew. 2018. "NPR's Move into Podcasting Analytics Raises Privacy Concerns." *Columbia Journalism Review* (blog). December 18, 2018. https://www.cjr.org/innovations/nprs-move-into-podcasting-analytics-raises-privacy-concerns.php.

Inside Radio. 2018. "NPR's New Podcast Measurement Metric Goes Live." *Insideradio.Com* (blog). December 12, 2018. http://www.insideradio.com/free/npr-s-new-podcast-measurement-metric-goes-live/article_e594129a-fddc-11e8-951e-17d28b048482.html.

Inside Radio. 2019. "Smartphones Still Dominate for Podcast Listening." *Insideradio.Com* (blog). May 30, 2019. http://www.insideradio.com/podcastnewsdaily/smartphones-still-dominate-for-podcast-listening/article_86163d48-82f7-11e9-a897-fb1ae4f18d37.html.

Inside Radio. 2020. "Edison Share of Ear Q3 2020: In-Car Audiences Rebound." *Insideradio.Com* (blog). November 10, 2020. http://www.insideradio.com/free/edison-share-of-ear-q3-2020-in-car-audiences-rebound/article_742967a6-232b-11eb-b1ae-4b5231251273.html.

Inside Radio. 2022a. "Listeners Like What They Bought from Podcast Ads. But They Have Ad Complaints Too." *Insideradio.Com* (blog). May 10, 2022. https://www.insideradio.com/podcastnewsdaily/listeners-like-what-they-bought-from-podcast-ads-but-they-have-ad-complaints-too/article_8bc75fd0-d081-11ec-b8a0-a39518ae10c5.html.

Inside Radio. 2022b. "Acast Buys Podcast Database Podchaser, In Counterpoint To Paywalled Platforms." *Insideradio.Com* (blog). July 18, 2022. https://www.insideradio.com/podcastnewsdaily/acast-buys-podcast-database-podchaser-in-counterpoint-to-paywalled-platforms/article_d21c043a-06ba-11ed-9688-d73a7e484fac.html.

InsideRadio. 2018. "Castbox Launches Subscription Model For Podcast Publishers." *Insideradio.Com.* June 29, 2018. http://www.insideradio.com/free/castbox-launches-subscription-model-for-podcast-publishers/article_65c561c0-7b61-11e8-8967-23ebebdc9704.html.

Interactive Advertising Bureau. 2016. "IAB Podcast Ad Metric Guidelines." *IAB Tech Lab.* https://www.iab.com/wp-content/uploads/2017/12/Podcast_Measurement_v2-Final-Dec2017.pdf.

Interactive Advertising Bureau. 2017a. "Podcast Technical Working Group." 2017. https://iabtechlab.com/working-groups/podcast-technical-working-group/.

Interactive Advertising Bureau. 2017b. "IAB Podcast Measurement Technical Guidelines, Version 2.0." *IAB Tech Lab*. https://www.iab.com/wp-content/uploads/2017/12/Podcast_Measurement_v2-Final-Dec2017.pdf.

Interactive Advertising Bureau. 2021a. "Compliant Companies." *IAB Tech Lab* (blog). January 25, 2021. https://iabtechlab.com/compliance-programs/compliant-companies.

Interactive Advertising Bureau. 2021b. "U.S. Podcast Ad Revenues Grew 19% YoY in 2020; Set to Exceed $1B This Year and $2B by 2023." IAB. May 12, 2021. https://www.iab.com/news/us-podcast-ad-revenues-grew-19-yoy-in-2020-set-to-exceed-1b-this-year-and-2b-by-2023.

Interactive Advertising Bureau. 2022. "U.S. Podcast Advertising Revenue Report: FY 2021 Results & 2022-2024 Growth Projections." https://www.iab.com/insights/u-s-podcast-advertising-revenue-report-fy-2021-results-2022-2024-growth-projections/.

Jackson, David. 2018. "Anchor.Fm Terms of Service Compared to Other Media Hosts." *David Jackson - Podcast Consultant - Speaker - Author* (blog). August 12, 2018. http://davidjackson.org/anchor-fm-terms-of-service-compared-to-other-media-hosts/.

Jaffe, Sarah. 2021. "Union Bargaining at a Podcasting Giant." *The American Prospect*. March 11, 2021. https://prospect.org/api/content/39c38a10-81ef-11eb-8cee-1244d5f7c7c6/.

Jarrett, Kylie. 2022. *Digital Labor*. Medford, MA: Polity Press.

Jarvey, Natalie. 2018. "IHeartMedia to Acquire Podcasting Company Stuff Media." *The Hollywood Reporter*, September 13, 2018. https://www.hollywoodreporter.com/news/iheartmedia-acquire-podcasting-company-stuff-media-1143014.

Jarvey, Natalie. 2021. "Behind Podcasting's M&A Frenzy: 'Easier to Buy Than Build.'" *The Hollywood Reporter* (blog). January 6, 2021. https://www.hollywoodreporter.com/business/digital/behind-podcastings-ma-frenzy-easier-to-buy-than-build-4112069.

Jeffries, Adrianne. 2020. "Is Your Favorite Podcast Tracking You?" *The Markup* (blog). October 8, 2020. https://themarkup.org/ask-the-markup/2020/10/08/podcast-privacy-tracking-listener-data?utm_source=adtech.podnews.net&utm_medium=web&utm_campaign=adtech.podnews.net:2020-10-13.

Jenkins, Henry. 2006. *Convergence Culture: Where Old and New Media Collide*. New York: New York University Press.

Jenkins, Henry, Sam Ford, and Joshua Green. 2013. *Spreadable Media: Creating Value and Meaning in a Networked Culture.* New York: New York University Press.

Johnson, Lauren. 2016. "With Second 'Podcast Upfront,' IAB Hopes Brands Will Buy into Audio Advertising." *AdWeek.* July 21, 2016. http://www.adweek.com/digital/second-podcast-upfront-iab-hopes-brands-will-buy-audio-advertising-172601/.

Jones, Dave A. 2022. "It's Not Really about RSS." Substack newsletter. *Podcasting 2.0* (blog). June 13, 2022. https://podcasting20.substack.com/p/its-not-really-about-rss.

Jones, Dave A. 2020. "Podcastindex-Org/Podcast-Namespace." HTML. *Podcastindex.org.* https://github.com/Podcastindex-org/podcast-namespace/blob/303a40f1881af6928c71adc25dcb23e6ff3abd40/podcasting2.0.md.

Jurgensen, Anne Steele and John. 2022. "Inside Spotify's Joe Rogan Crisis." *The Wall Street Journal.* February 4, 2022.sec. Tech. https://www.wsj.com/articles/spotify-joe-rogan-neil-young-covid-vaccine-11643987429.

Kafka, Peter. 2017a. "Apple Is Going to Let Podcast Creators—and Advertisers—See What Listeners Actually Like." *Recode.* June 10, 2017. https://www.vox.com/2017/6/10/15774936/apple-podcast-analytics-wwdc.

Kafka, Peter. 2017b. "VCs Don't Love Podcasting, but Gimlet Media Has Raised Another $15 Million Anyway." *Recode* (blog). August 2, 2017. https://www.recode.net/2017/8/2/16079634/gimlet-media-podcast-funding-stripes-laurene-powell-jobs-advertising-crooked-media-the-daily.

Kafka, Peter. 2017c. "Apple Has Finally Turned on Its Podcast Analytics Feature." *Recode* (blog). December 14, 2017. https://www.recode.net/2017/12/14/16778268/apple-podcast-find-listens-downloads-analytics-available.

Kafka, Peter. 2019. "Spotify Has Bought Two Podcast Startups and It Wants to Buy More." *Recode* (blog). February 6, 2019. https://www.recode.net/2019/2/6/18213456/spotify-podcast-gimlet-anchor-q4-results.

Kastrenakes, Jacob. 2018. "Twitter Is Going to Make Third-Party Apps Worse Starting in August." *The Verge* (blog). May 16, 2018. https://www.theverge.com/2018/5/16/17362138/twitter-api-third-party-apps-changes-explained.

Kelty, Christopher M. 2008. *Two Bits: The Cultural Significance of Free Software.* Durham: Duke University Press.

Kessler, Sarah. 2018. *Gigged: The End of the Job and the Future of Work.* New York: St. Martin's Press.

Kilkenny, Katie. 2021. "The Ringer, Gimlet Media Ratify First Collective Bargaining Agreements with Spotify." *The Hollywood Reporter* (blog). April 7, 2021. https://www.hollywoodreporter.com/business/business-news/the-ringer-gimlet-media-ratify-first-collective-bargaining-agreements-with-spotify-4162245.

Kilkenny, Katie. 2022. "Parcast Union Reaches Tentative Deal with Spotify, Management on First Contract." *Billboard* (blog). April 7, 2022. https://www.billboard.com/business/streaming/parcast-union-spotify-management-deal-first-contract-1235056924/.

Kitchin, Rob, and Martin Dodge. 2011. *Code/Space Software and Everyday Life*. Cambridge, MA: MIT Press.

Kosterich, Allie, and Philip M. Napoli. 2016. "Reconfiguring the Audience Commodity: The Institutionalization of Social TV Analytics as Market Information Regime." *Television & New Media* 17 (3): 254–71. https://doi.org/10.1177/1527476415597480.

Kuehn, Kathleen, and Thomas F. Corrigan. 2013. "Hope Labor: The Role of Employment Prospects in Online Social Production." *The Political Economy of Communication* 1 (1). http://www.polecom.org/index.php/polecom/article/view/9.

Kumar, Sangeet. 2019. "The Algorithmic Dance: YouTube's Adpocalypse and the Gatekeeping of Cultural Content on Digital Platforms." *Internet Policy Review* 8 (2). https://policyreview.info/articles/analysis/algorithmic-dance-youtubes-adpocalypse-and-gatekeeping-cultural-content-digital.

Kurtz, Brian. 2019. *Overdeliver: Build a Business for a Lifetime Playing the Long Game in Direct Response Marketing*. Carlsbad, CA: Hay House Inc.

Lafayette, Jon. 2020. "Scripps Sells Podcasting Unit to SiriusXM for $325M." *Broadcasting & Cable*. July 13, 2020. https://www.nexttv.com/news/scripps-sells-podcasting-unit-to-siriusxm-for-dollar325m.

Lambert, Thomas, and Armin Schwienbacher. 2010. "An Empirical Analysis of Crowdfunding." *Social Science Research Network* 1578175 (1): 23.

Lang, Michael N. 2006. "The Regulation of Shrink-Wrapped Radio: Implications of Copyright on Podcasting." *CommLaw Conspectus* 14 (2): 463–502.

Larson, Magali S. 1977. *The Rise of Professionalism: A Sociological Analysis*. Berkeley, CA: University of California Press.

Latour, Bruno. 2005. *Reassembling the Social: An Introduction to Actor-Network-Theory*. Oxford; New York: Oxford University Press.

Leadbeater, Charles, and Paul Miller. 2004. *The Pro-Am Revolution: How Enthusiasts Are Changing Our Economy and Society*. London: Demos. http://www.demos.co.uk/publications/proameconomy.

Lebow, Sara. 2021. "Spotify Poised to Overtake Apple Podcasts This Year." *EMarketer Insider Intelligence* (blog). September 20, 2021. https://www.emarketer.com/content/spotify-poised-overtake-apple-podcasts-this-year.

Lee, Wendy. 2021. "Why 'Last Podcast on the Left' Will No Longer Be a Spotify Exclusive." *Los Angeles Times*. October 12, 2021. sec. Company Town. https://www.latimes.com/entertainment-arts/business/story/2021-10-12/last-podcast-on-the-left-spotify-stitcher.

Lenhart, Amanda, and Susannah Fox. 2006. "Bloggers: A Portrait of the Internet's New Storytellers." *Pew Internet and American Life Project*. Washington, DC: The Pew Charitable Trusts. http://www.pewtrusts.org/our_work_report_detail.aspx?id=21106.

Lewis, Daniel J. 2021. "Apple Podcasts Statistics." *Podcast Industry Insights* (blog). November 28, 2021. https://podcastindustryinsights.com/apple-podcasts-statistics/.

Lindgren, Mia. 2016. "Personal Narrative Journalism and Podcasting." *Radio Journal: International Studies in Broadcast & Audio Media* 14 (1): 23–41. https://doi.org/10.1386/rjao.14.1.23_1.

Littleton, Cynthia. 2016. "Fox Backs Wondery Podcast Network Launched By Former Exec Hernan Lopez." *Variety* (blog). January 13, 2016. https://variety.com/2016/biz/news/wondery-podcast-network-fox-hernan-lopez-1201679146.

Llinares, Dario. 2018. "Podcasting as Liminal Praxis: Aural Mediation, Sound Writing and Identity." In *Podcasting: New Aural Cultures and Digital Media*, edited by Dario Llinares, Neil Fox and Richard Berry, 123–45. London: Palgrave Macmillan.

Llinares, Dario, Neil Fox, and Richard Berry, eds. 2018. *Podcasting: New Aural Cultures and Digital Media*. London: Palgrave Macmillan.

Lobato, Ramon, and Julian Thomas. 2015. *The Informal Media Economy*, 1st edn. Cambridge, UK ; Malden, MA: Polity.

Lobato, Ramon, Julian Thomas, and Dan Hunter. 2012. "Histories of User-Generated Content: Between Formal and Informal Media Economies." In *Amateur Media: Social, Culturual and Legal Perspectives*, edited by Dan Hunter, Ramon Lobato, Megan Richardson and Julian Thomas, 3–17. New York: Routledge.

Locke, Charley. 2017. "Where Is Hollywood Looking for the Next Hit? Podcasts." *WIRED* (blog). July 20, 2017. https://www.wired.com/story/podcasts-getting-tv-adaptations/.

Locker, Melissa. 2018. "Apple's Podcasts Just Topped 50 Billion All-Time Downloads and Streams." *Fast Company*. April 25, 2018. https://www.fastcompany.com/40563318/apples-podcasts-just-topped-50-billion-all-time-downloads-and-streams.

Locker, Melissa. 2019. "Meet the Startup Turning Your New Favorite Podcast into Your Next TV Binge." *Fast Company* (blog). March 9, 2019. https://www.fastcompany.com/90316661/meet-the-startup-turning-your-new-favorite-podcast-into-your-next-tv-binge.

Madsen, Virginia, and John Potts. 2010. "Voice-Cast: The Distribution of the Voice via Podcasting." In *Voice: Vocal Aesthetics in Digital Arts and Media*, edited by Norie Neumark, Ross Gibson and Theo van Leeuwen, 33–60. Cambridge, London: The MIT Press. https://mitpress.universitypressscholarship.com/view/10.7551/mitpress/9780262013901.001.0001/upso-9780262013901-chapter-3.

Main, Sami. 2017. "Podcast Revenue Will Jump 85% This Year to Hit $220 Million." *Adweek* (blog). June 26, 2017. http://www.adweek.com/digital/podcast-revenue-will-jump-85-this-year-to-hit-220-million/.

Mallenbaum, Carly. 2015. "The 'Serial Effect' Hasn't Worn Off." *USA Today*. April 13, 2015. https://www.usatoday.com/story/life/2015/04/13/serial-podcast-undisclosed/25501075/.

Manley, Mackenzie. 2021. "Popular Podcast Welcome to Night Vale Brings Live Show the Haunting of Night Vale to the Taft Theatre Stage in Cincinnati." *Cincinnati CityBeat* (blog). June 16, 2021. https://www.citybeat.com/arts/popular-podcast-welcome-to-night-vale-brings-live-show-the-haunting-of-night-vale-to-the-taft-theatre-stage-in-cincinnati-12266751.

Markman, Kris M. 2012. "Doing Radio, Making Friends, and Having Fun: Exploring the Motivations of Independent Audio Podcasters." *New Media & Society* 14 (4): 547–65. https://doi.org/10.1177/1461444811420848.

Markman, Kris M., and Caroline E. Sawyer. 2014. "Why Pod? Further Explorations of the Motivations for Independent Podcasting." *Journal of Radio & Audio Media* 21 (1): 20–35. https://doi.org/10.1080/19376529.2014.891211.

Marsal, Katie. 2015. "Thanks to 'Serial' & Apple's Podcasts App Baked into IOS 8, Podcast Listens Grow 18%." *AppleInsider* (blog). February 25, 2015. http://appleinsider.com/articles/15/02/25/thanks-to-serial-apples-podcasts-app-baked-into-ios-8-podcast-listens-grow-18.

Marwick, Alice E. 2013. *Status Update: Celebrity, Publicity, and Branding in the Social Media Age*, 1st edn. New Haven: Yale University Press.

Mayer, Liz. 2023. "Edison's 'Share Of Ear' Q4 2022: Streaming Is Now 20% of AM/FM Radio Listening, Podcasts Have Surged, and AM/FM Radio Dominates Ad-Supported Time Spent." *Westwood One* (blog). March 6, 2023. https://www.westwoodone.com/blog/2023/03/06/edisons-share-of-ear-q4-2022-streaming-is-now-20-of-am-fm-radio-listening-podcasts-have-surged-and-am-fm-radio-dominates-ad-supported-time-spent/.

Mayer-Schönberger, Viktor, and Kenneth Cukier. 2013. *Big Data: A Revolution That Will Transform How We Live, Work, and Think.* Boston: Eamon Dolan/Houghton Mifflin Harcourt.

McChesney, Robert Waterman. 2013. *Digital Disconnect: How Capitalism Is Turning the Internet against Democracy.* New York: The New Press.

McHugh, Siobhán. 2016. "How Podcasting Is Changing the Audio Storytelling Genre." *Radio Journal: International Studies in Broadcast & Audio Media* 14 (1): 65–82. https://doi.org/10.1386/rjao.14.1.65_1.

McHugh, Siobhán. 2022. *The Power of Podcasting: Telling Stories through Sound.* Sydney, NSW: NewSouth Publishing.

Meehan, Eileen R. 1993. "Commodity Audience, Actual Audience: The Blindspot Debate." In *Illuminating the Blindspots: Essays Honoring Dallas W. Symthe*, edited by Janet Wasko, Vincent Mosco and Manjunath Pendakur, 378–97. Norwood, NJ: Ablex Publishing Corp.

Mehta, Ivan. 2022a. "Spotify Testing In-App Podcast Creation Tools." *TechCrunch* (blog). July 1, 2022. https://techcrunch.com/2022/07/01/spotify-is-testing-in-app-podcast-creation-tools/.

Mehta, Ivan. 2022b. "Spotify Asks Users to Record Reaction Podcasts to Playlists." *TechCrunch* (blog). August 16, 2022. https://techcrunch.com/2022/08/16/spotify-prompts-some-users-to-record-reaction-podcasts-to-playlists/.

Menduni, Enrico. 2007. "Four Steps in Innovative Radio Broadcasting: From QuickTime to Podcasting." *Radio Journal: International Studies in Broadcast & Audio Media* 5 (1): 9–18. https://doi.org/10.1386/rajo.5.1.9_1.

Meyers, Alyssa. 2022. "Podcast Brand-Safety Tools Are Trying to Demystify the Space for Wary Advertisers." *Marketing Brew* (blog). September 12, 2022. https://www.marketingbrew.com/stories/2022/09/12/podcast-brand-safety-tools-are-trying-to-demystify-the-space-for-wary-advertisers.

Mickle, Tripp. 2017. "Apple Readies $1 Billion War Chest for Hollywood Programming." *Wall Street Journal*, August 16, 2017. sec. Tech. https://www.wsj.com/articles/apple-readies-1-billion-war-chest-for-hollywood-programming-1502874004.

Miller, Peter. 1994. "Made-to-Order and Standardized Audiences: Forms of Reality in Audience Measurement." In *Audiencemaking: How the Media Create the Audience*, edited by James S. Ettema and D. Charles Whitney, 57–74. Thousand Oaks, CA: Sage Publications.

Mills, Adam J., Christine Pitt, and Sarah Lord Ferguson. 2019. "The Relationship between Fake News And Advertising: Brand Management in the Era of Programmatic Advertising and Prolific Falsehood."

Journal of Advertising Research 59 (1): 3–8. https://doi.org/10.2501/JAR-2019-007.

Misener, Dan. 2019a. "App Listening vs. Web Listening." *Medium* (blog). August 15, 2019. https://blog.pacific-content.com/app-listening-vs-web-listening-da8ece1a0d2.

Misener, Dan. 2019b. "The Promise of Podcast Playlists." *Pacific Content* (blog). August 29, 2019. https://blog.pacific-content.com/the-promise-of-podcast-playlists-c39961f35393.

Misener, Dan. 2021. "The Most Crowded Categories in Apple Podcasts (April 2021 Edition)." *Medium* (blog). April 1, 2021. https://blog.pacific-content.com/the-most-crowded-categories-in-apple-podcasts-april-2021-edition-273b3d59866e.

"Mobile Operating System Market Share Worldwide." 2022. *StatCounter Global Stats*. January 9, 2022. https://gs.statcounter.com/os-market-share/mobile/worldwide.

Mocigemba, Dennis, and Gerald Riechmann. 2007. "International Podcaster Survey: Podcasters—Who They Are How and Why They Do It." https://www.yumpu.com/en/document/view/6343724/international-podcastersurvey/3.

Moore, Dene. 2020. "COVID-19 Crisis Forces Small Businesses to Get Creative." *The Globe and Mail*. October 1, 2020. https://www.theglobeandmail.com/featured-reports/article-covid-19-crisis-forces-small-businesses-to-get-creative.

Morris, Jeremy Wade. 2017. "Saving New Sounds: Podcasts and Preservation Jeremy Wade Morris." *Flow: A Critical Forum on Media and Culture* (blog). October 30, 2017. https://www.flowjournal.org/2017/10/saving-new-sounds-podcasts.

Morris, Jeremy Wade. 2020. "Music Platforms and the Optimization of Culture." *Social Media + Society* 6 (3): 1–10. https://doi.org/10.1177/2056305120940690.

Morris, Jeremy Wade. 2021. "Infrastructures of Discovery: Examining Podcast Ratings and Rankings." *Cultural Studies* 35 (4–5): 728–749. https:// doi.org/10.1080/09502386.2021.1895246.

Morris, Jeremy Wade, and Eleanor Patterson. 2015. "Podcasting and Its Apps: Software, Sound, and the Interfaces of Digital Audio." *Journal of Radio & Audio Media* 22 (2): 220–30. https://doi.org/10.1080/19376529.2015.1083374.

Morris, Jeremy Wade, and Sarah Murray, eds. 2018. *Appified*. Ann Arbor, MI: University of Michigan Press. https://www.press.umich.edu/9391658/appified.

Mullin, Benjamin. 2018. "Public Radio Organizations Buy Pocket Casts." *Wall Street Journal*. May 3, 2018. sec. Business. https://www.wsj.com/articles/public-radio-organizations-buy-pocket-casts-1525366680.

Murray, Simone. 2009. "Servicing 'Self-Scheduling Consumers' Public Broadcasters and Audio Podcasting." *Global Media and Communication* 5 (2): 197–219. https://doi.org/10.1177/1742766509341610.

Nadora, Mikhaela. 2019. "Parasocial Relationships with Podcast Hosts." In *Bachelor of Arts (B.A.) in Communication Studies and University Honors*. Portland, OR: Portland State University. https://pdxscholar.library.pdx.edu/honorstheses/771/.

Nagy, Evie. 2015. "Is Howl The 'Netflix of Podcasts' We've Been Waiting For?" *Fast Company* (blog). August 17, 2015. https://www.fastcompany.com/3049750/is-howl-the-netflix-of-podcasts-weve-been-waiting-for.

Napoli, Philip M. 2003. *Audience Economics: Media Institutions and the Audience Marketplace*. New York: Columbia University Press.

Newton, Casey. 2018. "Google Launches a Podcast App for Android with Personalized Recommendations." *The Verge* (blog). June 19, 2018. https://www.theverge.com/2018/6/19/17475878/google-podcast-app-android-download-launch-date.

Nicas, Jack. 2018. "Alex Jones's Infowars Is Removed from Apple's App Store." *The New York Times*. September 9, 2018. sec. Technology. https://www.nytimes.com/2018/09/07/business/infowars-app-alex-jones-apple-ban.html.

Nieborg, David B. 2016. "From Premium to Freemium: The Political Economy of the App." In *Social, Casual and Mobile Games: The Changing Gaming Landscape*, edited by Michele Willson and Tama Leaver, 225–40. New York: Bloomsbury Academic. http://dx.doi.org/10.5040/9781501310591.ch-016.

Nieborg, David B., and Thomas Poell. 2018. "The Platformization of Cultural Production: Theorizing the Contingent Cultural Commodity." *New Media & Society*. April, 1–18. https://doi.org/10.1177/1461444818769694.

Nieborg, David B., Chris young, and Daniel Joseph. 2019. "Lost in the App Store: The State of the Canadian Game App Economy." *Canadian Journal of Communication* 44 (2): 57–62. https://doi.org/10.22230/cjc.2019v44n2a3505.

Nielsen Media Research. 2020. "Host-Read Podcast Ads Pack a Brand Recall Punch." *Nielsen*. October 1, 2020. https://www.nielsen.com/insights/2020/host-read-podcast-ads-pack-a-brand-recall-punch/.

Nuzum, Eric. 2019. *Make Noise: A Creator's Guide to Podcasting and Great Audio Storytelling*. Illustrated edn. New York, NY: Workman Publishing Company.

O'Connell, Michael. 2015. "The 'Serial' Effect: Programmers Ramping Up on Podcasts." *The Hollywood Reporter*. April 13, 2015. http://www.

hollywoodreporter.com/news/serial-effect-programmers-ramping-up-786688.

Ortner, Sherry B. 2009. "Studying Sideways: Ethnographic Access in Hollywood." In *Production Studies*. New York, NY: Routledge.

Ortner, Sherry B. 2010. "Access: Reflections on Studying up in Hollywood." *Ethnography* 11 (2): 211–33. https://doi.org/10.1177/1466138110362006.

Osgood, Heather. 2020. "Direct Response versus Brand Awareness Podcast Ad Campaigns. Which Is Best For You?" Podcast Advertising Playbook. https://www.podcastadvertisingplaybook.com/direct-response-versus-brand-awareness-podcast-ad-campaigns-which-is-best-for-you.

Owen, Laura Hazard. 2015. "How Did the GE-Branded Podcast the Message Hit No. 1 on ITunes? In Part, by Sounding Nothing :Like an Ad." *Nieman Lab* (blog). November 30, 2015. https://www.niemanlab.org/2015/11/how-did-the-ge-branded-podcast-the-message-hit-no-1-on-itunes-in-part-by-sounding-nothing-like-an-ad/.

Owen, Laura Hazard. 2016. "The New York Times Launches a Podcast Team to Create a New Batch of Wide-Reaching Shows." *Nieman Lab* (blog). March 31, 2016. https://www.niemanlab.org/2016/03/the-new-york-times-launches-a-podcast-team-to-create-a-new-batch-of-wide-reaching-shows.

Paasonen, Susanna. 2010. "Labors of Love: Netporn, Web 2.0 and the Meanings of Amateurism." *New Media & Society* 12 (8): 1297–312. https://doi.org/10.1177/1461444810362853.

Parsons, Talcott. 1951. *The Social System*. New York: Free Press.

Passy, Mathew. 2020a. "So Begins the Podcast Tracking Wars with Rob Walch." *Podcast Me Anything*. https://www.podcastmeanything.com/40.

Passy, Mathew. 2020b. "Podcast Me Anything – Podcasting Your Brand with Fatima Zaidi of Quill." *Podcast Me Anything*. https://www.stitcher.com/show/podcast-me-anything/episode/podcasting-your-brand-with-fatima-zaidi-of-quill-79341354.

Perez, Sarah. 2021. "Apple Unveils Podcast Subscriptions and a Redesigned Apple Podcasts App." *TechCrunch* (blog). April 20, 2021. https://techcrunch.com/2021/04/20/apple-unveils-podcast-subscriptions-and-a-redesigned-apple-podcasts-app/.

Perlberg, Steven. 2016. "E.W. Scripps Buys Podcast Company Stitcher." *Wall Street Journal*. June 6, 2016. sec. Business. https://www.wsj.com/articles/e-w-scripps-buys-podcast-company-stitcher-1465239600.

Peterson, Mike. 2021. "Apple Reveals the Top Paid and Free Podcast Subscriptions." *AppleInsider*. September 30, 2021. https://appleinsider.com/articles/21/09/30/apple-reveals-the-top-paid-and-free-podcast-subscriptions.

Petre, Caitlin. 2015. "The Traffic Factories: Metrics at Chartbeat, Gawker Media, and The New York Times." New York: Tow Center for Digital Journalism. https://towcenter.org/research/traffic-factories.

Petre, Caitlin, Brooke Erin Duffy, and Emily Hund. 2019. "'Gaming the System': Platform Paternalism and the Politics of Algorithmic Visibility." *Social Media + Society* 5 (4): 2056305119879995. https://doi.org/10.1177/2056305119879995.

Pinch, Trevor J., and Wiebe E. Bijker. 1987. "The Social Construction of Facts and Artifacts: Or How the Sociology of Science and the Sociology of Technology Might Benefit Each Other." In *The Social Construction of Technological Systems: New Directions in the Sociology and History of Technology*, edited by Wiebe E. Bijker, Thomas P. Hughes, Trevor Pinch and Deborah G. Douglas, 17–50. Cambridge, MA: The MIT Press.

Plantin, Jean-Christophe, Carl Lagoze, Paul N. Edwards, and Christian Sandvig. 2018. "Infrastructure Studies Meet Platform Studies in the Age of Google and Facebook." *New Media & Society* 20 (1): 293–310. https://doi.org/10.1177/1461444816661553.

Podtrac. 2020. "Podtrac's Podcast Measurement Service Methodology Summary." http://analytics.podtrac.com/measurement-methodology.

Porch, Scott. 2018. "Is the 'Netflix of Podcasts' Moment Finally Here?" *Fast Company* (blog). June 27, 2018. https://www.fastcompany.com/40589660/these-companies-are-trying-to-build-the-netflix-of-podcasts.

Prey, Robert. 2020. "Locating Power in Platformization: Music Streaming Playlists and Curatorial Power." *Social Media + Society* 6 (2): 2056305120933291. https://doi.org/10.1177/2056305120933291.

Quah, Nicholas. 2015. "Hot Pod: The Netflix-YouTube-Twitter-Starbucks of Podcasting." *Nieman Lab* (blog). August 18, 2015. https://www.niemanlab.org/2015/08/hot-pod-the-netflix-youtube-twitter-starbucks-of-podcasting/.

Quah, Nicholas. 2017. "Apple's New Analytics for Podcasts Mean a Lot of Change (Some Good, Some Inconvenient) Is on the Way." *Nieman Lab* (blog). June 13, 2017. https://www.niemanlab.org/2017/06/apples-new-analytics-for-podcasts-mean-a-lot-of-change-some-good-some-inconvenient-is-on-the-way/.

Quah, Nicholas. 2018a. "Two Key Things to Note about Podcast Measurements." *Hot Pod News* (blog). June 27, 2018. https://hotpodnews.com/two-key-things-to-note-about-podcast-measurements/.

Quah, Nicholas. 2018b. "Enough with the 'Netflix for Audio.' Podcast Companies Should Take a Cue from Meditation Apps Instead." *Nieman Lab* (blog). July 3, 2018. http://www.niemanlab.org/2018/07/

enough-with-the-netflix-for-audio-podcast-companies-should-take-a-cue-from-meditation-apps-instead/.

Quah, Nicholas. 2018c. "How I Cheated the Apple Podcast Charts for $5." *Nieman Lab* (blog). October 23, 2018. https://www.niemanlab.org/2018/10/how-i-cheated-the-apple-podcast-charts-for-5/.

Quah, Nicholas. 2018d. "A Year in, Apple's Podcast Analytics Have Been an Evolution, Not a Revolution." *Nieman Lab* (blog). December 4, 2018. https://www.niemanlab.org/2018/12/a-year-in-apples-podcast-analytics-have-been-an-evolution-not-a-revolution/.

Quah, Nicholas. 2020. "The State of Collective Bargaining in Podcasting." *Hot Pod News* (blog). August 25, 2020. https://hotpodnews.com/the-state-of-collective-bargaining-in-podcasting/.

Quah, Nicholas. 2021. "Yes, Podcast Listenership Is Still on the Rise." *Vulture* (blog). March 16, 2021. https://www.vulture.com/2021/03/podcast-listenership-download-data-on-the-rise.html.

Quah, Nicholas, and Caroline Crampton. 2020. "Coronavirus Is Changing Podcasting, Fast." *Vulture* (blog). March 17, 2020. https://www.vulture.com/2020/03/coronavirus-changing-podcast-industry.html.

Quill. 2019. "Quill Launches World's First Marketplace to Help Aspiring Podcasters Launch Shows." *PRWeb*. November 25, 2019. https://www.prweb.com/releases/quill_launches_worlds_first_marketplace_to_help_aspiring_podcasters_launch_shows/prweb16746418.htm.

Quirk, Vanessa. 2015. "Guide to Podcasting." New York: Tow Center for Digital Journalism. https://towcenter.org/research/guide-to-podcasting.

Rainie, Lee. 2005. "Tech Terms and Internet Users." In *Pew Internet and American Life Project*. Washington, DC: Pew Research Center. http://pew.org/2yIvrG9.

Rainie, Lee, and Mary Madden. 2005. "Podcasting Catches On." Washington, DC: Pew Research Center. https://www.pewresearch.org/internet/2005/04/03/podcasting-catches-on/.

RAJAR. 2020. "MIDAS Survey of Internet Delivered Audio Services." London: Radio Joint Audience Research. https://www.rajar.co.uk/docs/news/MIDAS_Spring_2020.pdf.

Rao, Sonia. 2018. "'Alex, Inc.' Is a Sitcom about a Podcast about a Podcast Company. How Did That Get on TV?" *Washington Post*. March 26, 2018. https://www.washingtonpost.com/news/arts-and-entertainment/wp/2018/03/26/alex-inc-is-a-sitcom-about-a-podcast-about-a-podcast-company-how-did-that-get-on-tv/.

Resler, Seth. 2020. "Podcast Dynamic Ad Insertion 101 for Radio Broadcasters." *Jacobs Media Strategies* (blog). November 30, 2020. https://jacobsmedia.com/podcast-dynamic-ad-insertion-101-what-radio-broadcasters-need-to-know.

Reuters. 2019. "Spotify to Buy Third Podcast Company Parcast." *Reuters* March 26, 2019 sec. Technology News. https://www.reuters.com/article/us-spotify-tech-parcast-idUSKCN1R714O.

Roettgers, Janko. 2017. "Spotify Launches Three New Original Podcasts." *Variety* (blog). February 23, 2017. https://variety.com/2017/digital/news/spotify-original-podcasts-1201994875.

van Rooden, Stephan. 2020. "The Emergence of the Value for Value Model." *Entrepreneurability* (blog). December 4, 2020. https://www.entrepreneurability.nl/2020/12/04/the-emergence-of-the-value-for-value-model/?lang=en.

Roof, Katie. 2017. "Anchor Raises $10 Million for Podcast Platform." *TechCrunch* (blog). September 28, 2017. http://social.techcrunch.com/2017/09/28/anchor-raises-10-million-for-podcast-platform/.

Rose, Bill, and Larry Rosin. 2006. "The Infinite Dial 2006: Radio's Digital Platforms." Somerville, NJ: Arbitron Radio & Edison Research.

Rosenblatt, Bill. 2018. "'Netflix For Podcasts' Looks Doubtful Despite Steadily Growing Listenership." *Forbes* (blog). March 23, 2018. https://www.forbes.com/sites/billrosenblatt/2018/03/23/podcast-listenership-continues-to-grow-but-revenue-growth-may-be-challenging/.

Rosenblatt, Bill. 2019. "New Study Shows Limits of Ad Revenue For Podcasts." *Forbes* (blog). June 9, 2019. https://www.forbes.com/sites/billrosenblatt/2019/06/09/podcast-ad-revenue-continues-to-grow-but-growth-is-slowing-down/.

Rosenthal, Nicole. 2020. "The Real Reason Microsoft's Zune Was Such a Huge Failure." *Grunge* (blog). June 9, 2020. https://www.grunge.com/216047/the-real-reason-microsofts-zune-was-such-a-huge-failure/.

Rosman, Katherine, Ben Sisario, Mike Isaac, and Adam Satariano. 2022. "Spotify Bet Big on Joe Rogan. It Got More Than It Counted On." *The New York Times*. February 17, 2022. sec. Arts. https://www.nytimes.com/2022/02/17/arts/music/spotify-joe-rogan-misinformation.html.

Rosman, Katherine, and Reggie Ugwu. 2021. "What Really Happened at 'Reply All'?" *The New York Times*. March 11, 2021. sec. Style. https://www.nytimes.com/2021/03/10/style/reply-all-test-kitchen.html.

Ross, Andrew. 2009. *Nice Work If You Can Get It: Life and Labor in Precarious Times*, 1st edn. New York: NYU Press.

Rottgers, Janko. 2019. "Luminary Podcast Subscription Service to Launch With Exclusive Shows From Lena Dunham, Trevor Noah." *Variety*. March 4, 2019. https://variety.com/2019/digital/news/luminary-podcast-subscription-service-1203154250/.

Rowe, Adam. 2017. "Why the 'Netflix of Podcasts' Is the Biggest Media Battleground of 2017." *TechCo* (blog). May 5, 2017. https://tech.co/netflix-podcasts-biggest-media-battleground-2017-2017-05.

RSS Advisory Board. 2021. "RSS History." 2021. https://www.rssboard.org/rss-history.

Salvati, Andrew J. 2015. "Podcasting the Past: Hardcore History, Fandom, and DIY Histories." *Journal of Radio & Audio Media* 22 (2): 231–9. https://doi.org/10.1080/19376529.2015.1083375.

Salzman, Avi. 2022. "Spotify Saw Podcasting as a Panacea. Instead, It Produced Lots of Costs." *Barron's* (blog). May 1, 2022. https://www.barrons.com/articles/spotify-stock-podcasting-51651270060.

Saponara, Michael. 2018. "Joe Budden's 'The Joe Budden Podcast' Lands Partnership with Spotify." *Billboard*. August 22, 2018. https://www.billboard.com/articles/columns/hip-hop/8471655/joe-budden-joe-budden-podcast-spotify-deal.

Sarkar, Samit. 2016. "Amazon Picks up Horror Podcast Lore for TV Series." *Polygon* (blog). October 6, 2016. https://www.polygon.com/tv/2016/10/6/13191332/lore-podcast-tv-series-amazon.

Sawers, Paul. 2018. "Castbox Raises $13.5 Million as Podcast Investment Boom Continues." *VentureBeat*. April 25, 2018. https://venturebeat.com/2018/04/25/castbox-raises-13-5-million-as-podcast-investment-boom-continues/.

Schlütz, Daniela, and Imke Hedder. 2021. "Aural Parasocial Relations: Host–Listener Relationships in Podcasts." *Journal of Radio & Audio Media* 0 (0): 1–18. https://doi.org/10.1080/19376529.2020.1870467.

Schneider, Mark. 2018. "Apple and Spotify Remove Alex Jones' Podcast; Other InfoWars Shows Remain." *Billboard* (blog). August 6, 2018. https://www.billboard.com/articles/business/8468722/apple-spotify-remove-alex-jones-podcast-infowars-shows.

Scholz, Trebor. 2016. *Uberworked and Underpaid: How Workers Are Disrupting the Digital Economy*. Cambridge, UK ; Malden, MA: Polity.

Schultz, Don E. 2020. "From Direct Mail to Direct Response Marketing." In *A Reader in Marketing Communications*, edited by Philip Kitchen, Patrick de Pelsmacker, Lynne Eagle and Don E. Schultz, 116–32. London: Routledge. https://doi.org/10.4324/9781003060420.

Schwartz, Barry. 2020. "Google Podcasts Manager Shows You Search Impressions and Clicks from Google Search." *Search Engine Land* (blog). October 13, 2020. https://searchengineland.com/google-podcasts-manager-shows-you-search-impressions-and-clicks-from-google-search-342023.

Scolere, Leah, Urszula Pruchniewska, and Brooke Erin Duffy. 2018. "Constructing the Platform-Specific Self-Brand: The Labor of Social Media Promotion." *Social Media + Society* 4 (3): 1–11. https://doi.org/10.1177/2056305118784768.

Shah, Rajiv C., and Christian Sandvig. 2008. "Software Defaults as de Facto Regulation: The Case of the Wireless Internet." *Information, Communication & Society* 11 (1): 25–46. https://doi.org/10.1080/13691180701858836.

Shah, Rajiv C., and Jay P. Kesan. 2008. "Setting Online Policy with Software Defaults." *Information, Communication & Society* 11 (7): 989–1007. https://doi.org/10.1080/13691180802109097.

Shapiro, Ariel. 2022. "YouTube Launches a Dedicated Page for Podcasts." *The Verge* (blog). August 22, 2022. https://www.theverge.com/2022/8/22/23316907/youtube-podcast-page-spotify-apple.

Sharma, Shreya. 2022. "YouTube Is the Most Used Platform for Podcast Listening, per C ... " *Inside Podcasting* (blog). May 19, 2022. https://inside.com/podcasting/posts/youtube-is-the-most-used-platform-for-podcast-listening-per-cumulus-media-s-spring-22-report-286092.

Shaw, Lucas, and Priya Anand. 2020. "Podcaster Luminary Seeks Fresh Cash to Buoy Struggling Business." *Bloomberg.Com*. May 13, 2020. https://www.bloomberg.com/news/articles/2020-05-13/podcaster-luminary-seeks-fresh-cash-to-buoy-struggling-business.

Sheikholeslami, Goli. 2017. "Changes at This American Life." *This American Life*. December 12, 2017. https://www.thisamericanlife.org/about/announcements/changes-at-this-american-life.

Shields, Mike. 2005. "New Firm to Count Podcast People." *Adweek* 46 (44): 9–9.

Shirky, Clay. 2008. *Here Comes Everybody: The Power of Organizing without Organizations*. New York: Penguin Press.

Shontell, Alyson. 2016. "Investors Can't Stop Talking about a One-Month-Old App Called Anchor." *Business Insider* (blog). March 16, 2016. https://www.businessinsider.com/what-is-anchor-fm-and-how-to-use-the-app-2016-3.

Silberling, Amanda. 2021. "Patreon Says It Will Double Its Company Size Next Year." *TechCrunch* (blog). December 21, 2021. https://social.techcrunch.com/2021/12/21/patreon-cpo-interview-double-in-size-2022/.

Silberling, Amanda. 2022. "Get Ready to Find out Your Follower Count on Apple Podcasts." *TechCrunch* (blog). March 22, 2022. https://techcrunch.com/2022/03/22/apple-podcasts-followers-subscription-features.

Sisario, Ben. 2015. "WNYC to Open New Podcast Division." *The New York Times*. October 12, 2015. http://www.nytimes.com/2015/10/13/business/media/wnyc-to-open-new-podcast-division.html.

Skinner, Oliver. 2021. "Your Guide to Social Audio: Clubhouse and Other Voice-Based Social Media." *Voices* (blog). May 28, 2021. https://www.voices.com/blog/guide-to-social-audio/.

Sophus Lai, Signe, and Sofie Flensburg. 2020. "Appscapes in Everyday Life: Studying Mobile Datafication from an Infrastructural User Perspective." *MedieKultur: Journal of Media & Communication Research* 36 (69): 29–51.

Soto, Gabriel. 2022. "How Many Shows Must One Buy to Reach the Majority of Podcast Listeners in the U.S.?" *Edison Research*(blog). May 25, 2022. https://www.edisonresearch.com/how-many-shows-must-one-buy-to-reach-the-majority-of-podcast-listeners-in-the-u-s/.

Spangler, Todd. 2018. "IHeartMedia to Buy HowStuffWorks Podcasting Parent for $55 Million." *Variety* (blog). September 13, 2018. https://variety.com/2018/digital/news/iheartmedia-stuff-media-howstuffworks-podcast-acquisition-1202939938/.

Spangler, Todd. 2019. "Spotify Paid Nearly $340 Million to Buy Podcast Startups Gimlet and Anchor." *Variety*. February 15, 2019. https://www.iheart.com/playlist/variety-power-of-women-2019-312064750-EvupBB7c7woZYHEkWHpV79/.

Spangler, Todd. 2020. "Wondery Launches Its Own Podcast App, Aiming to Drive Up Subscriptions (EXCLUSIVE)." *Variety* (blog). June 23, 2020. https://variety.com/2020/digital/news/wondery-app-podcast-subscription-1234646024/.

Spangler, Todd. 2021a. "Spotify Clinches $60M-Plus Deal with Alex Cooper for 'Call Her Daddy' Podcast, Yanking It Away from Barstool." *Variety* (blog). June 15, 2021. https://variety.com/2021/digital/news/spotify-call-her-daddy-alex-cooper-exclusive-1234996840/.

Spangler, Todd. 2021b. "Second Annual 'Next Great Podcast' Contest Kicks Off from IHeartRadio, Dan Patrick." *Variety* (blog). August 24, 2021. https://variety.com/2021/digital/news/next-great-podcast-contest-iheartradio-dan-patrick-1235047285/.

Spangler, Todd. 2023. "Podcast U.S. Ad Revenue Projected to Hit $2.3 Billion in 2023, up 25%." *Variety* (blog). May 11, 2023. https://variety.com/2023/digital/news/podcast-ad-revenue-2023-forecast-study-1235610164/.

Spinelli, Martin, and Lance Dann. 2019. *Podcasting: The Audio Media Revolution*. New York, NY: Bloomsbury Academic.

Spotify. 2019. "A Quick Guide to Spotify's Podcast Metrics – News – Spotify for Podcasters." *Spotify News* (blog). November 27, 2019. https://podcasters.spotify.com/blog/a-quick-guide-to-spotifys-podcast-metrics.

Spotify. 2020. "'The Joe Rogan Experience' Launches Exclusive Partnership with Spotify" Spotify Newsroom. May 19, 2020. https://newsroom.spotify.com/2020-05-19/the-joe-rogan-experience-launches-exclusive-partnership-with-spotify.

Spotify. 2021. "Spotify Ushers in New Era of Podcast Monetization with New Tools for All Creators." *Spotify*. April 27, 2021. https://newsroom.spotify.com/2021-04-27/spotify-ushers-in-new-era-of-podcast-monetization-with-new-tools-for-all-creators/.

Spotify. 2022a. "Spotify's Platform Rules and Approach to COVID-19." *Spotify*. January 30, 2022. https://newsroom.spotify.com/2022-01-30/spotifys-platform-rules-and-approach-to-covid-19.

Spotify, dir. 2022b. *Investor Day 2022: CEO Daniel Ek's Opening Remarks*. https://www.youtube.com/watch?v=e4E5cvG8C_c.

Spotify, dir. 2022c. *Investor Day 2022: Podcasts and Audiobooks*. https://www.youtube.com/watch?v=17grJ3euyJw.

Spurlock, John. 2021. "Podcast Host Rankings by Episode Share (September 2021)." *Livewire Labs* (blog). October 7, 2021. https://livewire.io/podcast-hosts-by-episode-share/.

Srnicek, Nick. 2016. *Platform Capitalism*. Cambridge, UK: Polity.

Statista Research Department. 2021a. "Most Popular Podcast Devices in the U.S. 2019." *Statista*. April 9, 2021. https://www.statista.com/statistics/712230/popular-podcast-devices-in-the-us/.

Statista Research Department. 2021b. "Number of Podcast Listeners in the U.S. 2017–2024." *Statista*. June 29, 2021. https://www.statista.com/statistics/1123105/statista-amo-podcast-reach-us/.

Statista Research Department. 2022. "Number of Podcast Listeners Worldwide 2024." *Statista*. February 18, 2022. https://www.statista.com/statistics/1291360/podcast-listeners-worldwide/.

Steele, Anne. 2020. "Spotify Strikes Podcast Deal with Joe Rogan Worth More than $100 Million." *Wall Street Journal*. May 19, 2020. sec. Business. https://www.wsj.com/articles/spotify-strikes-exclusive-podcast-deal-with-joe-rogan-11589913814.

Steinberg, Brian. 2017. "Nielsen Says It Will Measure Audiences for TV Episodes That Stream Via Netflix." *Variety*. October 18, 2017. https://variety.com/2017/tv/news/nielsen-measurement-netflix-1202592985/.

Sterne, Jonathan. 2006. "The Mp3 as Cultural Artifact." *New Media & Society* 8 (5): 825–42.

Sterne, Jonathan. 2012. *MP3: The Meaning of a Format*. SST: Sign, Storage, Transmission. Durham, NC: Duke University Press.

Sterne, Jonathan, Jeremy Morris, Michael Brendan Baker, and Ariana Moscote Freire. 2008a. "The Politics of Podcasting." *The Fibreculture Journal* 13. http://thirteen.fibreculturejournal.org/fcj-087-the-politics-of-podcasting/.

Sturges, Fiona. 2018. "Podcast: Casting Call—Online Audio's Answer to 'The Apprentice.'" *Financial Times*. September 16, 2018. https://www.ft.com/content/c1e07f7e-b7fe-11e8-a1d8-15c2dd1280ff.

Sullivan, John L. 2018. "Podcast Movement: Aspirational Labour and the Formalisation of Podcasting as a Cultural Industry." In *Podcasting: New Aural Cultures and Digital Media*, edited by Dario Llinares, Neil Fox and Richard Berry, 35–56. London: Palgrave Macmillan.

Sullivan, John L. 2019. "The Platforms of Podcasting: Past and Present." *Social Media + Society* 5 (4): https://doi.org/10.1177/2056305119880002.

Swiatek, Lukasz. 2018. "Podcasting as an Intimate Bridging Medium." In *Podcasting: New Aural Cultures and Digital Media*, edited by Dario Llinares, Neil Fox and Richard Berry, 173–87. London: Palgrave Macmillan.

Tandoc, Edson C. 2019. *Analyzing Analytics : Disrupting Journalism One Click at a Time*. London: Routledge. https://doi.org/10.4324/9781138496538.

Terranova, Tiziana. 2000. "Free Labor: Producing Culture for the Digital Economy." *Social Text* 18 (2): 33–58. https://doi.org/10.1215/01642472-18-2_63-33.

The People's Choice Podcast Awards. 2018. "Podcast Awards—The People's Choice." *Podcast Awards*. 2018. https://www.podcastawards.com/.

Thorpe, Shawn. 2016. "Stitcher Launches Stitcher Premium Subscription Service." *Podcaster News* (blog). December 18, 2016. http://podcasternews.com/2016/12/18/stitcher-launches-stitcher-premium-subscription-service.

Titlow, John Paul. 2015. "Spotify Launches Podcasts, Video, and Context-Based Listening." *Fast Company* (blog). May 20, 2015. https://www.fastcompany.com/3046504/spotify-launches-podcasts-video-and-context-based-listening.

Trew, J. 2021. "Apple's Podcast Subscriptions Are a Mixed Blessing." *Engadget* (blog). April 23, 2021. https://www.engadget.com/apples-podcast-subscriptions-are-a-mixed-blessing-133008360.html.

Triton Digital. 2023. "Triton Digital Releases Inaugural U.S. Year-End Podcast Report." *Triton Digital* (blog). January 25, 2023. https://www.tritondigital.com/press-releases/January-24-2023/triton-digital-releases-inaugural-u-s-year-end-podcast-report.

Tsioulcas, Anastasia. 2022. "Joe Rogan Has Responded to the Protests against Spotify over His Podcast." *NPR*. January 31, 2022. sec. Business. https://www.npr.org/2022/01/31/1076891070/joe-rogan-responds-spotify-podcast-covid-misinformation.

Turchiano, Danielle. 2018. "'Dirty John' Team Talks Expanding Perspective of Bravo Adaptation." *Variety* (blog). August 8, 2018. https://variety.com/2018/tv/news/dirty-john-connie-britton-eric-bana-point-of-view-interview-tca-1202899927/.

Turner, Fred. 2006. *From Counterculture to Cyberculture: Stewart Brand, the Whole Earth Network, and the Rise of Digital Utopianism.* Chicago: University of Chicago Press.

Turow, Joseph. 1997. *Media Systems in Society: Understanding Industries, Strategies, and Power,* 2nd edn. New York: Longman.

Turow, Joseph, and Nick Couldry. 2018. "Media as Data Extraction: Towards a New Map of a Transformed Communications Field." *Journal of Communication* 68 (2): 415–23. https://doi.org/10.1093/joc/jqx011.

Tushnet, Rebecca. 2007. "User-Generated Discontent: Transformation in Practice." *Columbia Journal of Law & Arts* 31 (497): 101–20.

Ugwu, Reggie. 2021a. "SiriusXM Is Buying '99% Invisible,' and Street Cred in Podcasting." *The New York Times* April 26, 2021. sec. Arts. https://www.nytimes.com/2021/04/26/arts/siriusxm-99-invisible-roman-mars.html.

Ugwu, Reggie. 2021b. "'Podcast Movies'? Feature-Length Fiction Stretches the Medium." *The New York Times.* December 24, 2021 sec. Arts. https://www.nytimes.com/2021/12/24/arts/podcast-movies-fiction.html.

Ulanoff, Lance. 2015. "Podcasting: A Decade outside the Mainstream." *Mashable* (blog). August 29, 2015. http://mashable.com/2015/08/29/podcasting-mainstream.

Verma, Neil. 2012. *Theater of the Mind.* Chicago, IL: University of Chicago Press.

Vernon, Pete. 2018. "Alex Jones Forces Tech Giants to Act Like Media Companies." *Columbia Journalism Review* August 7, 2018. https://www.cjr.org/the_media_today/infowars-facebook-youtube.php.

Von Hippel, Erich. 2005. *Democratizing Innovation.* Cambridge, MA: MIT Press.

Wang, Jules. 2019. "Google Podcasts In-Episode Search Is Coming, Shows Now Being Fully Transcribed." *Android Police* (blog). March 26, 2019. https://www.androidpolice.com/2019/03/26/google-podcasts-in-episode-search-is-coming-shows-now-being-fully-transcribed.

Wang, Shan. 2016. "Public Radio Staffers across the U.S. Lay out New Guidelines for Podcast Audience Measurement." *Nieman Lab* (blog). February 3, 2016. http://www.niemanlab.org/2016/02/public-radio-staffers-across-the-u-s-lay-out-new-guidelines-for-podcast-audience-measurement/.

Watkins, Elizabeth Anne. 2019. "Guide to Advertising Technology." New York: Tow Center for Digital Journalism. https://doi.org/10.7916/d8-9aep-r971.

Webster, James G., Patricia F. Phalen, and Lawrence W. Lichty. 2014. *Ratings Analysis: Audience Measurement and Analytics,* 4th edn. New York, NY: Routledge.

Webster, Tom. 2017. "The Partially-Filled Glass of Apple's New Podcast Statistics." *Medium* (blog). June 18, 2017. https://medium.com/@webby2001/the-partially-filled-glass-of-apples-new-podcast-statistics-7bc8e273bf9b.

Webster, Tom. 2021. "The Crux of the Kerfuffle." *I Hear Things* (blog). October 29, 2021. https://tomwebster.media/the-crux-of-the-kurfuffle/.

Webster, Tom. 2022. "The State of Podcasting in 2022: Back to Work." *Medium* (blog). March 30, 2022. https://webby2001.medium.com/the-state-of-podcasting-in-2022-back-to-work-2b21583c33bc.

Welch, Chris. 2019. "BBC Pulls Its Podcasts from Google Podcasts and Assistant." *The Verge* (blog). March 26, 2019. https://www.theverge.com/2019/3/26/18282436/bbc-podcasts-google-assistant-home-block.

White, Peter. 2018. "British Podcast 'My Dad Wrote A Porno' to Be Adapted for U.S. Television, Deal Imminent." *Deadline* (blog). August 26, 2018. https://deadline.com/2018/08/my-dad-wrote-a-porno-us-tv-series-1202452427/.

White, Peter. 2020. "The Sound & The Flurry: How Podcasts Are Becoming a Hollywood Gold Mine." *Deadline* (blog). December 7, 2020. https://deadline.com/2020/12/podcasts-hollywood-film-tv-adaptations-trend-deals-1234636040.

Willens, Max. 2017. "What You Need to Know about Apple's New Podcast Analytics." *Digiday* (blog). June 12, 2017. https://digiday.com/media/need-know-apples-new-podcast-analytics/.

Willens, Max 2018. "The Washington Post Has Launched a New, 20-Minute Daily News Podcast." *Digiday* (blog). November 26, 2018. https://digiday.com/media/washington-post-launched-new-20-minute-daily-news-podcast/.

Williams, Wil. 2019. "Podcasters Are People: The Intimacy of Medium vs. Parasocial Relationships." *Wil Williams Reviews* (blog). January 4, 2019. https://wilwilliams.reviews/2019/01/04/podcasters-are-people-the-intimacy-of-medium-vs-parasocial-relationships/.

Winer, Dave. 2019. "What Is a Podcast?" *Scripting News* (blog). April 9, 2019. http://scripting.com/2019/04/09/135711.html.

Wittenbrink, Heinz. 2005. *RSS and Atom: Understanding and Implementing Content Feeds and Syndication*. From Technologies to Solutions. Birmingham: Packt Publ.

Wohn, Donghee Yvette, Peter Jough, Peter Eskander, John Scott Siri, Masaho Shimobayashi, and Pradnya Desai. 2019. "Understanding Digital Patronage: Why Do People Subscribe to Streamers on Twitch?" In *Proceedings of the Annual Symposium on Computer-Human Interaction in Play*, 99–110. New Jersey: Institute of Technology Newark, NJ, USA.

Zhang, Sonya, and Neal Cabage. 2017. "Search Engine Optimization: Comparison of Link Building and Social Sharing." *Journal of*

Computer Information Systems 57 (2): 148–59. https://doi.org/10.1080/08874417.2016.1183447.

Zinsli, Christopher. 2014. "'This American Life' Producer Raises $1.5 Million for Podcast Startup Gimlet." *Wall Street Journal*. November 11, 2014. sec. Venture Capital Dispatch. https://www.wsj.com/articles/BL-VCDB-15872.

Zohrob, Dave. 2018. "What's Really the Top Podcast Hosting Service?" *The Chartable Blog* (blog). August 29, 2018. https://chartable.com/blog/whats-really-the-top-podcast-hosting-service.

Zohrob, Dave. 2021. "Why Branded Podcasts Are Exploding (and Why We Built Chartable for Brands)." *The Chartable Blog* (blog). May 13, 2021. https://chartable.com/blog/why-branded-podcasts-are-exploding-and-why-we-built-chartable-for-brands.

Zuboff, Shoshana. 2019. *The Age of Surveillance Capitalism: The Fight for a Human Future at the New Frontier of Power*. New York: Public Affairs.

Zuraikat, Laith. 2020. "The Parasocial Nature of the Podcast." In *Radio's Second Century: Past, Present, and Future Perspectives*, edited by John Allen Hendricks, 39–52. New Brunswick, NJ: Rutgers University Press.

INDEX

Acast 168, 198, 200, 213
acquisitions 8, 11, 33, 46, 72–4, 80, 83, 96, 98, 147, 196, 199, 201, 204–5, 207, 215–17
Adler Berg, Freja 222
AdsWizz 73, 168, 198, 200
ad tech 11
AdvertiseCast 196
advertising/advertisers 1–2, 8, 13, 17, 31, 56, 80, 130, 136–8, 152, 170, 174, 180, 190–1, 194, 218
    accountability 205
    brand 13, 17, 22, 70, 181, 190, 192–6, 204–5
    branded content 17, 56, 190, 201–3, 205
    DAI, algorithmic surveillance and programmatic 196–201, 204–5
    direct response 13, 147, 190, 192–3, 204
    engagement 191
    firms 2, 38, 70, 207
    as influencers 212
    and marketers 27
    medium 71, 154
    monetization via 17, 179, 180, 220, 224
    sponsorship 112, 118, 138, 140, 147, 192
AdWeek 152, 157
affective labor 112–15, 119–20

AIR 54
Airr 67, 213
Alex, Inc. 71
The Alex Jones Show 99
algorithmic surveillance 196–201
alliances, platform 95–7
amateurs/amateur media 2, 4–7, 10, 12–13, 15, 19, 24, 28, 42, 46, 49, 51, 53, 101, 105, 120, 127, 141, 173, 223
    educating 127
    professionalism of 104, 106
Amazon 11, 16, 20–2, 35, 71, 80, 102, 143, 146, 167, 194, 196, 205, 209, 214–17, 220, 223–4
    Amazon Music 143, 209, 214
    Amazon Prime 31, 71, 89, 97, 185
    Amazon Turk 118
    Audible audio book service 193
Anand, N. 148, 153
Anchor (Spotify for Podcasters) 17, 31, 63–4, 67, 70, 72, 91, 98–9, 101, 162, 166, 180, 198, 205, 211, 217–18, 219 n.5, 220
    TOS 99
Anderson, Chris 6
Android 68, 95–6, 143, 167
Another Round with Heben and Tracy 129
app-ification 69, 96, 169

INDEX

Apple 16, 19, 21, 31, 34, 67, 93, 99, 100, 102, 133, 143, 147, 151–2, 162, 167, 169, 185, 190, 214, 220
   consumption metrics 163–6
   iOS mobile platform 68
   iOS Version 8.0 96
   iPhone 3, 11, 68, 95, 160, 164
   iPod 3, 16, 19, 30, 35, 65, 95
   subscription service 187
   top podcasts 82–3, 219
Apple Podcasts (iTunes) 9, 11, 19–20, 30, 35, 38–9, 43, 64, 66–7, 81, 83, 86, 89, 93–4, 101, 145, 162–5, 185, 187, 190, 202, 210–11, 214, 223–4
   "Arts" 39
   and early podcast platformization 87–9
   "Education" 39
   iOS 96
   rankings 82
   "Religion & Sprituality" 40
   "Society & Culture" 39–40
   TOS 98
Apple Worldwide Developers Conference (2005) 87
Application Programming Interfaces (APIs) 67, 94, 100, 151
Arie, India 200
Armchair Expert with Dax Sheppard 31, 74, 188, 208
Arment, Marco 170
Arvidsson, Adam 124
aspirational labor 122, 124, 133–5, 176
atomization, podcasting 212–13
Attig, Christiane 53
The Audacity to Podcast 16, 104, 108, 110, 118–19, 134
Audacy 73

Audible 70, 143
audience 3, 6, 10, 19, 21–2, 28, 46, 69–70, 84, 111, 113–14, 141, 146, 170, 188, 191, 209–10, 218, 224
   datafication 101, 146, 171
   imagined 119, 144
   market 190, 204
   maximization 97, 104, 120, 171
   measurement services 70–1, 151, 175
   metrics 13–14, 17, 136, 140–1, 145, 147–50, 157–8, 163, 168–9, 171
   producers and 49, 190
   studies 152–5
audio distribution 16, 32, 51, 111
AudioHook 198
authenticity 12, 119, 123, 135, 138, 204
   artistry and 128–31
   and creative empowerment 4
   and creative freedom 16
   and meritocracy 104
   and self-actualization 115–17
authorization 74
autonomy 102, 117–18, 131–3, 135, 138, 140, 171, 222

Barlow, John Perry, "Declaration of Independence for Cyberspace" 30
Barrett, Jason 139
Barstool Sports 57
Baym, Nancy K. 119
BBC Sounds 144–5
Benjamin Walker's Radio Diaries 182
Benkler, Yochai 5, 45, 105
Bermejo, Fernando 149
Berry, Richard 24–30
Big Tech 7
Billboard 76

BIPOC podcasts 221
Bishop, Sophie 199–200, 219
Bitcoin Lightning Network 184
Black podcasters 29
blogging 9, 15, 28, 108, 119
BlogTalkRadio 91
Blubrry 62, 76, 90, 136, 148, 159, 162, 168, 173, 189
Blumberg, Alex 10, 55, 71–2, 105, 121–2, 202
Bonini, Tiziano 14, 24, 211
Bottomley, Andrew 32
　Sound Streams 23
bottom-up formalization 46, 69, 74–5, 78, 80, 105
　facilitators 75–7
　unions 77–9
Braff, Zach 71
BrainStuff 58
brand advertisers/advertising 13, 17, 22, 70, 181, 190, 192–6, 204–5
brand communications 201
branded content 17, 56, 190, 201–3, 205
brand safety 199–200
Branson, Richard 124
Braun, Joshua 64, 84
Bravo network 72
British Broadcasting Corporation (BBC) 13, 51, 54, 62, 144–5, 167, 216
broadcast radio advertising 195, 205
Bruns, Axel 45, 106
Budden, Joe 56, 73, 95, 220
The Bungie Podcast 202
business-to-business podcast publishers 56
buying and selling advertising 17, 70–1, 155, 197, 199, 201, 205
Buy Me A Coffee 181, 183
BuzzCast 77, 189

Buzzfeed 129
Buzzsprout 64, 67, 162, 189
Byrne, Conal 208

Cadence13 72
Caldwell, John Thornton 7–8
California Consumer Privacy Act (CCPA) 170
Call Her Daddy 74, 198, 208, 215
Captivate Insider 189
Carlin, Dan 26
Carman, Ashley 196, 203
Casper Mattress 193
Castbox 97, 186
Casting Call 56
Chartable 151, 159, 159 n.1, 162, 175, 202
Clayton, Tracy 129
ClickRabbit 118
ClickWorker 118
clients 70, 153, 163, 168, 176, 198
Clifton, Kieran 144
Clubhouse 212
CNBC 130
Cochrane, Todd 160–1
codification 74
commercialization 130, 209, 224
ComScore 137, 162, 200
conferences, conventions, and communities 5, 8, 16, 23, 59, 75, 77–8, 87, 98, 104, 107, 112–15, 122–3, 125–6, 141, 178, 188, 211–12, 221
consulting agencies 54, 76
consumption apps 93, 95–7, 100
consumption metrics 150–1, 156, 168, 170–1
　Apple 163–6
　apps and future of podcast 166–7
　storage platforms and 90–2

content delivery network (CDN) service 156–8
content exclusivity 102, 214–16
content market 190, 204
content networks 57–60, 67
controls 50, 74
conviviality 211
Cooper, Alex 74
Corrigan, Thomas F. 103, 135
Couldry, Nick 146
COVID-19, podcasting during 40–2, 126
Craig, David 178, 203
  Social Media Entertainment 177–8
creative labor 77, 131, 174, 177, 210, 219–22
The Creators 53
creators and audiences 11, 14, 17, 22, 31, 177, 183
creator studies 178
Cridland, James 31, 62, 76, 82, 219 n.5, 223
critical media industry studies 7, 46, 64
Critical Role 187
cross-licensing of podcasting content 71–2, 215
crowdfunding platforms 75, 122, 181–5, 204
cryptocurrency 184
C Suite 203
cultural industry 15, 48, 86
  structural formation of 9–11
cultural production 8, 15, 17, 47–8, 97, 102, 104, 118, 123, 224
  democratization 104, 106
  diversity of 5
  industrialized 48–9
  industrial tradition 47
  macro and micro 7
  mass amateurization 5, 105
  modes of analysis 7
  monetization of online 176–9
  platforms and 85–7
  and professionalism 107–8
  self-branding 17
cultural shift 5, 105
cultures, podcasting 27–30, 104
Cumulus Media 212
Cundil, Matt 139
Cunningham, Stuart 178, 203
  Social Media Entertainment 177–8
Curry, Adam 34–5, 37, 64, 214
  Daily Source Code 3
  iPodder software 30, 35
  Value 4 Value system 184–5
custom audience studies 152–4
cyberlibertarianism 30

Dann, Lance 14–15, 30–1
  Podcasting: The Audio Media Revolution 14, 30
datafication 101, 146, 170–1
The Dave Ramsey Show 96
Deal, Mark 78
Death, Sex, and Money 129
demand-side platforms (DSPs) 197–8
Diehn, Erik 164
digital advertisers/advertising 139, 191, 197–8, 205, 210
digital advertising insertion (DAI) 171, 210
digital labor 118–19
  and entrepreneurism 123–5
digital patronage 182–3
digital platforms 84, 86, 183
Dillon, Tim 183
directories, podcast 35–6, 38, 43, 64–5, 67, 87, 89–91, 93, 95, 100, 109, 169, 216

direct response advertising 13, 147, 190, 192–3, 204
Dirty John 72, 215
discoverability 83, 210, 218–19
discovery platforms 92–6, 100–1
Disney/Disney+ 185, 198
distinct industries 10
distribution 3–5, 7, 15–16, 24–5, 30–2, 34–5, 37, 42, 49–51, 57, 80, 84, 86, 88–9, 93, 95, 100, 109, 118, 120, 147, 156–8, 174, 186, 192, 208–9, 214–15
   battles and future 209–14
   information 94
   online digital 105, 148
   podcast directories 64–5
   second-class 102
distributors 64–5, 80, 101, 122, 151, 160, 162, 219
do-it-yourself (DIY) 177
   DIY spirit 25
   production ethos 12, 23, 105
Dornfest, Rael 34
downloads per episode (DPE) 59–60, 91, 137–8, 148, 150–1, 157–8, 160, 169, 181
Dragons 188
Dr. Death 215
duality, podcasting 222–4
Duffy, Brooke Erin 111, 115, 131, 135
Dumas, John Lee 189–90
Dungeons 187
Duolingo 202
dynamic advertising insertion (DAI) 196–201

Earwolf 65, 215
Easley, Jared 75, 125

ecosystem, podcasting 2, 6, 8, 11, 13, 16, 22, 24, 29, 31–3, 37, 45–6, 64, 72, 82–3, 121–3, 135, 143, 163, 165, 168, 170–1, 198, 223
   advertising-supported revenue models 138–9
   platform governance 97–100
Eddings, Eric 79
Edison Research 2, 6, 20, 40, 53, 59, 70, 136, 154–5, 213 n.3, 217
   Infinite Dial (2023) report 20, 33, 38
   "Share of Ear" 6
   US podcast listeners (2021–2) 40–1
educational podcasts 57–8
effects 50, 129, 175
Ek, Daniel 72, 207–8, 216
Elledge, Josh 134
eMarketer 20
enclosure 25, 34, 36, 92–5, 97, 100, 158
entrepreneurialism (PM16) 124–5, 127–8
   artistry and authenticity 128–31
   autonomy 131–3
entrepreneurism 16, 30, 33, 124, 126, 212
   digital labor and 123–5
   and professional standards affective labor 112–15
   passionate podcaster 115–17
   production and marketing advice 109–12
Entrepreneurs on Fire (EOF) 189
exhibitors/exhibition 9, 46, 52, 64, 65–9, 80, 84

Facebook/Facebook groups 11, 35, 54, 86–7, 94–5, 99–100, 107–8, 133, 139, 146, 152, 157, 170–1, 197, 199, 201, 205, 211
facilitators
　audience measurement services 70–1
　hosts, podcast 60, 62–4
　industry 60
　podcast journalism 76–7
　professional organizations 75–6
Fast Company 186
The Feed 77, 189
female podcasters 53
first party monetization. *See* micro-monetization
Fiverr 54, 118
Flickr 89
formal economy 7, 49–50
formalization 9–11, 13, 15–17, 23, 45–6, 49–50, 55–6, 78, 80, 107, 117, 122–3, 140, 151, 158, 203, 212, 224
　of advertising markets 175
　audience data 17
　bottom up (*see* bottom-up formalization)
　industry 14, 45, 140, 147, 174, 215
　microcosm 126
　monetization and market information regimes 147–50
　of production practices 133–5
　standardization and 136–7
　top down (*see* top-down formalization)
　of user-generated content 105–7
Fox, Kim 29

Franks, Dan 75, 122, 125
freelancers 50, 52–4, 77–8, 80, 117, 123
functions 50, 213

General Data Protection Regulation (GDPR) 170
General Electric (GE) 202
genres 26–7, 36, 38–42, 156, 196, 219
gig economy 10, 104–6, 119, 124
Gillespie, Tarleton 85–6, 97
"Gilmore Guys" 4
Gimlet Media 27, 55–6, 58, 72, 79–80, 83, 121–2, 171, 176, 202, 215–16, 222
Global Alliance for Responsible Media (GARM) 200–1
Global Podcast Editors 221
Goldberg, Kevin 81–2
"Gold Rush" mentality 20
Goldstein, Steven 223
Google 11, 16–17, 20–2, 35, 37, 59, 70, 83, 100, 102, 139, 143–7, 151, 167, 169, 177, 197, 205, 209, 214, 216, 223
　AI Assistant 144
Google Podcasts 64–5, 68, 83, 109, 144–5, 166, 214
　Google Podcasts Creator Program 59
　Google Podcasts Manager 166
Graphtreon 183
Great Feeling Studios 58
Green, Joshua 5
Group M "Interaction 17" report 139
Guha, Ramanathan V. 34

Hackable? 203
Halo 202
Hammersley, Ben 3, 6

Hansen, Samuel 25, 36
Hardcore History 26
Hardy, Jonathan, *Branded Content* 201
Hark 213
"The Haunting of Night Vale" 188
Havens, Timothy 48
The Heard 58
Hearsay Audio Festival, Ireland 126
Heeremans, Lieven 58
Herbert, Daniel 48
Herring, Richard 188
Hesmondhalgh, David 48
Holt, Courtney 72
Homecoming 27, 122
Hook, Sandy 99
hope labor 103, 120, 135, 176
"Horse Radio Network" 26
host-read advertising 17, 112, 186, 195–6, 204
hosts, podcast 13, 26, 54, 60, 62–4, 67, 69, 71, 90–1, 93, 111–13, 118, 128–30, 149–50, 157–8, 162, 166, 191, 202, 205, 210, 212
  and audience/listener 28, 112, 180
  hosting companies 30, 60, 62–4, 76, 78, 90–2, 96, 98–100, 136–7, 148, 150–1, 157–8, 160, 162, 164–5, 167–70, 173, 189, 196
  top rankings 63
Hot Pod 76
Howl 65, 186
The HowStuffWorks podcast network 57, 97, 199
How to Start a Podcast 189
Hulu 97
Hunter, Dan 53
hybrid media industry 6–7, 47–51

IAB Working Group 161
iCloud 164
I Hear Things 77
iHeartMedia 2, 11, 13, 16, 22, 24, 37, 55–6, 58, 60, 73, 79–80, 143, 147, 175, 180, 199–200, 208, 216, 224
iHeartRadio 83, 97, 167
independent/indie podcasters 8, 23, 53, 56–9, 62, 76, 93–4, 101–2, 105, 107, 122, 134, 136, 138, 176–7, 180, 203, 210, 219, 221–2, 224
Independent Podcast Convention 126
Indiegogo 150, 181–2
indirect monetization 189
industrialization of culture 43, 48, 175
industry facilitators 60, 71
The Infinite Dial (2023) report 20, 33, 38, 154–5
informal economy 7, 49–50, 74, 175–8, 203
informal media systems 53
Infowars 99–100, 216
Inner Sanctum 27
In Our Time 51, 144
Instagram 170, 178, 199, 201, 211, 216
institutional structure 7, 28–9, 52, 75, 106, 222
integrated cultural-historical method of analysis 7
Interactive Advertising Bureau (IAB) 14, 70–1, 91, 95, 137, 147, 151, 160–2, 166, 168–9, 174, 193
  Podcast Technical Working Group 160
  Report (2016) 161
  version 1.0 standard 160
  version 2.1 162

International PodFest 212
Invisibilia 26
IQ-Notecast/Inflo 213
iTunes. *See* Apple Podcasts (iTunes)
iTunes 4.9 87–8

Jackson, Dave 16, 99, 104, 108–20, 212
Jarrett, Kylie 123
Jenkins, Henry 5, 45
Jobs, Steven (Steve) P. 19–20, 87–8, 124
Joe Budden Podcast 95
The Joe Rogan Experience (JRE) 31, 56, 74, 160 n.2, 196, 198, 208, 216
Jones, Alex 99–100, 216
Jones, Dave 37, 64, 208
Jones, David 214
journalism 76–7
"just in time" advertising 197

Katz, Dan "Big Cat" 57
Kessler, Sarah, *Gigged* 103
keynotes 126–9
Kickass News 82–3
Kickstarter 75, 122, 125, 150, 181–2
Kinzen 201
Kosterich, Allie 148
Krimitsos, Chris 75, 126
Kuehn, Kathleen 103, 135
Kurtz, Brian, *OverDeliver: Build a Business for a Lifetime Playing the Long Game in Direct Response Marketing* 192
KYCY 51

labor 33, 51, 104
  affective 112–15, 119–20
  aspirational 122, 124, 133–5, 176

authenticity and self-actualization 115–17
autonomy 118, 222
contradictions of professional 117–19
creative 77, 131, 174, 177, 210, 219–22
digital 118–19, 123–5
formalization 78
hope 103, 120, 135, 176
online 78, 119, 132
organizing 77–9, 106
specialization of 11–13, 16–17, 49, 77–9, 224
landscape of distribution 16, 64, 84, 100, 147–8, 222
Laporte, Leo 1–2, 105
Last Podcast On the Left 220
Leadbeater, Charles 106, 127
legacy media companies 2, 6–7, 12, 20, 22, 24, 36, 43, 46, 50, 96, 148
legacy media industry studies 10, 47
Leland, Gary 75, 122, 125
Lewis, Daniel J. 16, 104, 108–20, 134, 212
Libby, Dan 34
Libsyn 59–60, 64, 91, 96, 138, 148, 162, 170, 173, 189, 196
Lieber, Matt 55, 164
Lindgren, Mia 26
linking pins 71–2
listeners 4, 11, 19–21, 25–9, 31–3, 35, 38, 40, 66, 84, 99, 111, 113, 138, 141, 154–5, 162, 170, 175, 210, 218
  audio-realism and tension 27
  centralized repositories 101
  community 29, 114
  data 17, 101, 205

podcaster/creators and 11, 15, 26, 42, 183, 191
producer-listener relationship 24, 28
Listennotes 67, 213
live events 188
Llinares, Dario, *Podcasting: New Aural Cultures and Digital Media* 14
Lobato, Ramon 49–50, 53, 69, 74, 80, 124, 176
Long Tail market 6, 59, 68, 175, 179–80, 217
Lopez, Hernan 55
Lord of the Rings trilogy 49
Lore 2, 71
Lotz, Amanda 48
Luminary 65, 186–7, 214–15

Magellan AI 201
Mahnke, Aaron 2, 71
Mailchimp 193
market information regimes 147–50
  market viability 152–5
  shifting 150–1
Markman, Kris M. 4, 174
Maron, Marc 12, 105
Mars, Roman 74, 215
Marwick 124, 129
mass amateurization, cultural production 5, 105
Maximum Fun 185
McAfee Security 203
McCrery, Mark 137, 158, 162
McDonalds 17, 175
McGowan, Claudette 203
McHugh, Siobhán 173
McLaughlin, Amanda 58
media-hosting services 92
media industries 2, 12, 46, 59, 70, 80, 84, 136. *See also* formalization
  critical studies 7, 46
  hybrid 6–7, 47–51
  interactions in 50
  producers 52, 64
Mediamark Research Inc. (MRI) 159
medium, podcasting as 22–4, 53, 70, 80, 107, 125, 130, 140, 152, 154, 156, 161, 205, 209–14, 224
  cultures 27–30
  platforms and 30–3
  production practices of 42
  technology and sonic qualities 24–7
Megaphone 198, 210
  "Spotify Audience Network" 210
Menduni, Enrico 24
merchandising 187–8
mergers 8, 46, 72–4, 147, 204–5. *See also* acquisitions
meritocracy 12, 104, 118–20, 124
The Message 202
Meta 211
method and scope of analysis 7–9
metrics 35, 70–1, 151–2, 158, 160, 162, 175, 207
  client-side 163–9
  consumption (*see* consumption metrics)
  monetization and audience 13–14, 17, 135–9, 149
micro-monetization 175, 180–1, 190, 203
  crowdfunding/direct support 181–5
  indirect monetization 189
  live events 188
  merchandising 187–8
  paywalls, subscriptions, and bonus content 185–7, 204
Midroll 2, 96, 164, 186
mid-roll advertisements 195

Miller, Paul 106, 127
Miller, Peter 153
  syndicated studies 153
Misener, Dan 39–40, 66
Mitchell, Joni 200, 216
mobile personalization 146
mobility of podcasting 24
Momento 67, 213
monetization 2, 9, 17, 32, 46, 58, 62, 101, 111–14, 118, 130, 139, 141, 173, 175, 203, 220, 224
  and advertising support 137–9
  audience maximization 97, 120
  and audience metrics 13–14, 141
  freemium model 31
  industrialization 175
  legitimation 130
  and market information regimes 147–50
  metrics and 135–7, 141
  micro-monetization 175, 180–90
  of online cultural production 176–9
  third-party monetization 180, 190–203
Morris, Jeremy Wade 32, 69, 170, 219
The Moth 188
Mulder, Steve 137
Multitude Productions 58, 221
My Dad Wrote A Porno 71
My Favorite Murder 188

namespaces 36–7, 183–4, 214
Napoli, Philip M. 148, 190
National Election Poll 154
National Public Radio (NPR) 4, 10, 13, 16, 22, 40, 50, 54, 60, 62, 121, 136, 160–2, 167–9, 188, 224
  RAD technology 167–70

native advertising 138, 195, 212
netcasting 1
Netflix 89, 97, 185
  Netflix-ization 94
  Netflix of podcasting moment 94, 186
Netscape 34
networks 10, 16, 31, 46, 57–69, 71, 83, 87, 101, 122, 133, 138, 141, 160, 171, 187, 196, 203, 215, 217–18, 224. *See also specific networks*
New Media Show 77
New Oxford American Dictionary 33
The New York Times 55, 60, 81, 95, 185
"The Next Great Podcast" 56
Nieborg, David B. 86, 89, 93, 97, 100, 102
Nielsen 137, 152–3, 160, 162, 164, 196
99% Invisible 74, 182, 215
Notecast 67
Nuzum, Eric 37

oligopolization 74, 102
Omny Studio 62
online media 4, 10–11, 15, 21, 24, 49, 71, 95, 135, 137, 149, 152, 170, 203. *See also specific online media platforms*
  storage and distribution 6
  video conferencing platforms 42
Online News Association Conference (2009) 1
OnlyFans 183
optimization, platform 83, 149, 205, 219 n.5
  economy of attention 217–19
  gaming and 83–4

O'Reilly Media 34
Osgood, Heather 193
outdated technology 208
Overcast 96, 101, 170

Panoply 202
paratexts 49
Parcast 55, 79, 222
Pardo, Joe 126
Pardon My Take 57
Patreon 150, 181, 183–4, 204
patronage 182–3. *See also* digital patronage
Patterson, Eleanor 69, 170
paywalls, subscriptions, and bonus content 46, 185–7, 204, 214
paywall wars 65
"The Pen Addict" 4
people-catching technologies 69
personal and emotional connection 112–13
personal epiphany moment 129
Peterson, Richard A. 148, 153
Petre, Caitlin 171
The Pew Research Center 33, 70, 154
Planet Money 26, 55
platform-centric listening 210, 223
platform governance
   content exclusivity 214–16
   in fragmented ecosystem 97–100
platformization 9–11, 15, 23, 33, 80, 83, 85–6, 100, 146, 196, 209, 217, 222
   Apple's iTunes and early podcast 87–9
   mobile apps and client-side metrics 163–9
   network effects 101
platform-mediated workers 123

platforms 5–6, 9–11, 16–17, 21–2, 30–3, 35–8, 42–3, 46, 83–4, 99, 123, 145, 161, 169, 175, 179, 181, 198–9, 201, 205, 209, 212, 216, 220, 224
   alliances 95–7
   apps and 65–9, 168
   and cultural production 85–7
   discovery 92–6, 100–1
   enclosure 34, 36, 92–5, 97, 100
   optimization (*see* optimization, platform)
   storage 90–2, 100–1
   "winner take all" functions 95
playlists 211, 213
Podbean 67, 90, 167
PodcastAlley.com 87
Podcast Editor Academy 78, 221
Podcast Editors Conference (2021) 78
podcasters 6, 8–9, 16, 32, 42, 53, 59, 83, 94, 123, 125, 130, 139–40, 150, 166, 171, 183, 185, 195, 204, 223
   amateur 10, 12, 46, 105, 111–12, 116, 118, 122, 127–8, 135, 140, 223–4
   best practices for 108, 110
   Black 29
   and listener 15, 26, 42, 114, 119, 149, 191, 206
   passionate 115–17
"Podcasters Paradise" 189
The Podcast Index 63–4, 67, 217, 223
Podcast Influencer 82
Podcasting 2.0 4, 9, 37, 184, 204, 208, 214
Podcasting Smarter 189
Podcast Junkies 77
Podcast Magazine 76

Podcast Movement convention
    2016 (PM16) 8, 16, 75,
    107, 122, 125–7, 135,
    139–41, 162, 212
  keynotes 126–9, 133, 140
  logo 132
PodcastPickle.com 87
podcast/podcasting 3–4, 12, 22,
    26, 33–4, 45, 77, 80, 107,
    115, 117, 156, 183, 185,
    203, 223–4
  benefits of 3–4, 58, 129
  distribution battles and future
    of 209–14
  as distribution model 4, 186
  DNA of 156
  download distribution per
    episode 60
  growth 20
  listening 20, 28, 38, 66, 71,
    136, 144, 154–6, 158,
    163–5, 169, 209, 211,
    223–4
  oligopoly 74, 102
  and politics of spreadable
    media 4–7
  studies 14–15, 222
Podcast Pontifications 77, 189
Podcast Reader 77
PodcastRE project 32
Podcasts in Color 221
Podcast Taxonomy 78
Podcast Technical Working
    Group 160
podcatchers 3, 36, 66, 87–8, 101,
    156–7, 161, 163
podcatching apps 66–8, 169, 213
Podchaser 78, 213
podfading 223
PodFest Expo 75, 126
  Guinness Book of World
    Record 126
Podimo 222

Podland News 77
PodMov Daily 76
Podnews 77
Pod Save America 188
Podsights 159, 170, 175
Podtrac 59, 71, 151, 158, 164,
    168–9
  prefix analytics 159
  proprietary algorithms 158
  standardization 158–62
Podverse 67, 213
Poell, Thomas 86, 89, 93, 97, 100,
    102
post-roll ads 166, 195
PowerPress 90
power roles 16, 46, 48, 51–2, 66,
    70, 77, 80, 140
practices, podcasting 8, 12, 14, 23,
    28, 42, 48, 51, 77, 107–8,
    110, 152, 189, 222
practitioners, podcasting 7–8, 22,
    133, 173, 209, 211
  and ethnographic observations
    8–9
  and professionals 125
pre-professionals 28
pre-roll advertisements 195
Prey, Robert 219
Printful 187
Printify 187
pro-ams 11–13, 106–7, 127
producer-listener relationship 24, 28
production and consumption,
    podcasting 9, 11, 13, 16,
    35, 38, 40, 42, 51, 72,
    75, 77, 80, 84, 86, 91,
    101, 105, 108, 113, 118,
    128, 151, 174, 182, 212,
    215–16, 218, 223
  content networks 57–60
  distribution 64–5
  exhibition 65–9
  facilitators 60, 62–4

independents and freelancers 52–4
and marketing advice 109–12
practices 133–5
publishers 54–7
produsers 5, 11–13, 106
professionalism 16, 33, 103, 105–6, 127, 219–22
of amateurs 104, 106
contradictions of professional labor 117–19
cultural production and 107–8
entrepreneurism and professional standards 108–17
modes of 109
professionalization 12–13, 104–6, 117–18, 123, 126, 177, 220–1
professional organizations 46, 75–6, 80
programmatic advertising 17, 70, 196–201, 204–5
progressive downloading 161
Prohovnik, Maya 208, 210
proliferation, post-2005 platform 89–90
consumption apps and platform alliances 95–7
discovery platforms and enclosure threat 92–5
storage platforms and consumption metrics 90–2
proof of concept 136, 153, 155, 190
Pruchniewska, Urszula 115
public broadcasters 13, 22
Public Radio Exchange (PRX) 59
public radio organizations 96
publishers 54–7, 59–60, 62, 79–80, 196–9, 203, 214, 216
rankings 61

pull model 33
Punathambekar, Aswin 48
Pushkin Industries 187
push model 33

Q'd Up Podcast 77
Quah, Nicholas 40, 76, 79, 147, 165–6, 186
Quill 54, 78
Quirkos 108
Quirk, Vanessa 58, 188
Guide to Podcasting 179

radio 6, 12, 14, 24, 26–8, 30, 38, 40, 42, 51, 57–8, 66, 88, 121, 130, 144, 148, 152, 159, 190, 194–5, 199, 205–6, 216, 220
advertising revenue (US) 190
dissemination and radiophony 51
networks 4
remediation 22–4
TiVO for 19, 87
Radio 2.0 24
Radiotopia 182
RAJAR 28
Ramsey, Dave 180
RCA 88
The Read 29
reality check 8, 139
Really Simple Syndication/Rich Site Summary (RSS) 9, 14–16, 25, 33, 43, 45, 50, 57, 66, 84, 94, 100, 147–8, 152, 179, 183, 190, 204, 209–10, 214, 223. *See also* RSS feeds
content exclusivity 214–16
distribution mechanism 32, 42, 57, 64, 89, 102, 147, 208–9, 214
Google search interest 95

infrastructure of openness 33–8
online podcast content 32
open architecture of 15, 30, 42, 57, 85, 94, 147, 192, 210, 223
  protocol 9, 156
  standard 16, 34, 158, 169
  version 0.90 34
  version 2.0 37
  Web 1.0 technology 29
Redbubble 187
Reddit.com 1
relational labor 119, 177, 183
Remote Audio Data (RAD) 167–9
Reply All 79, 122
restriction 74
retail hosts 62
Richard Herring's Leicester Square Theatre Podcast (RHLSTP) 188
The Ringer 79–80, 215–16, 222
Rogan, Joe 12, 56, 200, 215–16
Rolling Stone 76
Rosin, Larry 136
RSS feeds 3, 14, 25, 35, 62–6, 87–8, 90–1, 109–10, 156, 185, 195, 197–8, 219 n.5
  as container technology 93
  decentralized control 37–8
  distribution technology 35
  flexibility 36–7
  syndication 35–6
  transparency 36
  URL 158

Sale, Anna 129
Sarnoff, David 88
Saturday Night Live 19
Sawyer, Caroline E. 4
School of Podcasting 16, 104, 108, 110, 118–19
Schumpeter, Joseph 124
Scripps, E. W. 2, 96, 140

search engine optimization (SEO) 83
second age 14, 75
self-actualization 104, 115–17, 119
self-branding 17, 118–19, 133–5, 224
self-theorizing 107
Serial 2, 12, 26–7, 45, 55, 103, 160, 164, 190, 194, 219
seriality 35, 43, 156, 214
The Shadow 27
"Share of Ear" 6
Shepard, Dax 56, 74
Shirky, Clay 5, 105
Simplecast 162
Simpler Media 189
SiriusXM 2, 11, 13, 16, 22, 24, 37, 55, 73, 80, 83, 140, 143, 147, 167, 174–5, 180, 194, 215–17, 220, 224
Slack 203
Slate 198
small-scale monetization 187, 218
Smith, Kevin 129, 131–2, 138
Snap Judgment 128, 182
Snipd 213
social audio services 36, 211
social media 5, 11, 15, 24, 27, 32–3, 49–50, 54, 67, 75, 83, 85, 87, 94, 99, 119, 144, 152, 159, 171, 177, 179, 201, 211–12, 223
  analytics 148
  entrepreneurs 111, 115
  followers 211
  marketing 119
social media entertainment (SME) 177–8
sociocultural environment 24–5, 27, 29, 33
soft self-promotion 115
Sollenberger, Eric 57

So Money 130
SoundCloud 63, 91, 101
Sounder 200
Sounds Profitable 53, 76–7
Spanish 202
specialization of labor 9, 11–13, 16–17, 49, 77–9, 224
Spinelli, Martin 14–15, 30–1
   Podcasting: The Audio Media Revolution 14, 30
spoken word audio 38–40, 42, 185
Spotify 4, 11, 13, 16–17, 20–2, 31, 35, 37, 55–6, 63–5, 67–70, 72–4, 79–80, 83, 91, 93–5, 98–102, 122, 143–5, 147, 151, 157, 161–3, 166–7, 169, 174–5, 180, 186–7, 194, 198, 200–1, 205, 207–10, 211–12, 213 n.3, 214–18, 220, 222–4
   Investor Day presentation 208
   Live 208, 212
   "Platform Rules" 216
   playlists 213
   podcasting growth 69
   subscription service 187
spreadable media 5
Spreaker 64, 67, 91, 96, 99, 162, 167
Squarespace 70, 193
Srnicek, Nick 84, 100
   tendencies 100
standard, download 155–8
   IAB 160–2
   Podtrac and 158–9
Start Up 71, 121–2, 202
Statista 217
Sterne, Jonathan 29, 35
Stewart, Steve 78
Still Processing 29
Stitcher 2, 65, 96, 167, 186
   Stitcher Premium 65

storage platforms 90–2, 100–1
S-Town 2
Stuff Media 58
Stuff You Missed in History Class 58
Stuff You Should Know 57–8
Super Listeners 191
supply-side platforms (SSPs) 197–9
surveillance capitalism 146

Tandoc, Edson C. 171
Taylor Nelson Sofres (TNS) 159
TD Bank 203
technology and sonic qualities 1, 3, 9, 22, 24–7, 72, 104, 122, 156, 168, 170, 208
TechSurvey (2019) 66
"Tech TV" 1
terms of service (TOS) 97–100
Terra, Evo 189
Terranova, Tiziana 119
Third Coast International Audio Festival (2016) 58, 107, 126
third-party monetization 180, 190–203
This American Life 2, 26, 55, 71–2, 96, 121
This Week in Tech (TWiT) 1–3
Thomas, Julian 49–50, 53, 69, 74, 80, 124, 176
Threadless 187
The Tim Dillon Show 183
TiVO for radio 19, 87
Todd, Mitch 75, 125
top-down formalization 46, 69, 80
   clients 70
   facilitators 70–1
   linking pins 71–2
   mergers and acquisitions 72–4
Torabi, Farnoosh 130
"Tossed Popcorn" 56

The Trade Desk and Basis 198
Trader Joe's 17, 175
Trader Joe's Inside 202
transformation 9–11, 209
Triton Digital 2, 20, 70, 154–5, 198
Tumblr 97
Turow, Joseph 16, 48, 52, 60, 64, 66, 70, 71, 77, 146
   Media Systems in Society 48, 77
   power roles 16, 46, 48, 51–2, 66, 70, 77, 80, 140
Twitch 183
Twitter 54, 82, 87, 94, 99–100, 211
   Audit 82
   Spaces 212

unionization 75, 77–9, 222
UpWork 78
user-generated content (UGC) 2, 5–6, 25, 28, 50, 86, 99
   digital content 140
   formalization of 105–7
   monetization 99, 217
   SSPs of 197
UserLand Software 34

Value4Value system 184–5, 204
The Verge 76
vidcasting 15, 50, 183
video streaming services 31, 178
Voices 191
Vox Media 76, 198
Voxnest 91

Wait Wait … Don't Tell Me 188
Walch, Rob 81, 181
Washington, Glynn 128, 182
The Washington Post 55
"Wayne's World" 19
Web 2.0 era 4, 9, 86, 89, 113, 129, 133

web hosting 89–90, 109–10, 157
Webster, Tom, optimization trap 149
web syndication 16
Welcome to Night Vale 27, 188
White Paper 79
Wikipedia 50
Winer, Dave 25, 34–5, 37
WNYC, New York City 2, 176
Wondery 55, 58, 60, 67, 72, 80, 167, 171, 187, 215–16
Wordpress 90, 97
workers' rights 219–22
Work in Progress 203
World Wide Developers Conference (WWDC) 19–20, 164
World Wide Web 30
Writers Guild of America East (WGAE) 79, 222
WTF with Marc Maron 2

Yahoo! 83
Yarusso, Chris 138
Young, Neil 200, 216
YouTube 4, 6, 11, 28, 50, 52, 69, 72, 86, 89, 93, 100, 143, 152, 157, 170–1, 177, 183, 187, 209, 211–12, 216–17, 223
   Red premium subscription service 185
   vidders 178, 187, 203

Zaidi, Fatima 78
Zeitgeist 22
Zencastr 42
Zillow 202
Zuboff, Shoshana, utopia of certainty 205
Zuckerberg, Mark 124
Zune player, Microsoft 66